M000205106

GAINING CONTROL
MANAGING CAPACITY & PRIORITIES

3rd Edition
JAMES G. CORRELL & KEVIN HERBERT

John Wiley & Sons, Inc.

Copyright © 2007 by James Correll & Kevin Herbert. All rights reserved.

Published by John Wiley & Sons, Inc., Hoboken, New Jersey.
Published simultaneously in Canada.

For general information on our other products and services or for technical support, please contact our Customer Care Department within the United States at (800) 762-2974, outside the United States at (317) 572-3993 or fax (317) 572-4002.

Wiley also publishes its books in a variety of electronic formats. Some content that appears in print may not be available in electronic books. For more information about Wiley products, visit our web site at www.wiley.com.

Library of Congress Cataloging-in-Publication Data

Correll, James G.
    Gaining control : managing capacity and priorities / James G. Correll, Kevin Herbert.
    — 3rd ed.
      p. cm.
    Includes index.
    ISBN-13: 978-0-471-97992-0 (cloth : alk. paper)
    ISBN-10: 0-471-97992-9 (cloth : alk. paper)
    1. Production scheduling. 2. Manufacturing resource planning. 3. Just-in-time systems.
4. Industrial capacity—Management. I. Herbert, Kevin. II. Title.
TS157.5.C67 2007
658.5′3—dc22

                                                                              2006017529

Printed in the United States of America

10 9 8 7 6 5 4 3 2 1

Contents

Acknowledgments

Upgrading this book that focused on the basics of capacity management and shop-floor control to one that still maintained those basics, brought it up to date with current technology and processes, and looks into the future, was no easy task. The learning that went on in that process was invaluable to both of us. We would like to extend our heartfelt thanks to the many people who played a part in bringing the original, second, and now this third edition to fruition.

First and foremost, our thanks to our wives, Donna Correll and Carol Herbert. The hours that we spent pounding away on the computer instead of spending time with them were countless. Our love and thanks go to them for all their patience and support. In addition, Carol was our proofreader. Her effort took two engineers' attempts at the English language and turned it into something readable.

We would like to give special thanks to Norris Edison, who wrote the original edition with Jim but, because he had retired and wanted to maintain his sanity, decided to forgo being an author again and provide Kevin the opportunity to lose his sanity. We would also like to recognize David Goddard for his assistance in some of the graphics. In addition we would not like to lose some of the people who made the original and second edition possible, especially our original editor and publisher, Dana Scannell. Thanks also to Terry Tuttle of Nutrilite Products, Inc., Ron Hawkins of Kop-Flex Company, Sue Mazzio of the Boeing Company, and Mike Laker of Douglas Aircraft Company for their help in reviewing the original manuscript.

Thanks to our publisher of the third edition, John Wiley & Sons, and to Matt Holt and Kate Lindsay of the John Wiley editorial staff. Your patience is appreciated.

Finally, we would like to acknowledge all of the people we have worked with over the years who have operated in the informal environment, and especially those who have pulled themselves out of the chaos to get control of their businesses. This is really their story, and they seldom receive recognition for what they accomplish, or gratitude for getting the product out the door in spite of all the obstacles. To them, we say thanks a million for your unknowing contributions to the book.

James G. Correll
Sandy, Oregon

Kevin Herbert
Watford, England

Introduction

Throughout our professional careers, while working in industry, teaching seminars, and consulting with companies, we have been troubled by the apparent inability of manufacturing departments to get control of their operations. It's like the story that one company president related not long ago. He said that, as president of a very large enterprise, people believed that he had a great deal of control over what the company did. But, he admitted, he felt a lot like the little boy in the circus parade riding the big elephant. The boy had a little stick. When tapped on the back, the elephant speeded up; tapped on the forehead, he slowed down; tapped on the right ear, he'd turn right. They forgot, said the president, that the elephant could go anywhere he pleased and the little boy was merely making suggestions. This was how the president felt: He was not in control of the company but was merely making suggestions.

Have you ever felt that way? Or, even worse, has the elephant been doing what it wants to do and not what you want it to do? There are two things you can do: Get a bigger stick or educate the elephant. This book is aimed at educating the elephants.

One of the big hurdles we face constantly in industry is understanding terminology. We have tried to be consistent in our terminology, and have for the most part adopted the terminology of the American Production and Inventory Control Society (APICS). We are aware that you may use different terminology in your company. Since the original publication of this book, new methods and techniques and terminology have been introduced. Enterprise Resource Planning (ERP), Agile, Lean, and Six Sigma have earned their place in industry and will play a key role in the future. New concepts, software, and processes such as Finite Capacity Scheduling (FCS), and Advanced Planning and Scheduling (APS) are starting to make their mark on industry with both bad and good results. We explore each of these so there is a clear understanding of both their potential and their pitfalls. There are many publications on each of them and we encourage you to research them further, while being careful to understand their capabilities and constraints.

This book takes you on the journey of the Hayes Tractor Company, where they have to learn the fundamentals of capacity management and shop-floor control and then begin to reap the rewards as they apply these fundamentals. Unlike many companies, Hayes continues its quest for improvement and ventures into the future, following Effective Management's path to success—Class A. In this book, you will follow the story of Brian Miller, a manager in the out-of-control Hayes Tractor Company. All characters and companies in the book are fictitious, but they are composites of the people and companies we have worked with over the years. The situations are based on actual events: You may find many of the characters and situations to be familiar! The education and consulting firm, Effective Management, and its Class A process are also fictitious, but they follow all the teachings and philosophy of the Oliver Wight Company, where both of the authors are currently employed.

Although the story takes place in the Hayes Tractor Company, which is a metal fabrication and assembly shop, we take numerous side trips to many other companies to expose the reader to a variety of industries, including electronic assembly, food processing, aerospace and defense, and electronics. Our intent in doing this is to show how the concepts and principles explained in this book are applicable to any industry.

Our objective in writing this book is to help you understand what you have to do to get real benefit from the various processes and software that exist today. The answer lies in gaining control of the company, which is often referred to as "'closing the loop.'" This book shows you how.

We want the book to be fun and interesting to read and we hope we have accomplished this through the use of the Hayes story. Its true-to-life examples show how easy it is to be out of control and how problems can be solved by understanding and perseverance. Crucial to this is educating people to gain understanding so that they can change their behaviors. In applying this knowledge and these techniques to your company, we wish you every success.

Cast of Characters

HAYES TRACTOR COMPANY

Pete Smith	General Manager
Ralph Barnard	Production Manager
Brian Miller	Machine Shop Manager
Dan Milkosky	Fabrication Manager
Mickey Issacson	Assembly Manager
Joan Van Schot	Production Control Manager
Jose Garcia	Machine Shop Supervisor
Larry Placarde	2nd Shift Machine Shop Supervisor
Hank Jones	2nd Shift Welding Supervisor
Jim Romero	Grinding Supervisor
Cecil Nickerson	Machinist
Roy O'Brien	Materials Manager
Harold Bloom	Purchasing Manager
Mac Helm	Personnel Manager, ex-Machine Shop Manager
Tony Alonso	Expeditor, machine shop capacity planner
Alex Handly	Engineering Manager
Elliot Hathaway	Manufacturing Engineering Manager
Lloyd Adams	Design Engineering Manager
Sharon Levy	Controller
Carol Barrow	Quality Control Manager
Lenny Youngman	VP, Sales and Marketing
Jennifer Westlund	Demand Manager

Ivan Solokov	Maintenance Manager
Laura Sanderford	IT Systems Analyst
Carl Mueller	Material Planner
George Turner	Corporate Business Improvement Group
Mark MacDowell	Executive VP

Outside Contacts

Dennis Jones	Effective Management Coach/Capacity Planning
Roxanne Barnes	Effective Management Coach/Integrated Business Management
Les Johnson	Effective Management Coach/Lean
Amy Shinn	Effective Management Coach/Advance Planning Systems
Frank Snider	Teacher, local junior college
Sue Corey-Smith	Production Manager, Missile Systems Company
John Hall	General Supervisor, Precision Air Components
Hal Beckman	Materials Manager, Good Health Vitamins
Marty Bloch	Plant Supervisor, Beartone Manufacturing
Harvey Piscoli	Production Manager, ERON Technology
Rob Ericson	Production Manager, Mercury Electronics
Buster Jones	Manufacturing Manager, McNally Machine Tool
Joe Crowe	Production Manager, Supreme Enterprises
Tom Kirk	Master Scheduler, Supreme Enterprises

Chapter One

Out of Control

Brian Miller rebuilt the 1957 Chevy convertible for his wife as he had planned. She loved old cars and especially the 1957 Chevy. Her dad drove one when she was little and she never forgot it. Brian knew what parts he needed and had them there when it was time to install them. He figured out the proper sequence in which to reconstruct his pride and joy. He even scheduled his weeknights and weekends to ensure that he would complete the car in time to coincide with his wife's 30th birthday, yet not interfere with his family life, and work—in that order. Because things never seemed to work out exactly as planned, he constantly rescheduled his time to get things done. He met his target date a day early. On her birthday night, he ceremoniously opened the door of the Chevy for his wife. She seated herself, turned the key, and took Brian for a ride in her new car.

His planning and execution had resulted in a project completed on time. Why then, he thought from his office at the Hayes Tractor plant, couldn't he get his three production shifts running smoothly? He was the manager of the machine shop. He had a computerized planning and scheduling system that was supposed to provide schedules with which he could run the machine shop. Why was it that he couldn't achieve the same success he'd had rebuilding the Chevy?

Brian had only been at the West Coast plant for two months, having transferred from the company's Midwest division. He was the new guy on the block, and he was learning how to survive in this good-ol'-boy environment. As he looked out over the shop, he was not a happy man. The plant was in real trouble. Product was never delivered on time, lead times were unpredictable, and productivity was atrocious. The schedule that was generated by the computer was unusable and may as well have been thrown in the trash as soon as it arrived. Things were simply out of control.

It had been 6 months since Pete Smith was promoted from the Midwest plant to replace the retiring general manager. Pete had slowly begun to prune the ranks of the old-guard managers, replacing them with a group of more forward-thinking people.

Brian was one of these, replacing the Machine Shop manager who had been with the company for 45 years and had been moved over to the Human Relations department. Brian came from Quality Control to the Machine Shop, which didn't make the people in the shop too happy. They thought the new manager should have been elevated from within their own ranks, as was the tradition. Ralph Barnard, the Production Manager, had thought so, too.

On Brian's first day on the job, he was called into Ralph's office. Pete had known Brian at the Midwest plant and had arranged for his transfer, feeling that Brian's management style and quality perspective were needed at Hayes. Ralph, on the other hand, didn't know Brian at all. Ralph, who was in his early sixties, wore a constant sour smile as if his stomach were continually in revolt. He closed the door and sank heavily into the high-backed chair behind his desk.

His desk was covered with production reports, shipping schedules, product drawings, engineering changes, and memos about missed schedules. What caught Brian's attention, however, was a statue of a steel-gloved hand with a lightning bolt struck through it. The inscription read: "Cause it to happen!" This exemplified Ralph's attitude.

"All right, it's as simple as this," Ralph said, leaning back in his chair. "You've been brought in here as the Machine Shop manager. But here's the deal, Miller: You've got three months to get productivity up and shortages down. Nobody expects you to meet the schedules that come out of Production Control. That would be virtually impossible, since they're so screwed up. What I want you to concentrate on is the hot list from Mickey in Assembly. That'll tell you the real priorities, and that's what I want you to work on. If you don't, I'll find someone who will!"

Brian slowly lifted himself from his chair and thought to himself, "What have I gotten myself into?" He said, "Well, Ralph, I appreciate your vote of confidence. And I guarantee you I'll work hard to get the job done. I know I can do it."

"I hope so, kid." Ralph couldn't suppress his smile.

Needless to say, Brian left the office concerned about his lukewarm welcome, but even more determined to make a difference at Hayes. He had little idea of what he was up against.

He knew his first move was to try to establish a working relationship with his people, so Brian had his supervisors take him around and introduce him to everyone. He wanted to let these people know that he was a friendly sort and not one to just stay squirreled away in his office.

The second part of Brian's plan was to enroll quietly in a Machine Shop class at the local community college. Since his knowledge about machining parts was limited, he figured it'd probably be in his best interests to get some hands-on experience.

It was after the third class session that his teacher, Frank Snider, came up to Brian, having noticed that his hands weren't exactly the hands of a machinist. "Where do you work, Brian?" he asked.

"Hayes."

"Oh, yeah? What's your position there?"

"I'm the Machine Shop manager," Brian said.

Frank just about fell over. He had retired from Hayes' machine shop and now was teaching this class to stay busy. "I'll give you all the help I can," was Frank's generous reply. Fortunately Brian liked working with the equipment and proved himself to be a quick learner.

Several weeks later, Frank returned to Hayes to pick up some scrapped parts that Hayes had agreed to give the college for its students' use. Brian was on the shop floor, expediting a past-due part, when he found Frank chatting with a group of Brian's machinists who were some of Frank's old buddies. Frank made a point of telling them all about his new star pupil. Brian was embarrassed. But, contrary to his fear that it would lower his workers' estimation of him, it earned Brian a good deal of respect. The old timers were really impressed that the "kid" would take the time to try to learn the trade.

Brian, however, had bigger problems to face with his new job than just earning the respect of his workers. First, there were the daily 8:30 A.M. part-shortage meetings.

Some years ago the company had installed an Enterprise Resource Planning system to generate information that told the material planners when to release orders. The computer was also providing Brian with schedules and machine-load reports for each of the work centers. The only problem was that they were completely worthless. They didn't reflect the work that really needed to be done, and a large percentage of the scheduled orders were already past due. Consequently, everyone was using hot lists to communicate the real priorities.

The supply chain organization constantly told Brian that there wasn't anything wrong with the computer system. The problem was with the people, who were simply not following the schedules. Brian knew that they were including him in their comments, but he had no idea what he was doing wrong.

Brian also knew there were problems with management. It was as if top management didn't understand the limitations of the manufacturing process. It seemed they just wished things would happen and then expected Brian and the other managers to get them done on time. Sales was continually promising new orders with less than normal lead-time and expecting them to be shipped on time. To say the least, the job ahead of Brian was not going to be easy or fun.

Brian arrived at the factory each morning around 6:30. He wasn't expected to be in the office until 8:00, but expectation and reality had already proven to be two different things. His first action was to find his third-shift supervisor to see what went on the night before. Then, he would track down the expeditor. "Tony," he would yell through the constant noise that permeated the plant, "where's the hot sheet? Get me an update, will ya?" Thank God Tony was devoted and arrived even before Brian.

The next half hour or so would be spent going through the parts on the hot list, checking their status with Tony, and, at the same time, trying to assess what progress had been made and where he needed to concentrate his effort to "cause it to happen." Brian would walk into the plant and check with his own eyes to make sure that the hot parts were running on the machines.

Built in the 1920s, the Hayes facility was an old shop, with a smattering of new state-of-the-art equipment mixed in with mostly older machines. Even though they'd been painted and repainted over the years, there was no escaping the age of the plant and its equipment.

At 8:30, the managers gathered for the shortage meeting: Ralph; Dan from Fabrication; Mickey from Assembly; Joan from Production Control; Roy, the Materials Manager; and Harold from Purchasing. It was Dan and Mickey who made Brian's life difficult. But, then, they probably felt the same way about Brian.

Dan was in his mid-forties and had been a buddy of Ralph's for years. They were regular golfing partners, football couch potatoes, and they'd been known to enjoy a beer or two together as well. Mickey was in his mid-thirties—the same age as Brian. Ralph's relationship with Mickey was also special. Ralph had a son of his own, but it was common knowledge that Ralph also looked upon Mickey as a son. The only problem in this little mutual-admiration society was that Dan and Mickey didn't like each other. Neither had any advantage over the other with the boss. Their only common ground was that they could both gang up on Brian.

On this particular day, the shortage meeting got under way right on schedule. It was one of the few things at Hayes that was consistently on schedule. As usual, they started at the top of the list of shortages, which was typically over 300 parts. The status of each and every part was reviewed. Brian was prepared. He'd done his homework and knew where most parts on the shortage list were, and when they should be delivered to Mickey or Dan. Invariably, Mickey's response was, "That's not good enough! I need that part at least two days earlier." Now, everyone in the room knew that Mickey always wanted everything before he really needed it. If a part from Dan's Fabrication department was late, Dan always pointed the finger at Mickey, saying, "The parts are in the paint shop," which was under Mickey's jurisdiction. It was how Dan always got off the hook. But on this particular day, Mickey had decided it was time to push back.

Reading down the list, Ralph came to a cover that was supposed to be coming out of Fabrication on its way to Assembly. Dan, without blinking, said, "It's in paint." Mickey was ready for this, and jumped right on Dan.

"That's a bunch of bull!" Mickey shouted. "I just came from there. That cover's *not* in paint! It's sitting in your hand-grind area."

This backlash infuriated Dan. "You're wrong, as usual, Mickey! We've completed enough on that order to cover the shortage, and they're in paint!" Ralph interceded and cooled the two men down. Brian shook his head in dismay. This was the daily atmosphere in which he now found himself.

After the meeting Dan had taken off immediately. Brian went looking for him to try to learn more about the Hayes environment and found him just leaving the grind area. Brian asked him if the covers he had so adamantly insisted were in paint were really there. Dan smiled, and said, "The parts are always there when Mickey goes back to look. And they were there this time, too. I saw to that long before the meeting was over. You don't think I have to go to the bathroom *that* much, do you?" Brian was beginning to realize that intimidation was the only way to survive in this environment. You tried to intimidate the boss. You tried to intimidate your peers, and you absolutely had to intimidate the people that worked for you.

It was surprising that anything got built in this factory. It did, but only through sheer brute force and the dedication of guys like Mickey in Assembly. Mickey battled against confusion and chaos, and was in constant communication with his people and the expediters. He knew what must ship and when. He also knew what was missing to make those shipments and he made sure he let everyone else know.

For Brian, that meant on average 150 different parts in his shop that were all past due and needed in assembly that week. Most of the parts had more than a six-week lead time. Each part had a specific day during the week when it was needed, and it took constant watching to make sure that Mickey got the parts that he needed when he needed them. Brian was continually checking, making sure the right parts were running on the machines.

Every day Mickey would come in with a list of additional parts that weren't on the original shortage list. "You know that motor mount we thought we had? Well, we had some screw-up and we need more." Brian loved to get half a page filled with extras. It just made his day.

Once the part-shortage meeting had been completed, everyone had a new set of priorities. Brian rounded up his supervisors and Tony to let them know about the additions. "Guess what, guys, more hot parts." No one seemed the least bit surprised. "What I live for," said one of the supervisors reviewing the list. Tony added these new items onto the original hot sheets and passed them around to the supervisors. Afterward, Brian was once again out on the floor making sure they were running the right parts.

With 170 employees in his machine shop to deal with, Brian's life was rarely dull. There were grievances to arbitrate, promotions to consider, attendance problems, fixture breakdowns, and industrial engineers plotting new equipment layouts. "The new Libiher hobb won't fit in the same position as the old hobb and the foundation for it is larger than we expected," said an engineer, looking over the drawing. "This means we'll have to move the horizontal broach." Next there were the personnel meetings to review all the problems about hiring new people. Then, it was time for lunch.

Brian closed the door to his office. He didn't want to see anybody. He just wanted to eat his sandwich in peace. The phone rang—it was his wife. "Yes, dear, just another day in paradise."

After lunch, it was more of the same: more meetings, more problems, more parts to expedite. The frustration level continued to rise. "All I want," Brian thought to himself, "is some decent, reliable information. At least then I might be able to come up with some sort of game plan." At 35 years old, Brian hadn't gotten to the point where he was ready to accept that things couldn't and wouldn't get better. He knew that lots of things were wrong at Hayes. He had graduated from college as an industrial engineer, and that had supposedly trained him to find better ways. Although he wasn't exactly sure just how it was supposed to be, he knew it was not supposed to be like this.

One day, while he was waiting in the expeditor's office, which was located in the middle of the shop, Brian picked up the computer-printed schedule. It listed everything that was supposed to be made in each work center for the next week, sorted by operation start date. He took it to Tony and asked, "Why don't we start using these instead of hot lists?"

Tony sighed disgustedly and told him that the first 12 items on the schedule for the lathes were parts nobody seemed to need. Then, he pointed out that the 23rd item on the schedule was the hottest job in the whole factory, according to the shortage meeting that morning. Brian was confused. He stared down at the computer printout. It was the right concept, but the information on it seemed useless. Not knowing where the information came from or how it was developed, he was at a loss.

Brian realized that the key to getting work done on time was having the right number of people, with the right skill sets, at the right time. To accomplish that, he needed visibility of what was required. All he had was a report that the computer generated every week. It showed the total amount of work in standard hours that were scheduled to be completed week by week for each work center. The trouble was that it always contained a lot of work that was already past due. The future wasn't any better. He knew he could not believe the amount of work the computer showed. In some cases there was very little work and in other cases the amount of work shown far exceeded what Brian knew was coming. The load was all over the place. He didn't know whether to hire additional people to take care of the past dues, or to lay people off. Brian decided to check it out with Mac, the ex-machine-shop manager, now manager of Human Relations. He must have had some way to predict when and where people and equipment were needed.

Brian walked into Mac's office. Mac was behind his desk, as gruff and grumpy as if he had never left the shop floor. He didn't really like being H.R. manager, but after 45 years, he wasn't about to leave Hayes. Brian put the capacity report on the desk before Mac. "I'm having a terrible time trying to plan the number of people I need. Is it really possible to plan with this capacity report?"

Mac let out an abrupt laugh. "You look at that thing and you tell me." Being his replacement, Brian knew Mac resented him, and no amount of charm was about to melt that girded exterior.

"Well, it seems obvious to me that it's useless. So what did you use to plan with?"

"Well," Mac drawled, enjoying the fact that Brian was having such problems, "when you get a little more experience, you'll get the gut feel, and you'll know."

Brian stared at Mac blankly. He had precious little time to turn things around. Mac had had 45 years, and Brian could see by the chaos on the shop floor that after all those years, Mac hadn't done very well at balancing capacity. Brian felt a deep emptiness.

He walked into his office like a condemned man, picked up the phone, and asked Tony to come to his office. Brian had confidence in Tony. He knew that a good expeditor was the key to survival, and Tony knew more than anyone about the machine shop at Hayes.

Tony entered the office tentatively. The tone of Brian's voice on the phone had suggested that he wasn't very happy. Tony pulled a chair out and sat down. "So, what's the story?" he asked. It was how Tony approached every encounter.

"Tony, what do I do about planning capacity in this place? I can't tell if we're coming or going."

"Is that all this is about?" Tony asked, having already assumed that Brian was going to want to reschedule the whole shop. "Man, that's a piece of cake."

"A piece of cake?"

"Sure. C'mon, I'll show you." Tony led Brian onto the shop floor amidst the constant roar and clatter. "A piece of cake," Brian thought. "Okay, maybe I will survive this place." He was starting to feel better.

Tony walked him over to a group of machining centers. A box was attached to a column nearby and it was jammed full of work orders to be completed. "You see that?" Tony asked, raising his voice over the noise, as one of machines peeled a string of metal chips from a part. "You can just look at the work-order box and know we're in big trouble on these machines. We gotta have more capacity, so we're going to have to work overtime." The two walked down the aisle to a drill press that had one work order. "See that?" Tony pointed to the only order in the box. "We don't have any capacity problems here."

"That's great, Tony. That's just great," Brian said as the sinking feeling returned. "But, it's all after the fact. It's too late to do anything about it. I mean, if I need to hire people, I need to do it a lot sooner than when the work goes past due."

Tony smiled. "When I said it was a piece of cake, I meant that I'd show you how we did it. I never said it worked, but that's the way we've always done it. The problem now is that we're just too big to operate like this any more."

"That's not all," Brian said. "Late shipments just aren't going to be tolerated anymore. Our jobs are on the line here."

Later, while leaning back in his chair and staring vacantly at the calendar on the wall, Brian counted the days he had left. He stared down at the schedule and the capacity reports on his desk. He had the tools that were supposed to be giving him the information he needed, but they weren't providing accurate information. "The computer can't be the answer," he thought. "Look what it produces—junk. If only I knew what I had to do to solve a problem. No matter how difficult the solution might be, at least I could apply myself and do it." But Brian didn't even know what the problem was. And the frustration continued to build.

Then he thought about his wife's Chevy, sitting in the garage at home. He remembered when he had finally finished it, turned the ignition key and it wouldn't start. Why wouldn't it start? He had had to go back and, without a clue, track down the problem. But once he found the problem, even though it meant additional hours of work, he knew what he had to do. He never minded the hard work. The frustration at Hayes was maddening because he couldn't find the problem.

The frustration didn't just stay at the factory. As the weeks and months passed, Brian began to bring it home more and more. He was tired, angry, and sick of all the endless problems without solutions. He'd snap at his wife, the innocent victim of his frustration. Then, there was her hurt and anger because her husband was never there, with all of his waking hours being consumed by a job that seemed without reward, a job that seemed to be tearing them apart. Maybe they should go back to the Midwest plant. Things had been better there.

Brian tried to explain how out of control things were, but he didn't have the words. All he had was this continual, unnerving agitation. It was often all he could do to keep himself in control. He wanted her to understand, but the problem was that he himself didn't understand. Something had to give.

Sitting in his office, Brian tried to sort through the problems he was encountering. He even thought back to a management problem-solving class he'd taken in college, and suddenly a vision of Harvey Piscoli's face appeared in his mind. Harvey! Why hadn't he thought of him earlier? Brian was on the phone in a second. Harvey was one of Brian's best buddies in college and he was now the Production Manager at ERON Technology, located a few blocks from Brian's old Midwest plant. Brian was never sure what it was that Harvey's company built, but it had something to do with scientific research instrumentation.

"Piscoli!" Brian said to Harvey on the other end. "I've gotta tell you, buddy, I think I've gotten myself in over my head by taking this transfer to the West Coast. And I'm afraid to admit it, but I think I need some help." It lifted Brian's spirits just to hear Harvey's laugh. Brian then explained his desperate and deteriorating situation. "I tell you, Harvey, I come to work each day wondering how I'm going to meet my schedules and productivity goals. I don't even know what the real schedule is. Everyone seems to have their own. I spend most of my time chasing after parts shortages."

Brian continued: "My schedule calls for 800 hours of output one week, 700 the next, and 900 the week after that. And my capacity report always has a bunch of past-due work, and the future is unrealistic. It's gotten so bad, Harvey," Brian said, "I don't have time to think about who is going to be on vacation next week or what tooling I need or which machines need maintenance."

"Brian, I've been in that situation before. What are you guys using for a scheduling system?" Harvey asked.

"We've got a new ERP system, but it certainly doesn't seem to be much help," said Brian. "I spend half my day trying to keep up with the changes."

"Sounds like you guys have to close the loop," Harvey said.

"Harvey, they've got me jumping through the loop. In fact, it kinda feels like that loop is getting tightened around my neck." Both Brian and Harvey laughed.

"Tell me, Brian, are you getting valid schedules for each work center every day?"

"We have a weekly schedule for the shop, but nobody uses it. The schedules I get now are unreliable; the dates either change constantly, or they're way past due."

"What about capacity planning? Are you guys doing that?" Harvey asked.

"I get that capacity report that I told you about every week," Brian said. "It's supposed to tell me how much capacity I need, but I haven't found it very useful either because it only shows me released work, not what is planned for the future."

"I'll tell you, partner," Harvey said, "Capacity planning has made an amazing difference for us. We're even able to anticipate capacity problems and take the actions necessary to avoid them. The visibility we're getting today has made this job one even you could probably do, Miller."

"Talk to me, Harvey. All I wish is that I had some idea of what was really going to happen tomorrow."

"Not to gloat, buddy, but we're able to tell what's happening months in advance. And if we don't think we can meet the schedule, we get together with the planners before the problem gets to the crisis stage and we work it out."

"Your system's supporting all that for you? How do you stay on top of it all? I tell you, Harvey, my boss is constantly monitoring the efficiency, utilization, and output of my departments. If we miss any of the goals he sets for us . . . well, you can guess what it's like. Then, if I try to talk to him about how far behind we are, he tells me, 'Put a little pressure on your people. They'll get the work out. They always have.'"

"Well, don't get too down on yourself, Brian. It sounds similar to this place a few years ago." Harvey went on to explain that ERON now had an overall operating plan and the schedules that supported that plan. The impact on his job was significant. His responsibility now was to meet the Master Schedule. That meant making sure he had the equipment, tooling, and manpower necessary to address that demand. "But, the most important part, Brian, is that we have all the information we need to run the factory and meet our schedules. Now, management expects me to make the schedule, but they've also given me the authority to make sure that we do."

All Brian could do was shake his head in disbelief. "Obviously, we're not getting the most out of our ERP system. And, I gotta tell you, Harvey, it's gonna be tough to get people at Hayes to change the way they do things. They've been doing them this way since creation. I also know they've been doing it wrong that long, too. So, where do we start?"

Harvey tried to reassure his friend. "You have to have accurate data to start with. When we first got going, our data was about as reliable as a stopped watch—it was only accurate twice a day. If I were you, I would make sure that the data feeding into ERP is accurate. Then, I would take a look at the routings."

"Piscoli, I knew you were the man I had to talk to. Now, all I got to do is figure out what you're talking *about* and go do it, right? Thanks, buddy."

Brian realized he still had a lot to learn and there would be a great deal of work involved. But, it was like he had always said: "Hard work isn't the problem." When you know what you've got to do, you do it. It's the not knowing that makes everyone crazy. Then, you're just working against yourself, and that's the hardest work you can do.

Chapter Two

Gaining Knowledge

A few days later, Brian was called up to Ralph's office. He wasn't sure what to expect. He did know things hadn't improved much since he had started, and he was never quite sure when the axe might fall. As he entered the office, Dan, Mickey, and Joan, the Production Control Manager, were already seated. "Have a seat, Brian," Ralph said, motioning to the remaining empty chair. "I realize that things are pretty hard for you guys with this scheduling system of ours, but I'm not accepting any excuses because of it. And Brian has been telling me that he doesn't have any way to predict what his capacity requirements are going to be. There's no question we gotta find a better way to run this place. That's why I want the four of you to attend a three-day course on capacity management next week. Roy tells me the instructors are well known and put on an excellent presentation. He thinks we would learn something from it. He also wants Joan to go along. He said his department will pay for it, so I figure it'll be worthwhile if you pick up a few points." He handed the course brochure to Dan.

Dan thumbed through it and handed it to Brian. As Brian opened the four-page spread, he remembered the last course that he had attended. The speaker spent the whole day talking about things that had little to do with Brian's immediate needs. He could tell Ralph was intent on sending him to this one, so he resigned himself to another three days lost. Ralph was always big on meeting his numbers. This time it was the education and training quota that the corporation imposed on him. He would just have to come in before the course each day and try to get things lined up and then drop by after the course to see what disasters had occurred each day.

The course was being held in a local hotel. The four members of the Hayes party found seats and filled out their name cards with their company name. Brian was seated next to a woman from Missile Systems, a large, local defense contractor. He looked around at the names of the other companies in attendance. There were people from Good Health Vitamins, Precision Air Components, Dorman Chemical, Beartone Manufacturing, and several other companies. Brian wasn't sure he could understand how all of these different companies with different products and different processes could use the same capacity planning techniques.

The speakers arrived at the front of the room. There were two speakers: a woman in her late forties and another man perhaps 10 years older—both casually dressed. The lady moved to the front of the group. "Hi, I'm Roxanne Barnes from Effective Management Inc., an education and consulting firm, and next to me is Dennis Jones." Dennis waved as Roxanne continued. "Our topic for the next three days is capacity management. As they say on the airlines, if this is not your intended destination, now would be a good time to deplane." Everyone laughed, helping to put them at ease. "We're here to talk about getting control of your manufacturing operations through capacity management and good scheduling."

Brian was ready to hear about the solution to his out-of-control problem at work. He listened as the speakers offered their manufacturing credentials and explained the areas that they planned to address that day. When they had finished their introduction, Brian looked across to Joan and nodded his approval. He could see that she agreed with his early assessment.

Roxanne described the material each student had. Among other things there was a book she referred to as the *Class A Checklist* and a course notebook with almost all the slides she and Dennis would be presenting. Each slide had space for notes.

Roxanne walked around the table where her computer and projector sat and said, "In order to for us to apply what we are going to learn about capacity management properly we need to see the whole picture. To accomplish that we will use a model we call the Integrated Business Model." She then flashed up on the screen Figure 2.1.

Figure 2.1 Integrated Business Model

© Oliver Wight

"As Albert Einstein once commented, 'All models are wrong, some are useful'; so too this model is a starting place for all companies to begin building their processes.

"As you can see the model starts at the top with Performance Improvement which means that you must start with performance metrics that drive the right behaviors and hold people accountable to meet them. We will cover the performance metrics for capacity management and shop scheduling in a lot of detail as we talk about the specific topic.

"We will also be referring to Class A as we proceed through the course. We will go into more detail at various points in the course but for now let me give you a very high-level definition. Class A is an industry standard that helps you compare your performance against the best practices as defined in the *Class A Checklist* I referred to earlier. The checklist is made up of nine chapters. If you receive a score of 5 then you are excellent in that process. Following that logic, if you receive a score of 4 you are very good, a 3 is good, 2 is fair, and 1 is poor. If you are not doing the process you receive a score of 0. Class A companies have achieved an average score of 4.5. We will be focusing on the Managing Internal Supply chapter. To say the least, to be considered a Class A company you really have to be good.

"In the 'Integrated Business Model' figure (see Figure 2.1) we are trying to depict the processes that need to be integrated for management to be able to control the business from top to bottom. It shows product management, demand management, and supply management as three 'legs' in the center of this diagram. Each of those is capped by a preparatory 'wheel' of activities that serves to prepare for reviews within the Integrated Business Management process, which I'll discuss in a few minutes. We won't get into detail about the activity within those preparatory wheels, with the exception of the Supply Review wheel. In the vast majority of companies we work with, we find the individual elements within each of the three legs to be poorly integrated, and more often we find competing internal objectives and turf battles going on. Integration across the legs is almost always weak, at best.

"In contrast, companies that follow Class A principles, exhibit Class A behaviors, and reach Class A standards of performance have these functions fully integrated, with a clear multifunctional focus on achieving the business strategy and continuously improving business results. That integration is accomplished through a process we call Integrated Business Management, shown here on the screen in Figure 2.2. This model is simply a more detailed view of part of the previous slide (Figure 2.1).

"I want you to notice that at the heart of Integrated Business Management, depicted by this ellipse, are strategic and business plans with continuous financial review and reconciliation of issues and imbalances. The Integrated Business Management process itself is what successful companies use to deploy their strategic plans and objectives throughout the entire company. In other words, they use Integrated Business Management to link strategy to execution activities. Senior managers review actual business results formally, regularly, and thoroughly in this process, to make sure all functional activities and results remain on target and on strategy. The process culminates in a single operating plan and empowers people at all

Figure 2.2   Integrated Business Management

© Oliver Wight

levels of the company to make good business decisions from day to day, week to week, and month to month. As a result more good decisions get made more quickly, and good information flows continuously both top down and bottom up and across all functional areas.

"At the very top of the Integrated Business Management ellipse is what we call the Management Business Review. This review is the culmination of the month-long Integrated Business Management process. It is a crisp and concise monthly executive review of recommended plans and allows presentation of recommended solutions to resolve significant issues. If all preliminary work is done well, it is a quick review and approval process. Often, however, there is important debate that allows senior management to test recommendations and evaluate current business conditions and strategies. In the end, it is a decision-making meeting that results in a single set of demand, supply, product management, and financial plans covering the next 18 to 24 months, and clear decisions to resolve current problems and avoid future problems. The approved plans are then quickly and broadly communicated throughout the company. Functional leaders are held accountable for executing the approved plans and for delivering the planned outcomes. With this model in place, everyone in the organization is on the same page and works with the same objectives. The company's strategy has been solidly linked with functional strategies and with planning and execution processes.

"The Management Business Review can be only as effective as the reviews that precede it each month. I want to spend just a few minutes talking about each of those reviews. The Integrated Business Management process begins each month with a Product Management Review that ensures Sales and Marketing ownership for all product portfolio plans, as well as currency of the plan's deliverables, timing, and cost. This is facilitated by the Product Coordinator (Manager, Director). The focus is normally on what has changed from the previous month's review and care is taken to ensure the resources are available to execute the plans successfully. This monthly review provides the Demand Manager with information that he or she can use to forecast increasing demand for new products and services, and reduced demand for replaced or cannibalized products and services. This critical input to the demand plan on new and changing products and necessary resources is often overlooked by companies doing traditional Sales & Operations Planning, yet is essential in developing accurate forecasts and flawlessly launching new products and product initiatives.

"Moving on to demand, you notice that the Demand Review considers all sources of demand, including non-revenue demand such as sales and professional samples. By this time, the forecasters have incorporated the plans of the Sales organization, Marketing plans, customer promotional events, field sales intelligence, economic trends, and a host of other inputs. Demand management also considers historical patterns, utilizes statistical forecasting tools, and draws information from everyone who has contact with the customers. In this step, performance is analyzed, ownership of all market and customer plans is reinforced, and commitments are made for volume, revenue, and margins.

"The Supply Review, which is where we will focus, is driven from the output of the Demand Review and takes into consideration the strategic and business plans and the operating strategy. Those involved in the Supply Review analyze all potential constraints through the lens of what we call Resource Requirements Planning, which we will go into in detail later on. The executive responsible for Supply Chain plans and performance (in many companies this is the

Supply Chain manager or director) reviews performance, capability, flexibility, and alternative supply strategies when supply constraints create an imbalance between demand and supply. He or she wants to be certain, especially in capital intensive companies, that underutilized equipment is identified as an issue so that plans can be developed either to increase sales of items produced on that equipment, to modify that equipment for other purposes, or to reduce that capacity. The Supply Manager facilitates and coordinates the preparation process leading to the Supply Review, working closely with the Demand Manager to balance demand and supply capabilities throughout the planning horizon. At the same time they maintain inventories as low as possible while simultaneously increasing customer service and minimizing costs. The output of this review is commitment to an achievable supply plan that supports demand and product management requirements, or an assessment of alternatives when a gap between demand and supply cannot be closed. Balancing supply and demand volumes is where the traditional Sales & Operations Planning processes end.

"But the Integrated Business Management process doesn't end there. It continues by integrating financial analysis continuously in the process and during each of these review steps. We no longer wait for that analysis until all the plans are reviewed in the formal Reconciliation Review, led by the Integrated Reconciliation process leader—usually one of the Leadership team—that follows the other reviews I've described. Reconciliation of differences, issues, and gaps is conducted continuously throughout the month. Having the ability to examine financial implications of alternative plans in the individual review meetings empowers people to make decisions at appropriate organizational levels and allows the leadership team to focus its attention on only the most important issues during the Management Business Review. There is normally a brief final reconciliation meeting chaired by the process leader to finalize the information for Management Business Review, but analysis and decision-making are accomplished throughout the month.

"Perhaps the most important thing about the Integrated Business Management process is how it directly links strategic planning, business planning, company-wide projects, and day-to-day detailed planning and execution activities. This linkage gives the Leadership team the ability to ensure that all the daily decisions and activities throughout the organization keep each of your Integrated Business

Management product families on strategy and in alignment with the plans approved in the Management Business Review. There is no ambiguity; everyone operates from the same set of authorized plans and numbers; accountability is unambiguous; and results are tracked and reported. The most eloquent yet simple endorsement we've heard about Integrated Business Management is that it enables senior management to 'hit the numbers' and 'deliver the strategy consistently.'

"On the surface, this linking of strategy to execution through Integrated Business Management appears to be a simple extension of the traditional Sales & Operations Planning process. It is a simple change conceptually, but it isn't easy to implement. And it's just one element of the culture change required on a journey to business excellence. It's a big effort, but it yields significant business benefits quickly.

"Let me quote a couple of specific endorsements for the Integrated Business Management process. At Effective Management we have been teaching and coaching companies on Sales & Operations Planning since 1984. In recent years the rest of the world has been waking up to the power of this process. In February 2004, AMR published the article, 'Sales & Operations Planning Bringing Order Out of Chaos.' The article stated, 'The only enterprise process that balances the supply- and demand-side equations optimally is Sales & Operations Planning. In fact, a formal well-executed Sales & Operations Planning process was identified as one of the top practices of performance leaders in AMR Research's studies.'

"Additionally, The Aberdeen Group published a survey in which they stated, 'Enterprises that deploy S&OP programs strategically consistently outperform by an average 20% in gross margin.'" Roxanne paused.

"Importantly, these findings are based upon the traditional S&OP process, not the Integrated Business Management process that incorporates the strategy and financial aspects to drive even greater benefits.

"If your company isn't ready to go as far as Integrated Business Management, I suggest you start with Sales & Operations Planning. The software needs are really simple and creating the data to support Resource Requirements Planning is a piece of cake in comparison to Detail Capacity Planning.

"Are there any questions about the Integrated Business Management process?"

"So you really expect the sales and marketing organization to forecast?"

Roxanne turned and focused on a man in the fourth row. "It's Sam isn't it? And you're the Production Control manager at Dorman Chemical."

"Well you got the name and company right, but the title is a misnomer. I've never been able to control production," Sam replied, which was followed by some knowing laughter.

Roxanne laughed also, "Well Sam, yes, we do expect people to forecast and do a reasonably good job of it. We know there is no such thing as a perfect forecast, but we find that if companies follow the best practices described in Chapter 6 of the *Class A Checklist*—Managing Demand—they are able to significantly improve the accuracy of their forecast."

"Ya gotta class on that? Because if you do I know a lot of sales and marketing people at Dorman that need that class," Sam responded.

"Yes we do. Please talk to me at break on that, Sam."

Brian could see Joan making notes and knew that she would be right there with Sam at break time.

"Let's go back to the Integrated Business Model (Figure 2.1). I have explained what basically happens in each of the three legs to support Integrated Business Management. We will of course go into much more detail on the Supply Review leg, but before we do that I want to point out that if we are doing the process properly we are operating to one set of numbers. That means there is only one demand plan and it drives all three legs. What isn't specifically shown on the model is finance. Finance uses the same set of numbers to drive all the financial planning and reporting. They simply add to cost portion and they have the financial plan. There is no problem keeping the plans in sync because they are all one plan.

"Lastly, let me direct your attention to the bottom of the model—People, Values, and Knowledge Management. We have all heard the line that a lot companies spout—people are our most-valued asset. People are not going to perform well unless there are values that are lived everyday in the organization. Stating them and living them are two entirely different issues. Taking it a step further, people need knowledge that is not restricted to the way the company operates today. For instance, this course will provide you with perhaps a completely different way to operate. Your company must have thought enough of each of you to spend money to expand your horizons. In the same way that values are worthless unless they are lived, knowledge is worthless unless it is used to make improvements. If you walk away from this course and have everything memorized but don't apply it, you have wasted your time and your company's money. If you walk away and apply only a few things, we believe that you will reap rewards that far surpass the cost of this course.

"Then the 'knowledge management' part of the model means that your company has a process to capture knowledge, leading to increased control and business improvement.

"With that little gem of knowledge I think we need a break. How about coming back in 10 minutes? Remember, this class is about capacity management and meeting schedules, so let's start if off right and be back on time. I will be handing the next portion of the course off to Dennis Jones."

At break Brian went over to Joan to get her impression about the course. "So what do you think?"

"I think it is great," she replied. "I'm not sure about Dan and Mickey, however. They don't look too impressed."

"You know those two. 'Not invented here' means it must not be any good. Anyway, could you see those two operating in any kind of structured environment? Certainly not Dan. He mumbled something to me about the instructors not even knowing what parts are—they keep calling them items.

"An 'item' is the generic term for parts. In the process industry you're not going to call chemicals parts. Same thing in the food industry and the list goes on. At Hayes, like most engineering companies, we call them parts."

"Can't he open up his mind a little?" Joan replied, really exasperated.

"Not in our lifetime," Brian chuckled.

"You got that right!" Joan replied. "Let's get back in so we're not late. Bet you, Dan and Mickey are late." She was correct.

"Okay," Dennis began. "Now I want to direct your attention to another more detailed diagram, the Supply Point Management Model (Figure 2.3), which builds on the Integrated Business Model's Supply Review leg.

"It all starts with the Supply Point Management box. Most Class A companies have what we call a Supply Manager. The Supply Manager's responsibility is to coordinate all the supply activities so there is an 'agreed-on' plan. The function is critical in the In-

Figure 2.3   Supply Point Management Model

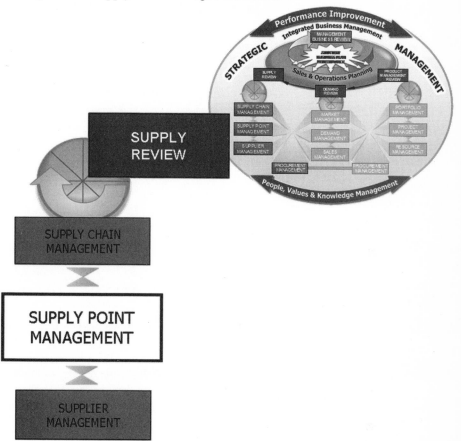

© Oliver Wight

tegrated Business Management process. How many of you have a person called a Supply Manager or someone that performs a function similar to that?"

As Dennis looked around the room a few people raised their hands but they were all from one of two companies.

"Well, that is typical," he continued. "Until you understand the importance of the integration of the processes, you really can't understand the importance of the function."

Brian looked over at Joan and saw that she was intently listening to the instructor, but Dan and Mickey seemed to be off in a dream world.

Figure 2.4   Detailed Supply Point Management Model

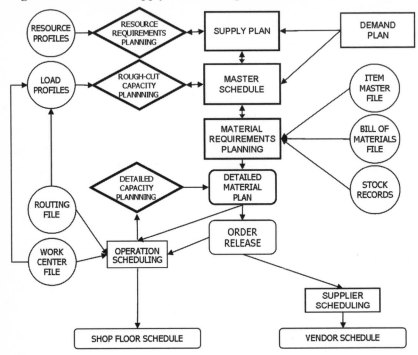

"Let's now look at the processes that operate within the Supply Point Management box (Figure 2.3). To do that let's look at a more detailed version of the Supply Point Management Model (Figure 2.4).

"The key driver is the Supply Plan, which is an output from Integrated Business Management meeting. It is what the supply organization has committed to making, summarized into families. We summarize them into product families because in most companies there would be far too many items for senior management to deal with if it were done at the end item or option level.

"The Supply Plan drives master scheduling. Here the families are broken down into end items or options. It is the master scheduler's job to assure that the full amount in the family is represented in the Master Schedule, but not more.

"The Master Schedule, in turn, drives Material Requirements Planning. In this process the end items or options are broken down automatically by the Enterprise Resource Planning system, using the Bills of Materials and stock records. In this process, called a Bill of Materials explosion, detailed material plans are created for every item needed to meet the Master Schedule, whether produced internally or externally. The material planner's job is to assure that the plans support the Master Schedule and the Supply Plan.

"To the left of each of these processes are, respectively, Resource Requirements Planning, Rough-Cut Capacity Planning, and Detail Capacity Planning processes. These are used to validate capacity availability at each stage from Supply Plan down to the Material Plan. Once we have a detailed material plan we can link these to the Shop Floor Schedules. These processes are the main topics of our discussion in this course. All four processes—supply planning, master scheduling, material planning, and capacity planning—are dependent on there being valid plans at each stage. When we say 'valid,' we mean that the item is required and that there is capacity to make it. To be valid, the information coming into the process must be valid. That means that the data that feed the input processes must also be accurate. In the case of the Master Scheduling and Material Requirements Planning, the four main sets of data that must be accurate are the demand plan, inventory (stock), item master, and bill of materials. How accurate and how to measure each one is in the *Class A Checklist.* The third requirement for the plan to be valid is that it must be appropriately managed. That means that supply and demand must be lined up to support not only the demand but also the internal and external supplier's capability to accomplish it. Taken another step, not only does the question of 'Can we do it?' need to be answered, but the question 'Should we do it?' also needs to be asked. The 'Should we do it?' revolves around cost. Even though we might lose money on the order, management may decide it is the right thing to do for a key customer. However, unless the question is asked every time, management can't give the correct answer. That is the way Class A companies behave. They are always astonished when they start asking the 'Should we do it?' question about how many times they are losing money on an order and didn't know it in the past. One of the main objectives of capacity planning is being able to answer the question for the short term, but also mid and long term. We will be asking the 'Should we do it?' question throughout the course. Just as a reference, how many of you ask the 'Should we do it?' question today?" Dennis queried.

Brian glanced around the room to see how many hands went up. None! Then he looked over at Dan. Dan seemed to have woken up and was nodding his head in agreement, but when Brian looked at Mickey he saw his arms were folded and he was leaning back in his chair. That was Mickey's way of indicating that this was a bunch of "bull" without saying it. Brian then looked over at Joan and met her eyes. She started shaking her head as she glanced back at Mickey. "This is really going to be fun," Brian thought as he turned his attention back to Dennis.

"Now let's take a look at the three processes on the left: Resource Requirements Planning, Rough-Cut Capacity Planning, and Detail Capacity Planning," Dennis continued.

"These are the three levels of capacity planning that should be employed. Resource Planning tests only key resource availability for aggregate family volumes over 18–24 months; Rough-Cut Capacity Planning tests only key resources at the individual Master Schedule item level. By contrast, Detailed Capacity Planning tests capacity of all supply work centers over the execution horizon of the complete material plan, in order to support achieving the Master Schedule. Any independent demand, such as making spares, will have been included in Master Schedule and Material Requirements Planning processes and therefore in the detailed capacity plan. These three levels of capacity planning provide assurance across the supply chain that we can execute our plans.

"Material Requirement Planning also drives the Shop Floor Schedules through the Operation Scheduling program. This provides detailed schedules to the shop floor when needed, to tell the individual work centers what, when, and how much product to produce.

"In the past, it was common for supply planning to be done top-down. Planners would say, 'Just give us the aggregate plan and we'll break it down to the item level using an historical average item mix of product shipments, and then do our supply planning.' With the advent of far more powerful computer systems, most companies now drive the detailed item forecasts down to the detailed capacity planning level over cumulative lead time, to uncover any capacity issues and develop alternative recommendations for capacity shortfalls. Resource and rough-cut capacity planning tools are often used for a quick 'what-if' analysis in the Integrated Business Management process. They are also utilized to make certain there are no obvious constraints before beginning more detailed planning activities. All necessary resources such as people, equipment, and facilities must be available to support the plans. We typically think 'our factory' when we think about capacity planning. The factory is an important user of capacity planning, but others such as marketing, sales, engineers, and the whole external supply chain need to be considered. We will be covering that late on the second day of the course." Dennis looked around the faces, but there were no questions, so he continued.

"What the entire process is trying to do is ask the following questions:

- What does the customer want?
- What do I have?
- What do I need to make, and when do I need to make it?
- What does it take to make it?
- What do I need to get, and when do I need to get it?

"We often refer to these as 'universal manufacturing questions,' first articulated by the late Oliver Wight. They are the same questions all companies ask, whether they're making automobiles or magazines, supplying patient care in a clinic, or planning a holiday dinner for your family. As you can see, the first question to be answered is always, 'What does the customer want?' That question sets the direction for the entire supply chain and is answered by the forecast from the Demand Planning Manager over the next 18–24 months.

"Each of the three capacity planning processes relies on receiving valid input data to drive the capacity plans. All three rely especially on the accuracy of Work Center and Routing data.

"Since these data are so important to supporting capacity planning and shop scheduling we will start there. We are going to begin with routings. These are the documents that describe the manufacturing process and contain the data necessary for capacity planning. When I was employed at Calber Manufacturing, one of the first things we had to do to get detailed capacity planning operational was to get our routings to accurately reflect what was actually happening on the production floor. How many of you here know how accurate your routings are?" A few people raised their hands.

"When I say 'know,' that means that you have a process in place to actually measure their accuracy." All the hands went down then except the people from Missile Systems. "Well, we have a few, and all from the same company. That is unusual. Normally, no one raises their hands when I ask if it is actually measured."

Brian felt that Dennis was talking right to him. "I wonder how accurate our routings are," he thought.

At the next break, Brian and Joan looked at each other and shook their heads. They knew that what they were hearing made more sense than they had ever imagined. By the third break, they had begun talking to some of the people sitting around them. The vast majority of them were in situations similar to the one at Hayes. They all had lots of problems. There were differences, however, in how they felt about what they were hearing. Some of these people had very positive attitudes and were excited about going back to their companies to begin fixing things. Others, on the other hand, weren't sure things would ever change in their companies. Some felt that the techniques that were explained were nice, but not worth their time and they could see no benefit. Unfortunately, Dan and Mickey fell into this latter category.

Over the next three days Roxanne and Dennis covered capacity management and shop scheduling in excruciating detail. "No pain, no gain," Brian often mused to himself. They explained how to measure and get accurate routing and work center data. They injected enough about Kanbans to provide a good understanding of where and how they could be used effectively. They described how detailed scheduling and capacity planning systems worked and how to manage with them, and then expanded that to how it could be applied to other departments. Once those basics were well understood they went on to explain advanced planning systems and their proper applications. They also explained the concepts of *lean* and *agile* and how they could be applied.

By the end of the course, Brian could see that there were a lot of things that had to be fixed at Hayes besides the routings, but that seemed like the best place to start. The course had also shown him that there were companies that were doing some things right. It gave him hope.

As Brian left he made sure he had his notebook. He knew that he could never remember all that was said over those three days, but the notebook would be a great reference guide. He noticed Joan had her notebook too and, like him, that she had also taken a lot of notes. "Between the two of us we should figure this out," he thought. He doubted that Dan and Mickey would be much help.

After the course, Brian pulled Joan aside. "You know, Joan, this stuff is starting to make a little sense to me. The speaker talked about some of the same things that a buddy of mine in the Midwest told me they were using successfully. Can our computer do capacity requirements planning?"

"Sure. The Enterprise Resource Planning software we bought has that capability," she said.

"Then why don't we use it?" Brian asked what seemed so obvious.

"As far as I can see, because no one has taken the initiative to get it running," Joan said. "I guess, after this, it looks like something we should pursue. It shouldn't be a big problem. Information Systems has asked several times if we want to use it. I've said no, because of a lack of time on my part."

"I think we should get going on it," Brian said, ready to start as soon as he got back to the plant.

"Sounds fine with me," Joan said, "but first we'll have to do something about our data accuracy. You heard what Dennis said. 'Dispatch lists and detailed capacity planning are useless without accurate data.'"

"Yeah, my buddy said the same thing," Brian said. "He also said that the information coming out of Material Requirements Planning needs to be accurate. Let's make a deal. I'll take the responsibility for the routings and scheduling data, and you work on the Material Requirements Planning stuff."

Joan agreed, but added, "You heard what Roxanne had to say about the Integrated Business Management process. It is where we really need to start. That means Resource Requirements Planning. You know we are attempting to do Sales & Operations Planning but it is really me working with the marketing folks. We really need the VPs to get involved in the process, and get Pete Smith, as the General Manager, to lead the process."

Brian shook his head and replied, "Okay, I'll try and work on Ralph, and you work on Pete and your boss. I think Roy will go for it, but getting Pete and Ralph to go along will be a real chore."

Chapter Three

Constructing Routings and Work Centers

The day after the class, back at Hayes, Brian was motivated. He got on the phone with Elliot in Manufacturing Engineering. "I just got back from the course Ralph sent me on and I want to start implementing some of the recommendations. To do it I need to get the routings right. I know you guys are busy. So am I. But how am I supposed to get things under control if the routings are wrong? Elliot, we're not talking about changing the production methods, just correcting the documentation. . . . Well, for instance, on this drive shaft, there's a second turning operation and a deburr missing. . . . I'm telling you, they're not on the routing. . . . They are needed too. We do them every time we run this job. The supervisor must write them in."

"All right, Brian, all right," Elliot responded. "We'll get around to looking at them as soon as we get a chance."

"When will that be?" Brian asked.

"I don't know. Just give me a break," Elliot said as he hung up.

Brian's frustration level was rising. It seemed like such a simple thing. The shop was supposed to follow the steps that were on the routing. However, for that to work, the routings needed to contain every step of the process. That shouldn't be so difficult to get right. Everyone at Hayes agreed that the routing should be accurate, but no one ever did anything but talk about it.

One of the primary messages Brian and the others had received at the course was that accurate routings were a prerequisite to doing a good job of planning capacities and executing schedules. How was he supposed to get the routings correct when everyone seemed to have a different opinion of what was correct? Brian rechecked his notebook from the class. He wanted to be certain he was using the same terms as he had heard.

Dennis Jones from Effective Management had said that the routings were a vehicle for communicating the manufacturing process to the shop floor as well as a foundation for the planning and scheduling processes. He used an example from a fictitious table and chair manufacturing company (see Figure 3.1).

Figure 3.1   Typical Routing

Part Number	Part Description					
173	Leg, Table					
OPN. No.	Dept.	Work Ctr.	Operation Description	Set Up	Run	
			Release			
			Pick			
10	M	01	Saw	0.10	0.01	
20	M	04	Turn	1.00	0.15	
30	S	07	Form Sand	0.50	0.20	
			Store			

Both uses were equally important. He said that the routings needed to contain the following minimum information:

• ITEM NUMBER—identifies the unique item to which this particular routing pertains.

• ITEM DESCRIPTION—the commonly used description of the item. This element makes it easier for the user to know what the item actually is.

• OPERATION NUMBER—identifies the sequence in which the operations are to be performed within an item's routing. The number should not be used to describe the operation in any way. The convention is to use increments of five or ten to allow for easy additions or alternate operations, although this is not a problem with today's modern computers.

- DEPARTMENT—a collection of work centers that is usually combined to reflect the organizational structure. It is often the cost center.
- WORK CENTER—one or more people and/or pieces of equipment that can be considered as one unit for purposes of capacity planning and detail scheduling.
- OPERATION DESCRIPTION—a simple description of the work to be performed. The key word here is *simple*. In some environments, instructions regarding item dimensions, tooling, and operation detail may be included. If this information is lengthy, it is better to place it on a referenced, separate text or specification sheet, rather than include it in the operation description. This will help keep the routing itself simple.
- SETUP TIME—the length of time required to convert a specific piece of equipment or work center from the production of one specific item to the first good piece of the next item.
- RUN TIME—the length of time required to produce one unit of an item at an operation. This information represents what it should take a typical operator to perform the operation under normal circumstances. This is usually expressed in "standard hours" per unit (such as piece, feet, pound, etc.) or in standard hours per 100 or 1,000 units. In some process industries this may be the standard process time for an order, where run time is process dependent, not number of pieces dependent.

Standard hours should always be used on the routings for both setup and run times because it eliminates the variability of item size, process difficulty, operator experience, and other factors. Standard hours are based on machine stroke rate, or process cycle, or may be determined based on industrial engineering where the work is labor paced. The standard hours for a job are calculated from the standard run time multiplied by number of pieces or units required to be processed, plus the set up time for that job. Standard hours are converted to real hours by dividing by "load factor." Load factor takes into account the demonstrated performance of a work center, which allows for variability referred to previously. This way, jobs for items with very different characteristics can be scheduled and capacity planned logically in standard hours, then converted to actual hours afterward, allowing for shift patterns.

Brian compared this information to the routing they used at Hayes (see Figure 3.2) and found it was almost identical.

Figure 3.2   Routing Used at Hayes Tractor Company

Part Number	Part Description					
163726	Hub, Front Wheel					
OPN. No.	Dept.	Work Ctr.	Operation Description	Set Up	Run
			Release		
			Pick		
10	Fab	16	Saw Blank	0.5	.10
20	Mach	24	Turn	3.0	.20
30	Mach	22	Drill	2.0	.10
40	Mach	19	Tap	1.0	.20
			Store		

His next task was to determine how accurate the routings were.

Brian got a random sampling of 20 machine-shop routings printed out from the computer file. He sat down with his supervisors and went over each routing in detail to see if they were correct. The main problems the supervisors found were in the time standards, although they also identified several other areas, including missing operations, unnecessary operations, wrong work-center callouts, and wrong sequences. After the review was finished, they realized that only 12 of the 20 routings were completely correct. Brian quickly calculated that the routing accuracy of this sample was 60%, far from the minimum of 95% that Dennis Jones the course leader from Effective Management had said was necessary for good capacity planning.

Brian knew that he would have trouble convincing Elliot that the routings were this bad. First off, he realized that his sample might not be representative of the entire routing file, and he didn't have time to do this kind of tabletop review for all the routings. Secondly, he knew that Elliot would think the results were biased, because they were based only on manufacturing's opinions of what was correct. And, of course, he knew that Elliot would stand steadfastly behind the standards. It seemed that manufacturing always griped to engineering that the standards were wrong.

There was no question in Brian's mind—the routings needed to be fixed. But how was he going to convince Elliot of that? Brian would have to get an independent audit done.

MEASURING ROUTING ACCURACY

Brian searched through the handouts from the course and found the attendance list. He decided to put in a call to Sue Corey-Smith, the woman who sat next to him from Missile Systems. She had indicated that their routings were in good shape. She had even made a few comments to Brian about the way Missile Systems had conducted their routing audits. Brian figured it might be worth his while to get in touch with her since she had offered to give him a tour of her facility and explain to him what they had done. Brian wasn't so sure that the process of making defense products really had anything in common with the way Hayes did business. Nonetheless, Sue had said that Missile System's average routing accuracy was 99% for the last 6 months. That thought alone was enough to make Brian interested in finding out more. Brian gave her a call and Sue was happy to set up the tour.

Two weeks later, as Sue and Brian sat in her office, she explained that determining routing accuracy began by examining an open order (shop order) on the shop floor and checking to see if the item was actually being made in accordance with the routing. The shop order was then checked against the computer file to make sure there hadn't been a change since the order was released. The operation number, the sequence of operations, and the work center needed to be verified, as well as the identification of any missing or unnecessary operations. The setup and run hours also needed to be verified.

She cautioned Brian not to get caught up in the debate over the accuracy of standard hours. There were times when people believed that standards were too loose or too tight. But the load factor calculation would take out any bias in setting the standards. What was important at the start was relative accuracy—a sense of reasonableness. Of course, standards have to be reliable and sufficiently accurate so that people will believe the schedules and capacity requirements that are based on them.

Sue told him that for the purposes of capacity planning and shop scheduling, standards that are within plus or minus 20% of the actual performance are accurate enough to start with. She explained how the use of a load factor (see Chapter 5) can compensate for the effect of actual-to-standard variance on capacity plans and schedules. In many cases, especially with computer-controlled machines, companies can get as good as plus or minus 5%.

Sue took Brian out onto the factory floor. He was introduced to an auditor from the Accounting group and the supervisor of the area. Sue emphasized that even though Accounting performed the audits, Manufacturing Engineering was still responsible for creating and maintaining routing accuracy. However, it was also Production's responsibility to report any known or suspected inaccuracies. "We just wanted an unbiased group to report the accuracy level as it was actually being performed. The audit is intended to have Accounting report the accuracy level of a statistically sound sample. It is Production's responsibility to identify the problems and Manufacturing Engineering's responsibility to fix them. The audit process makes sure the procedures that have been established to identify and correct routing errors are working. It is up to Manufacturing Engineering and Production to assure the 95% minimum accuracy, not the auditor. The auditor's only job is to verify the accuracy level in much the same way that a bank auditor verifies the accuracy of the bank's records. No matter what, it's still the bank's responsibility to assure its accuracy. The focus of the audit is to find out if the feedback and correction process is working."

Brian followed the auditor as she went through the process of checking the routings. Although Missile System's items, machines, and manufacturing operations were completely different from those at Hayes, Brian could see similarities in the way that the overall manufacturing process could be scheduled and managed. He realized that Hayes could probably learn a great deal from the successes of other companies.

Brian noticed that the auditor was checking only one operation and questioned Sue about it. "It's impractical for the auditor to follow a work order and catch it at every operation. So, we have her verify only that one operation and confirm the previous and next operation. In our company that works because the operators know the processes. If you're in an environment where the operators don't know, you would have to audit the whole routing," Sue told him.

"Dennis Jones, our instructor, said the 95% minimum objective was for the whole routing," Brian said.

"We did some comparisons on that," said Sue. "We found that our operation audit caught a lot more errors than just having someone review the routing from memory. We are doing a random sampling of the operations. By doing these audits monthly using a statistically sound sample, over time the probability of uncovering any errors that exist is quite high. I asked Dennis after the class and he said what we were doing was a good way to do it in our circumstances." Her reasoning made perfect sense to Brian.

Brian questioned the practice of just asking the operator. Sue responded that they are careful about the operators they interview. In case the operator doesn't know the process sufficiently well they make sure the operator is qualified and avoid new operators. The auditor always checks with the supervisor prior to the audit to assure the operators are qualified.

On the way home, Brian thought about who could do the audit at Hayes. He knew Accounting would not be a good choice, because they didn't have the staff to do it. Besides that, they would probably complain that "it's not our job to check your manufacturing documents." He also figured that Elliot in Manufacturing Engineering wouldn't want to cooperate, and if one of his people performed the audit, no one would believe it. "Who else is suffering from these bad routings as much as me?" he wondered. It suddenly dawned on him—Carol Barrow, the manager of Quality Control. Carol was constantly taking the heat for the low quality of the items being produced. Both Carol and Brian were well aware that the real problems were in the manufacturing processes themselves. Getting Quality Control to audit the routings would allow them to focus the proper attention on those real problems.

The next morning, Brian explained the situation to Carol. Even though Carol was hard pressed to spare an inspector even for a few hours a month, she was quick to realize the benefit of what Brian was proposing. This approach would not only help him fix some of his scheduling problems, it would also help her efforts to improve quality.

Brian's initial fear about conducting the audit was whether or not the operators would tell the truth. Sue had told him that Missile Systems had worried about that, too, but found that almost without exception, the operators were all very cooperative. They even devised a form to handle the operator's input. Sue dug one out of a file and Brian stuffed it into his briefcase. "The reality is," she said, "once people understand the need, all you have to do is ask for their help." When Brian eventually did ask his operators, he got plenty of feedback.

Carol and Brian started the audit process the next day. The auditor went into each work center and picked up the routing sheet for the job that each operator was working on. He asked the operator if the operations were performed exactly as specified on the routing. And were the operations done in listed sequence? Did the job come to the work center from the work center listed on the routing? Did it then go to the next work center on the routing when the work was completed? Were there any missing operations? Were the standards reasonable? If the answer to any of the questions was no, the auditor recorded the operation as a "miss." If the answers were all yes, the operation was considered accurate.

When the auditor finished the audit in the work centers, he compared the routing sheets with the routings in the computer file. If the computer file was the same as the routing sheet and no miss was recorded then it was considered good or a "hit." If the operation was recorded as a miss in the floor audit, it remained a miss. If the error had been corrected in the routing file, then the operation was considered accurate. The auditor then calculated the accuracy percentage by dividing the number of accurate operations by the total number of operations that had been audited.

Technically, an accurate routing is one that has no errors at any of its operations. This method of calculating routing accuracy by sampling operations is acceptable. Ultimately, however, the entire routing must be verified before it can be declared accurate.

The results of Carol's first audit were worse than Brian's earlier sample. It indicated 36% accuracy on the routings. However, prior to showing the results to Ralph and Pete, Brian asked Carol to sit on them for a while. He wanted to do a little investigation.

Manufacturing methods had changed over time. Improvements were made, technology changed, new equipment replaced outdated machines, and new tooling was introduced. But the routings had not been kept up to date with those changes.

Brian tracked down Jim, the supervisor of the grinding area, to ask him about one of the erroneous routings. "Listen, Jim," he said, thumbing the audit in his hand, "the auditor indicates here that you're not following the routing on the item #96458 gear shaft."

Jim shook his head from side to side with a smile. "Not for the last three months. We aren't able to get the required finish Manufacturing Engineering says we're supposed to get, so we had to add a grind operation after the lathe operation."

"Since it isn't called out on the routing, how do you remember those kinds of things?" Brian asked.

"Usually, it's not a problem if it's a job that runs frequently. If it's not, the operators try to keep notes. Sometimes when we put a new operator on a job or one of the more experienced operators forgets or there are no notes, we run into some problems. The last time we ran this job, it was originally set up on second shift by a new operator who spent the whole night trying to achieve the required finish level on the lathe. After making lots of scrap, he gave up, even though it was on the hot sheet. When Cecil Nickerson, who has been here at Hayes for 35 years, arrived in the morning, he immediately knew what the problem was, and he simply turned the shafts oversize to leave grind stock, and added a grind operation."

"Did you ever tell anyone that the routing's wrong?"

"We told Manufacturing Engineering several times, but they never got around to fixing it, so we quit trying. Now, we just do what we have to in order to get the items right and write in the operations on the work order."

Brian called Elliot in Manufacturing Engineering and asked him if he would come down and review the problem. Elliot reluctantly agreed.

Elliot asked Cecil, "Can you get that finish on the lathe operation if you're really careful?"

Cecil gave Elliot a disgusted look. "Used to be able to when the machine was new. But now she's worn beyond ever holding that finish requirement."

Elliot relaxed. "Well, there's your problem. It's not my fault. Go talk to Maintenance."

Brian headed down to Maintenance and asked Ivan, the maintenance manager, why the lathe hadn't been fixed.

"It's on the schedule," was Ivan's reply.

Looking over Ivan's shoulder at the schedule, Brian noticed the original request date. "It's been on the schedule for three months," blurted Brian.

Ivan just shrugged his shoulders. "I'm trying to get to it, guy. It's the best I can do."

Brian stomped away frustrated. Everyone was putting the blame someplace else. No one was willing to assume the responsibility for the problem, so it got dropped in his lap. It appeared that the only way he could protect himself at Hayes was to be as good at finger pointing as everyone else.

Brian returned to his office disgruntled and discouraged. How was he going to get the support departments to respond more quickly? He began thinking about Missile Systems and its 99% routing accuracy. Then, he remembered the feedback form that Sue had given him that he had stuffed into his briefcase. He immediately retrieved it. It was a three-part form called "Request for a Bill of Material/Routing Change" (see Figure 3.3).

Figure 3.3   Requesting a Bill of Material/Routing Change

Part #	Operation#	BOM ☐	RTG ☐
Problem:			
Recommended Action:			
Signed		Dept.	Date
Reply:			
Signed		Dept.	Date

Originator's Copy
Reply Copy
Replier's Copy

At the top of the form was a place to state the problem and recommendations for action. There was a place for the originator to sign it, which could be anyone in the company, but was usually a shop supervisor. The bottom third of the form was for the reply. Bill-of-material problems were sent to Design Engineering, and routing problems were sent to Manufacturing Engineering. Each respective group then investigated the requests and the solutions were implemented.

Brian went to Elliot's office and talked to him about using the form. Elliot was less than enthusiastic. Then, Brian showed him the results of the audit done by Carol's inspectors. Elliot almost jumped out of his seat. Both he and Brian knew that Pete would go through the ceiling if he saw those results. Elliot immediately realized Brian was right. Their only salvation would be to install a corrective-action plan as soon as possible. They quickly agreed on some minor changes to the form and Elliot arranged to have it printed right away.

When the new forms were ready, Brian brought his supervisors together and explained how to fill them out. He emphasized that they were to make sure that these forms were filled out whenever there was a problem. "This is how things get better," he promised. Nothing else had worked yet, and they were all ready for a change.

Over the next several days, the supervisors filled out 27 forms, keeping one copy and sending the other two to Manufacturing Engineering. Elliot had alerted his manufacturing engineers to expect the incoming forms.

Late during the third day that the new forms were being used, Elliot brought a stack of requests to Brian. One of them concerned item #96458, the gear shaft that Brian had previously discussed with Elliot. "Look, Brian," Elliot said in his most conciliatory voice, "I'll agree that we should add a grind operation until Maintenance gets the machine fixed. But adding an operation for deburring is ridiculous. There's enough time while the machine is running on automatic cycle for the operator to deburr the item that was just finished."

"It makes sense to me," Brian said. "See how easy I am? All you need to do is add a note on the routing so we'll know we're supposed to do it."

"That's simple enough," Elliot said. Both men smiled at how truly simple things could be when they worked together to resolve their problems. "There's one more thing, though," Elliot said, holding up the stack of forms, "wherever they can, the supervisors can help reduce the number of requests."

"How are they supposed to do that?" Brian asked.

"By taking some of the pressure off the operators. Several of these requests are for relaxing the standards. Instead of berating the operators every time they don't achieve a standard, have the supervisors get to the bottom of the problem. If it really is a problem with the routing, then send us the feedback form and we'll fix it."

"You got some idea how to convince them of that?"

Elliot had already anticipated Brian's question. "The standards are used to do much more than just measure shop-floor performance. They're going to be used to plan the operational priorities, to plan capacity, and to calculate the cost of the tractors. Realistic standards are required if we are going to accomplish that accurately," Elliot said to reemphasize his point.

"So I suppose you expect me to turn them around overnight," Brian said, realizing the enormity of the task. "What about Pete's insistence on productivity improvements?"

"There's no question, Brian," Elliot said fully understanding Brian's dilemma, "you have a big education job ahead of you. The real problem lies with Pete and Ralph. We've got to get them to understand that the standards impact more than just productivity."

In spite of the work ahead, Brian was becoming enthusiastic. For the first time real progress was beginning to happen. He took the material from the class and developed his own material regarding routing accuracy. He tailored it to fit Hayes, but that didn't take a lot of work. He really wanted to emphasize that the accurate routing would help them do a better job of scheduling the work centers and planning capacity. Since he had three shifts and wanted everyone to be together, he scheduled the education session two hours before the end of day shift. The routing-accuracy session went reasonably well. The supervisors pledged their support and help, even though a number of them were still skeptical about the standards.

Slowly, working together as partners on the same team rather than as adversaries, Production and Manufacturing Engineering began establishing rapport. They were also gradually documenting their actual manufacturing processes as well. During the subsequent audits, Carol's auditors asked the operators and supervisors if the routings were correct. If they said no, they were asked if an action request had been turned in. By following this procedure, accountability was established. If the form had been turned in, but the computer file had not been updated, it was Manufacturing Engineering's responsibility. If there were mistakes in the routings and no action request had been written, it was Production's responsibility.

The results of the first audit showed 78% of the misses had not been reported by Production. When Brian saw the results, he called his people together on each of the three shifts and explained the situation. He let it be known how unhappy he was that they had been complaining about the routings being inaccurate, but then, when they had been given the chance to fix the problem, they hadn't responded. "What are we?" Brian asked, challenging each of them with his disappointment. "Are we a bunch of cry babies or are we people who can get things done around here?" Brian must have hit home, because afterward, the machine-shop people started identifying problems and sending the reports into Manufacturing Engineering in floods. Elliot appealed to Brian for help. Working as a team, the supervisors and some of the lead operators came in on several Saturdays to assist the manufacturing engineers.

One of Brian's supervisors suggested that Brian should post the results of the audits on a big board right by the time clock so everyone could see the results. Another of the supervisors commented that if they were going to do that, it needed to be kept up to date. Everyone agreed that it was a good idea, and Brian committed to an updated board.

When Brian and Elliot showed the results of the first audit to Pete, he reacted just as they had expected. The heat was turned up red-hot. Fortunately, their plan for solving the problem calmed him down.

As things improved, Pete was heard to be bragging to some of the other Hayes plants about their routing accuracy. "It would never have happened without the Effective Management course and that visit with Sue at Missile Systems," Brian thought.

Now, whenever Production calls Manufacturing Engineering, they come right down and look at the problem in process and take care of it immediately. The 99% routing accuracy that Sue had talked about was gradually becoming a reality at Hayes, because if anything was wrong, both sides were communicating, and both sides were feeding back the information necessary to make the process work. They all realized that if the feedback/fix-it process was working properly, they should find no errors, because as fast as the factory found the problem, Manufacturing Engineering would fix it. They agreed that the ultimate goal was 100%, and everyone agreed not to slack off when they reached the 95% minimum threshold.

Having recognized the need for data accuracy and seen how the routing-data-accuracy effort had rallied his staff together, Pete started making the reporting of data accuracy a regular part of his monthly performance review meeting.

ALTERNATE ROUTINGS

Brian knew that there are times when the specified routing cannot be followed. The desired machine may be overloaded or broken down. The tooling may be damaged or in use on another job. At times like these, an alternate process often can be used. Rather than change the master routing, however, which would reroute all future jobs to the alternate process, he felt that a second routing option should be provided for anytime a situation occurs that requires an option method of manufacturing. The order could be switched for that order only.

One of Brian's supervisors approached him about a job that was scheduled to run on the multi-spindle drills the next week (see Figure 3.4).

Figure 3.4   Original/Prime Routing for Part #568321

Part Number	Part Description					
568321	Bracket					
OPN. No.	Dept.	Work Ctr.	Operation Description	Set Up	Run
			Release		
			Pick		
10	Fab	57	Weld	0.1	2.00
20	Mach	36	Mill	1.0	0.50
30	Mach	22	Drill, Multi-Spindle	1.5	0.02
			Store		

The supervisor told Brian that the drills were already overloaded with past-due work, and it was unlikely that this job would get done on schedule. Brian decided to run the job on the single-spindle drills, even though he knew it would take longer and increase the cost. He then needed to get the routing to reflect this. In the past, Brian would have just told the supervisor to go ahead, and he would not have worried about changing the routing. Now, however, Brian wanted the routing in the shop to represent what the work centers were really expected to do. So, he went to Tony, the shop scheduler, and asked him to delete the multi-spindle operation from the routing on the released order only and replace it with the single-spindle operation. Tony immediately updated the routing, using operation add-and-delete transactions (see Figure 3.5).

Figure 3.5   Alternate Routing for Part #568321

Part Number	Part Description					
568321	Bracket					
OPN. No.	Dept.	Work Ctr.	Operation Description	Set Up	Run
			Release		
			Pick		
10	Fab	57	Weld	0.1	2.00
20	Mach	36	Mill	1.0	0.05
30	Mach	21	Drill, Single-Spindle	1.0	0.06
			Store		

The software being used at Hayes had the capability of storing multiple routings for each item. Although Hayes had not been utilizing this feature, Brian recognized that he could put the primary routings into the file and also load in some commonly used alternates (see Figure 3.6). Whenever a problem was realized, Production Control could select which routing path they wanted to use based on the circumstances at the time with the approval of Production. That way, orders would be routed the way the shop was really planning to run them, and Brian could hold his people accountable for following the routing.

Figure 3.6   Master Routing for Part #568321

Part Number	Part Description					
568321	Bracket					
OPN. No.	Dept.	Work Ctr.	Operation Description	Set Up	Run
			Release		
			Pick		
10	Fab	57	Weld	0.1	2.00
20	Mach	36	Mill	1.0	0.05
30	Mach	22	Drill, Multi-Spindle	1.5	0.02
30A	Mach	21	Drill, Single-Spindle	1.0	0.06
			Store		

REWORK ROUTING

There are times when rework is required. If it's not going to be done immediately, rework should be handled on a work order so that it will get onto the schedules and the capacity plans. In this situation, a standard rework routing or a customized rework routing will be necessary for the proper rework steps to be scheduled and communicated. A rework routing can be created in one of two ways. The rework operations can be added to the existing routing (see Figure 3.7) if the portion of the job that is to be reworked is intended to be done immediately and follow the rest of the job through the remaining manufacturing steps. The second option is to split the rework pieces away from the original order and issue a new order. This allows the original job to proceed through the manufacturing process. The items that need to be reworked can then be rescheduled by the material planner to a new need date (see Figure 3.8). Both choices allow the additional capacity requirements to be generated and the rework to be scheduled. Rework routings can be stored as an alternate routing and selected as needed.

Figure 3.7   Routing for Rework Operations Included for Part #373904

Part Number	Part Description					
373904	Plate, Adapter					
OPN. No.	Dept.	Work Ctr.	Operation Description	Set Up	Run
			Release		
			Pick		
10	Fab	16	Saw	0.5	.01
20	Mach	36	Mill	2.0	.03
30	Mach	19	Drill	1.0	.02
40	Mach	19	Tap	0.5	.02
50	Fab	54	Plug	0.1	.01
60	Mach	19	Re-Drill	1.0	.02
70	Mach	21	Re-Tap	0.5	.02
			Store		

Figure 3.8   Separate Rework Routing for Part #373904

Part Number	Part Description					
373904	Plate, Adapter					
OPN. No.	Dept.	Work Ctr.	Operation Description	Set Up	Run
			Release		
			Pick		
10	Fab	54	Plug	0.1	.01
20	Mach	19	Drill	1.0	.02
30	Mach	21	Tap	0.5	.02
			Store		

WORK-CENTER IDENTIFICATION

The machine shop at Hayes was making great progress toward increasing the accuracy of its routings. One area that had not been considered was the impact that work-center identification would have on capacity planning. Unfortunately for Brian and Elliot's people, they did not uncover the work-center identification problem until they had already started to do capacity planning (see Chapter 5). The mistake was that the initial assignment of work centers was made without understanding all the reasons for work centers to be on the routing.

There are four basic reasons:

1. To direct the work to the proper place.
2. To allow appropriate cost calculation.
3. To specify sequence and timing in the work-center schedule.
4. To generate capacity requirements for the appropriate resource, whether it is people or machines.

A work center is the smallest unit for which we want to plan and measure capacity. Each machine, workstation, or person can be established as a work center, but this is usually an unnecessary level of detail. It can result in voluminous data and reports.

When establishing work centers, there are several considerations that must be taken into account. All of the workstations assigned to a work center must, in general, be interchangeable; that is, able to process any work that comes to the work center. A work center can be composed of one of the following:

1. A machine or a group of machines that perform similar operations

When specifying a group of machines as a work center, it must be determined if: (a) most of the work directed to the work center can be performed on any of the machines included in the work center group, and (b) the work center contains the necessary capabilities to do the work as defined on the routing. It is acceptable if a small percentage of the work must be done only on one specific machine in the group.

For example, turning machines and grinding machines should be in separate work centers because they do entirely different operations, unless they are grouped together in a manufacturing cell, which will be discussed later in Chapter 10. It is less obvious, however, that single-spindle turning machines should be separated from multi-spindle turning machines, or that machines that accommodate various work-piece sizes should be separated. Other considerations might include different output rates, capacities, colors, or materials. Again, the key issue is interchangeability.

2. A person or group of people who performs similar tasks

Manual operations, such as assembly, inspection, and packaging, can be grouped into work centers based on the interchangeability of the skills, where most people assigned to the work center can perform most of the work scheduled for it. Also, if the people in a group are cross-trained on the various steps of the work to be performed, a single work center is appropriate.

3. A group of machines or people who perform a sequence of operations

The tractor assembly line at Hayes fits this criterion, with different operations performed along the line in a prescribed sequence. On Hayes's transmission-case machining (see Figure 3.9), various stations perform their operations simultaneously. The transmission cases move on a conveyor from the milling station to the boring station and on to the drill and tapping station. As one case is being milled, another is being bored, and another is being drilled and tapped.

Brian recalled a conversation he had with an engineer from Castlebend Ceramics, a company that made china. The engineer described a work center that consisted of four different operations linked together in a continuous process (see Figure 3.10). A ribbon of glass was produced by the melting furnace, fed into a press where plates were formed, and passed to a shear where the plates were trimmed to a clean edge. They then went to an annealing furnace, which hardened the glass. Castlebend had arranged all four of these pieces of equipment into a single work center.

Figure 3.9   Transmission Case Machine Line

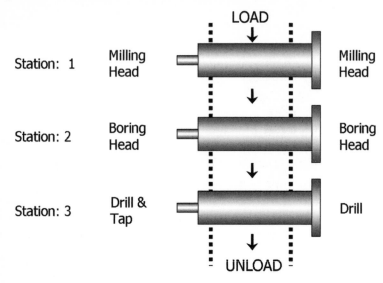

These three examples are called *flow lines* because the product always moves down the line in the same way, one piece at a time, in a continuous flow. None of these situations requires a detailed routing to identify the capacity or priority at any individual operation. From a priority standpoint, whatever starts at the first step determines the priority at the rest of the steps. The capacity of the line is determined by the slowest step. Plan the capacity of the bottleneck, and the capacity of the entire line has been planned. Schedule the starting or gateway operation, and all other steps on the line will be scheduled appropriately.

Automated flow lines are not the only cases where a group of dissimilar machines can be called a work center. Any grouping of machines or people, however large or small, can be considered a work center. These are often called manufacturing cells and should be considered as one work center, as long as the flow of work always follows the same path inside the cell for an established group of similar products. Individual operations are not performed within the cell on other products.

There are situations in some companies where operators are capable of running several different kinds of machines—for example,

Figure 3.10   Manufacturing China Plates at Castlebend Ceramics Company

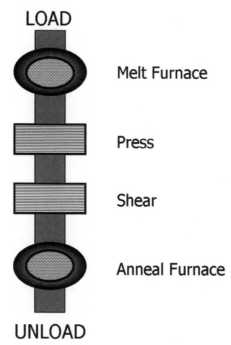

surface grinders, OD grinders, and centerless grinders—or several packaging lines manned by a single crew. When the equipment has been placed in a work center based on its capability, the planning of the capacity for the group of operators can be done by setting up a separate resource center for the operators and aggregating the capacity requirements for the individual machine work centers into that resource center. This requires a software feature that provides for the assignment of work centers to resource centers and the capability to aggregate the capacity requirements. This issue will be discussed in more detail in Chapter 5.

Mickey's assembly line is, in reality, a cell, even though at this time he doesn't realize it. Brian will also discover that cells can be set up in other areas relatively easily.

Brian considered making every machine a work center. When he added up the number of machines, he realized that to do so would create more than 150 work centers. Recalling what Dennis Jones had said at the course, Brian knew that meant he would have 150 capacity plans and dispatch lists to deal with—one for each machine. It didn't take much for him to figure out that trying to deal with that many capacity plans and dispatch lists would be a nightmare. Brian also knew that a lot of his work could be done on any of several similar machines; that is, the machines were interchangeable. He really needed to know the total capacity requirements and priorities on that group of machines.

The first problem regarding work centers in the machine shop appeared in the turning operation. Manufacturing Engineering had assigned two different sizes of lathes to the same work center. Two of the machines could perform work on bar stock up to two inches in diameter, and the third could perform work up to a three-inch diameter. It was possible to lump the capacity of the three machines together, as long as no more than one-third of the work was over two inches in diameter and their total capacity wasn't exceeded.

Trouble started when a mix change occurred and the amount of work over two inches in diameter exceeded the capacity of the larger machine. At that point, the three-inch machine became so overloaded that the work center fell behind schedule, even though the total workload on the work center had not changed. It became evident that something had to be changed. The solution was to set up the two-inch machines as one work center and the three-inch machine as a separate work center. This gave Brian the advantage of grouping the two-inch machines together, and, at the same time, provided him with visibility of the requirements for the larger machine alone. That way he could see the capacity constraint coming, and either have the work released early when capacity was available or subcontract it.

Dan ran into a similar situation with a group of four-punch presses. The newer presses in the group were capable of producing at nearly twice the rate as the two older models. The newer models were obviously the preferred machines, and most of the production, when possible, was directed through them. Manufacturing Engineering had set the standard times based on the capability of the new machines.

Unrealistic information immediately surfaced. The capacity planning system used the higher machine output rate, and showed that plenty of capacity was available. Unfortunately, when the new presses were completely loaded and the old presses had to be used, they could not produce at the scheduled rate. It didn't take long for Dan to realize that if he planned his labor to the scheduled rate, he would quickly fall behind schedule, even though the Manufacturing Engineering standard indicated everything was all right. This was the perfect excuse for Dan to blame the computer system when in fact it was the data—the improper grouping of work centers—that created the problem.

Once Elliot started digging around in the details of Dan's problem, the solution was clear. "I think we'd better subdivide these machines based on their output rates," Elliot told Dan. The new presses would comprise one work center, and the two older presses would be set up in another. Once this was done, Elliot's people saw that the new presses were overloaded. This meant they needed to reroute some of the work from the faster new machines to the slower ones. The work orders to be scheduled on the older presses would have their routings changed to reflect the slower process. Everyone recognized that the production costs would be higher on the slower machines, and running jobs there was not what they preferred to do, but it was what was happening anyway. The new grouping of machines now reflected reality.

In properly identifying and defining the work centers, the machine's capabilities have to be considered. In Brian's case, this meant that, because of the mix, the two- and three-inch lathes had to be separated. The output rate of the machines in a work center also must be considered. In Dan's case, by separating the new presses from the old and setting the time standard based on their new capabilities, we can see capacity constraints better.

A final factor in the assigning of work centers is the issue of supervisory control. If two supervisors each had the same types of machines, those two still may not be combined into one work center. For example, a prototype shop may have an identical piece of equipment as a production area. Although they pass the test of "identical capability," they must be assigned different work centers. The reason is accountability. When two supervisors try to manage one work center, neither is accountable.

In a multiple-shift situation where different supervisors manage different shifts, the accountability for the work center needs to be accepted at the next level up in the organization. This can present a problem in large companies where you must go up several levels in the organization before you find single accountability for all shifts. If you have to go too high in the organization, the person will not take the time to review the capacity plans for each work center every week. This was not a problem at Hayes because Mickey, Dan, and Brian had responsibility for the three shifts.

In the machine shop at Hayes, the morale started to improve. First, Manufacturing Engineering was responding to the problems on the routings. Second, the production people were reporting any discrepancies in the routings, and they were also building a great deal of confidence in their accuracy. There were fewer delays because the routings reflected what really had to be done, and no work had to be sent back. It was becoming clear to everyone on the production floor why accurate data were so important, and they knew they had taken a big step forward. They realized that the reliability of their planning and scheduling information was only as good as the data upon which it was based.

Brian was pleasantly surprised when Sharon Levy, the Controller, complimented him on the work he had done to clean up the routings. She explained that the Accounting department had always been concerned about how the routings were structured because they used that information to calculate product standard costs by "rolling up" the cost of each operation into the total cost. The roll-up process consisted of Finance applying the labor and overhead rates for each work center to the setup and run times on the routings. If there were missing or unnecessary operations on the routings, or if the setup and run times were wrong, then the standard cost calculations would be wrong. And since different work centers had different labor and overhead rates, if the work-center assignments were incorrect, the cost data would also be wrong. Sharon also pointed out to Brian that, since he was changing the routings on open work orders whenever a change in the process was necessary or rework had to be done, then the actual costs were also more accurate. She wanted Brian to know how excited her department was about the clean-up effort Brian was implementing because they knew that their cost data would now be a lot more accurate.

With accurate routings, the door was also open for Brian to take the next step into operation scheduling. It would be at this point that he would begin to gain control. Finally, he would be able to correctly establish what was expected from his department, so that he could produce what was really needed next.

Chapter Four

Mastering Dispatching and Scheduling

The factory was never really quiet, but there were times when it was at least calm. At 6:00 A.M., toward the end of third shift and an hour before the first shift started, Brian liked to walk through the nearly deserted machine shop. He wasn't always looking for something specific, just getting a feel for the shop and for the day ahead. It was as if he hoped that somewhere, hidden in the smell of that distinct machine-oiled air, a magical solution had been found that would straighten out the problems in his factory.

The answer, of course, was neither in the air nor in some miracle. It was, however, already present in his factory. As Brian was slowly discovering, his solution lay in understanding the basic elements of running a production area, learning what management tools were available, and then using those tools to manage his operations better.

He'd walk into his office after one of these moments in the shop and the reality would come rushing back. The number of emails was staggering. It wasn't just the emails but what was attached to them—an insurmountable number of reports. There was a time in the not-too-distant past when the majority of the information in those reports was simply wrong. Prior to improving the accuracy of the routings, data integrity had been a joke.

Brian recalled a typical recurring situation. A call would come in from a customer who wanted a tractor delivered in four weeks when the normal lead time was 10 weeks. Sales and the customer would compromise on a six-week delivery date. After the tractor assembly order was jammed into the Master Schedule, the parts orders would be sent out by the material planner onto the shop floor. No one was really sure if the shop could deliver the product in six weeks or not, but everyone knew that all the stops would be pulled out in an attempt to do so. The complaints from the shop about orders already being late when they finally got them were generally ignored. If the shop could do it in six weeks, everyone looked good. That often meant either working overtime or pushing other work aside. Brian and his colleagues were just expected to "work around or through the problems," and "do the best you can."

COMMUNICATING PRIORITIES

The role of the shop schedule is to provide information for the short-term control (a few days to a few weeks) of shop operations. It communicates the priorities required to convert the planned Master Schedule into deliverable product. Priority is the position a production order should take in the queue (waiting line). Priority in and of itself does not imply that an order should necessarily be expedited, but merely in what sequence the orders are needed to support the Master Schedule.

Hayes used the due dates assigned to the work orders to establish priorities in the shop. The order due dates were assigned by the material planners to coincide with the need dates calculated by the Material Requirements Planning system. These dates were then used by the scheduling system to establish due dates for each of the manufacturing operations. The trouble was that most of the shop orders were either already past due or had been released with less than the full planned lead time available. Consequently, many of the operations were also past due. In many cases, the order due dates did not reflect when the jobs were really needed. Of course, the past-due dates were particularly meaningless. Since nobody knew when the work was really supposed to be done, the shop would prioritize the work from their hot list.

One of the groups of parts for which Brian was responsible was the gears. The process to produce a gear began with Dan's Fabrication department sawing 20-foot steel bars in half so they would fit in Brian's bar lathes. The 10-foot bars would then be sent to Brian's machine shop. Since most of the scheduled dates were past due, Dan would decide the priority on the saws based on the Assembly hot list. If a part didn't appear on the hot list, Dan wouldn't saw the bars until he had some open time, which was when nothing on the hot list was waiting for the saws.

Since Brian's scheduled operation dates were also meaningless, Brian didn't know which orders he should be working on first. By the time Dan moved the sawed bars to Brian, the job was often more than 30 days into the total 60-day planned lead time for the gears, with the result that it was nearly impossible for Brian to complete the job by the time it was needed in Assembly. Then, it wouldn't be too long before those gears showed up on the hot list, and the machine shop would have to jump through hoops to get them done. The fact that Dan had consumed 30 days instead of the 2 days allocated in the schedule was now irrelevant.

Without having valid schedules for operations in his department, Dan had only the order due date (to stock or availability) to go by. Jobs that were not past due or near their due date didn't get much attention. Since all jobs don't have the same lead times, the same routings, or go through the same processes, the order due date alone doesn't prioritize the early operations. To really know what to work on, the supervisor needs to see the *priorities by operation*.

Brian remembered the advice given by Dennis Jones and Roxanne Barnes at the Effective Management course that, if he was ever to get his jobs from Dan in time to complete them on their scheduled due date, Dan needed a valid schedule that told him when he should have *his* operations completed. Brian also realized that a valid schedule by operation would be a great help to him in his own shop to help settle the conflicts over priorities with his own supervisors.

As he was going home one night, Brian drove by the airport. He had always loved watching the airplanes as they lifted off—the power thrust, the coordination of so many complex systems that seemed to defy all earthly boundaries. As a large commercial airliner cruised in for its landing, Brian wondered how in the world airline manufacturers ever scheduled parts for something as complicated as an airplane. Then he remembered John Hall, the general supervisor from Precision Air Components whom he had met at the course.

The next morning he pulled out the course attendance list and gave John a call. John told him he would be pleased to show Brian and some of his colleagues around Precision Air, provided Brian would return the favor and show him around Hayes at some later date.

Brian immediately contacted Joan to see if she wanted to go. She thought it was a great idea. They also agreed it would probably be worthwhile to take Tony, the machine-shop expeditor.

When they arrived at Precision Air, John took the three of them out onto the shop floor to show them how Precision's scheduling system worked. They walked to the closest work center, where John showed them a screen, which he called a Dispatch List. Brian noticed that it looked similar to the schedule he had seen in the expeditor's office earlier at Hayes in paper form and what Dennis Jones described in the course.

"Does this thing really work for you?" asked Brian.

"Sure," John said, "once we got the routings cleaned up and the Material Requirements Planning due dates correct."

Brian looked at the operation due dates and the order due dates. There were a few jobs behind schedule, but, by and large, they were in good shape. He looked over to Tony and pointed to the screen. "This looks pretty similar to our shop schedule, doesn't it?"

Tony shrugged, "Yeah, except for one thing. They obviously have dates the supervisors believe in."

Brian turned to Joan. "How are you doing in fixing the Material Requirements Planning data? Are our order due dates reliable?"

"For the most part, but I'm not so certain about operation dates," Joan said. "And I'm not sure how overloaded we are, but then neither is anyone else. There also could be some jobs in there that aren't needed when they are scheduled. But unless someone can help identify them, the material planner probably wouldn't catch it. Accurate dates can only be calculated by Material Requirements Planning if it has accurate data to begin with. We just haven't been able to ferret out all the problems yet. And there are a lot of them. However, we are making progress on bill-of-material accuracy and inventory accuracy. We certainly are not where we need to be yet, but since the Effective Management course we attended, we have gotten some of our stockroom supervisors off to a course on inventory accuracy and they have come back with good ideas that they are applying."

"Good for you," John interjected. "We sent people to that course also and got good results. How about your Routings?"

Brian smiled. "We're starting to get that under control," he said.

"Well, I'll tell you," John said, "the most difficult thing about a Dispatch List is getting people to use it and not rely on the hot list. I found that the only way to do that was to return to the basics and teach all the supervisors and operators how the whole scheduling system works. It was only after that that they really started using it."

Brian once again turned to Joan. "Now that the routing education is done, do you think you can put together that kind of program at Hayes and teach everyone?" he asked.

"Sure," said Joan.

"Hold on a second here," John jumped in. "That won't work unless you lead the training sessions in your department yourself, Brian. The words and actions have to come from you."

"Why's that? Joan knows more about this stuff than I do, and she's more capable of teaching it than I am," Brian said.

John shook his head. "We tried having the education and training department come out and teach everyone about how the Dispatch List works. Our problem was that the area manager and his area supervisors gave it lip service. Whenever there was an emergency, they reverted back to their old ways. It was the same old behavior. It wasn't until they really understood how the system worked that they took ownership of it. And only then did the shop people buy into the new system and start following the schedules. Let me tell you, having to teach it to others forces you to understand it yourself. It also sends a clear message to the troops when the boss says it. The second time around, when we used this 'boss-teaches' method, we got the behavioral change we were looking for."

"I guess that makes sense," Brian responded. "It worked really well for routing accuracy. There's something I've been meaning to ask," said Brian. "If you're doing things as well as it appears, why did you bother going to the course?"

John smiled. "Two reasons. First, we haven't gotten capacity planning working as well as we would like, so we thought we might pick up some pointers. Things may look good around here right now, but if we get any sizable change in business, we could end up right back where we were. Then, we would have to work our butts off to get back on schedule. The second reason we went was to find out how to schedule those work centers where there are capacity constraints. We don't have the luxury of overtime or adding people in some work centers. What about you?" John asked. "Are you doing any capacity planning?"

"We've got the software," Brian said, "but we can't get the numbers to come out right. The truth is we really haven't had the time to look into it seriously until now."

As Brian, Joan, and Tony drove home, they discussed the strategy that would be necessary to accomplish the education process that John had recommended.

"We have the training materials from the Effective Management course already," Joan said, "but I need some help to put them all together. If I could use Tony for a couple of weeks, we could probably pull it off."

"You have to be kidding," Brian replied. "I'd never survive without him out in my area."

"Hey, Brian," Tony piped up from the backseat, "you remember that 4-week vacation I asked for and you said 'No problem'? Well, maybe you and Joan should start training my replacement now. I don't want you not letting me have that time off."

"You have someone in mind?" Brian asked.

"How about one of our shop supervisors?" Tony suggested. "You can replace him with one of the team leaders. After all, Brian, you should be training them anyway."

As Brian was about to agree, Joan jumped in. "You may have to help me convince Roy. He's undoubtedly going to be reluctant to let me work on this full time for two weeks."

"Wonderful," Brian thought. "Wait until Ralph hears about this—he'll be furious." Brian knew, however, that he was going to have to step up to this issue sometime. He remembered something he had heard at a supervisor's training course: "Great leaders provide a vision and then move the obstacles so the task can be accomplished." Now he understood why great leaders were so hard to come by. He knew he was up against some real obstacles.

As they pulled into the Hayes parking lot, they put the final touches on their plan. Brian waited until after the shortage meeting the next morning to talk to Ralph. His timing couldn't have been better. Not only did Brian have fewer shortages than anyone else, but Ralph was in a hurry to catch a plane to Hayes's Midwest plant and was only half-listening to Brian's plan. Without giving it a second thought, he gave Brian his okay.

Later that same day, Brian sent Larry, one of his second-shift shop supervisors, to assist Tony. After a few days, Larry was handling the scheduling routines with only minor guidance from Tony. This allowed Joan and Tony to begin putting together Hayes's education and training sessions. In two weeks, they were able to complete the training material. During that time, Brian had spent his evenings going over what they had developed, so that he and Joan could start the process of teaching the supervisors and expeditors at once.

SHOP SCHEDULING

The educational material Joan and Tony tailored from the Effective Management course began with an explanation of shop scheduling. In the notes for the slides they wrote:

> *The way to determine shop priority is to employ an operation-scheduling system. The objective of operation scheduling is to communicate to the shop what jobs they should be working on and when those operations should be completed in order to meet the demands from Material Requirements Planning and, in turn, the Master Schedule. A prerequisite for shop scheduling is a valid—accurate and attainable—Master Schedule. An invalid Master Schedule will result in invalid Material Requirements Planning. Invalid Material Requirements Planning will then result in shop schedules that are unattainable. It is simply not possible to hold a shop supervisor accountable for meeting schedules under these circumstances.*

The training material went on to explain that operation scheduling establishes start and completion dates for each operation necessary to meet the material plans and provides a foundation to control the progress of work. The method by which the schedules are calculated is a process called backward scheduling. In this process, start and finish dates for each operation are calculated by offsetting activities backward from the order due date to arrive at the initial order release date.

The start date of an order that has been planned by Material Requirements Planning (MRP) is determined by offsetting the total lead time from the MRP Item Master File. This is not necessarily the same number as the lead time obtained by the backward scheduling process. The MRP lead time is a fixed number, often based on average order quantity, whereas the backward scheduled lead time is calculated from the specific order, its routing, and work-center data. In reviewing the training material, Brian thought that a major effort would be required to get the lead-time data right. Whenever the parts weren't delivered to the stockroom on time, the prevailing reason given was that there wasn't enough time provided to do the job. The typical response was to increase the lead time.

THE LEAD-TIME LOOP

Brian remembered an encounter that Dan had had earlier with Joan over lead times.

"I obviously don't have enough time to complete my jobs," Dan said, "because they're always late." This had become a continuing gripe of his at the morning meeting. "I need more lead time," he complained. He became relentless in his pursuit of this issue. His arguments with Joan continued for several weeks before she went against her better judgment and finally gave in.

"I'll add a week to the lead times on all your parts," Joan told him.

One reason Joan had been reluctant to increase the lead times was because, if she moved the components out one week, the parents in the bill of material would also have to be moved out a week. Ultimately that would end up at customer orders, and she didn't want to move all of the customer orders out a week. Dan understood that. It was agreed that Joan would increase Dan's lead times by one week, but the order due dates would remain the same. Unfortunately, because of the system's backward scheduling process, when Joan put that added week into the computer, all the orders that were scheduled to be released were now scheduled to be released a week earlier. All of the planned orders in Material Requirements Planning were impacted—their recommended start dates were all moved one-week earlier than before.

Suddenly, a week's worth of work had become past due in respect to its start date, plus there was a new week's worth of work scheduled to be released. Increasing the lead time by a week caused the release of two-weeks' worth of work in the next week's release cycle. When the two-weeks' worth of work hit the shop floor, the situation became even more confused.

At the next shortage meeting, Dan said, "My schedule is even worse than it was. Work is backing up, and I'm going to have to add more capacity if it doesn't improve soon. I'm now working at maximum overtime in most of my work centers. I tell you, Joan, I need more lead time."

Joan tried to explain that the week that she had added was compounding the problem, but Dan wouldn't buy it. Joan gave in and added another week to the lead time. Again, two-weeks' worth of work went out and again things got worse on the floor.

After the third lead-time increase, when Dan once again pleaded for more time, Joan smiled and, without any further argument, said, "Sure, Dan, I'll fix it."

Joan knew that continuing to increase the lead times would only make things worse. So, without telling Dan, she went into the database and deleted 1 week of the additional weeks of lead time. Consequently, all the start dates for the orders planned to be released that week were scheduled out a week, so there were no new orders to be released. Since no new work was released, the jobs already at the work centers got all the attention. They began to catch up to the schedule and the number of shortages went down. The following Monday, Dan came into the shortage meeting smiling. "You know, Joan," he said, "I think we're finally onto it here. I think we hit the magic point. Maybe what we should do is add another week."

Joan, still not letting on that she had decreased the lead time instead of increasing it, said, "Sure, Dan, I'll take care of it."

For the next two weeks the charade continued. Since only small amounts of work were being released, the load level was dropping rapidly. With the increased lead time the load had been growing, and Dan had been working maximum overtime to catch up. With Joan reducing the lead times, so reducing the short-term load on resources, Dan started to catch up on his late jobs. After Joan had cut out all the extra lead time she had added, she kept on cutting it until the total lead time was two weeks less than it had been originally. She knew that, through the years, Dan had been padding his lead times. She also knew that by taking out the additional two weeks, she had reached the point where most of Dan's unnecessary padding had been removed. Had she tried to subtract more, Dan really might not have enough time to do the jobs. From this point on, Joan understood that any further reduction should continue one day at a time, and only because they had actually done something in the factory to reduce the lead time. At some point she needed Dan's approval. The question was how to let him know what she had already done.

Sometimes, patience has its own rewards. The next morning in the shortage meeting, Dan said, "Joan, I have to tell you things are running great. We have fewer late jobs than we have ever had before, and since we are getting close to schedule I'm going to try and maintain it. That extra lead time really did the trick."

Joan broke the news. "Dan, it's not quite what you think." After Joan had explained what she had done, there was dead silence. Ralph could see that Dan was about to explode, and so he spoke before Dan could say anything. "Dan, don't knock it if it works, and you just said things were getting better."

"It was the only way I could get you to understand," Joan said. "The issue isn't lead times, Dan; it's whether or not you have the capacity to do the job. And you can't solve a capacity problem by increasing the lead time. Increasing the lead time simply increases the backlog of work."

One way to explain this is to use an analogy of a hose. Compare the planned lead time to a garden hose. If there's water (work) running through the hose, it doesn't make any difference how long the hose is, no more water is going to come out the end of the hose. Only a certain amount of water can flow out at any one time. To get more water to go through, the hose diameter has to be made bigger, not longer.

Does that mean the shorter the hose, the better? The answer is yes, if adequate time is given for the work to get done. Making the hose too long causes the water (work) to be released earlier than is necessary. With constantly changing priorities, the wrong jobs are often worked on first, thus consuming capacity that should have been used on another job with a higher need. Also, if engineering or customer changes are made when there are long lead times, scrap or rework may result. Long lead times confuse the issue of whether there is a priority problem or a capacity problem.

It was this encounter that made it clear to Brian and Dan how important it was to have realistic lead times. Joan and Tony explained in the training material that the best way to accomplish this is to take the total lead time for each part number and break it down into the individual operations that were performed by a work center. The lead time needs to include the functions of releasing the order to manufacturing, picking the required components from the stock-room, and storing the product in the stockroom when the order is complete. The time for each operation should be divided into queue, setup, run, and move times (see Figure 4.1).

Figure 4.1   Routing Lead-Time Elements

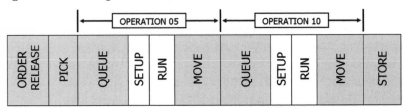

These elements could all be added together to calculate the total lead time for that part number. Since these calculations were based on the data in the production routings, they emphasized in the course why it was so important to have routing accuracy.

ACTUAL LEAD TIME

Tony and Joan's description of actual lead time was the amount of time taken from order release until a specific job was completed and arrived in the stockroom. This was fairly straightforward. However, when they went on to say that the actual lead time on the same part number might vary significantly from one order to the next because of many factors, particularly priority, Brian was puzzled.

Then he thought about when Pete, the General Manager, was pushing a product through the shop. Pete's particular order might take only 5 days to complete, even though the scheduled lead time on that same part might take 25 days. Brian had to laugh when he thought about how an order might stay open forever if it was never expedited.

PLANNED LEAD TIME

Another subject that Tony and Joan outlined for their training course dealt with planned lead times. They defined planned lead time as the elapsed time *expected* to get a production run from order release through to order completion, including all of the anticipated elements of production. In Figure 4.2, there are two operations.

Figure 4.2   Routing & Planning Lead Time

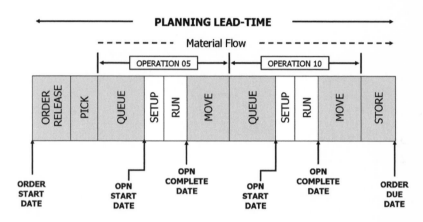

The planned lead time is calculated by starting with the amount of time it takes for the order-release process. Then, the standard pick time is added. Next, the standard queue time, the standard setup time, and the standard run time for the first operation are added. Then, the standard move time to the second operation is added. Following that, there is queue time, setup time, and run time for the second operation. Finally, the move time to the stockroom and the time required to put the parts away are included. The result is the Total Planned Lead Time.

At Hayes, Dan never knew what the real priorities were among the jobs on the floor. It seemed to him that he was always being pushed to complete a job in less than the normal amount of lead time planned for the job. In an effort to assure that he had enough lead time to do a job, Dan had wanted to pad his planned lead time. As Dan learned, this didn't solve the problem, but made it worse. Joan had discovered the right solution: minimize the amount of work-in-process, communicate valid priorities, and work to the schedules.

There are two aspects to valid schedules. First, a valid schedule should reflect what is really needed to support the Master Schedule. Secondly, a valid schedule needs to be one that can actually be met. If the schedule reflects the need, but can't be executed, it is invalid. Conversely, if the schedule reflects something that can be done, but is not needed, it is also invalid.

To maintain valid schedules for production operations, the Master Schedule must be relatively stable. If the Master Schedule is continually changing, the priorities in the factory, and at the suppliers, also will be continually changing. When a Master Schedule change is considered, the question must be asked: "What will making a change to the Master Schedule cost in terms of working overtime, finding alternate operations, inefficiencies, and increased purchasing problems?" A Master Schedule that is not a true representation of what can be accomplished in the shop is not realistic.

OPERATION SCHEDULING

The process of operation scheduling is based on the concept of backward scheduling. To perform backward scheduling, the Enterprise Resource Planning system needs some specific information. First, it needs data from Material Requirements Planning: the order number, part number, quantity, and due date for planned orders and the scheduled receipts (see Figure 4.3).

Figure 4.3   Operation Scheduling

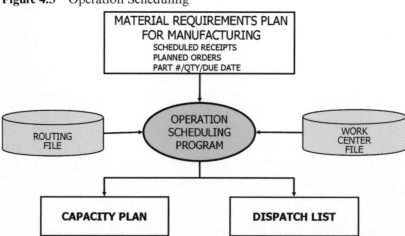

The second factor is the routing, which defines the steps necessary to produce the product: the operation sequences, the standard times required, and the work centers where the operations are to be performed (see Figure 4.4).

Figure 4.4   Routing Used at Hayes Tractor Company

163824	Adapter					
Part Number	Part Description					
OPN. No.	Dept.	Work Ctr.	Operation Description	Set Up	Run
			Release		
			Pick		
10	Fab	16	Saw Blank	0.5	.10
20	Mach	24	Turn	3.0	.20
30	Mach	22	Drill	2.0	.10
40	Mach	19	Tap	1.0	.20
			Store		

The third set of data is the work-center information, which includes planned queue times (see Figure 4.5) and scheduling rules (see Figure 4.6), such as shift length, number of shifts, move time, pick time, store time, and release time.

Figure 4.5   Planned Queues

Dept.	Work Centers	Queue (Days)
Fab	16 Saw	1
Mach.	19 Tap	1
Mach.	24 Lathe	2
Mach.	36 Mill	2
Mach.	22 Drill	1

A manufacturing calendar aids in backward scheduling. It identifies regularly scheduled workdays. Days such as weekends and holidays are not used to plan work schedules. Overtime—such as

Figure 4.6   Scheduling Rules

— 8 hours / shift
— Work center 19 & 36:   1 shift
   All other work centers: 2 shifts
— Move times:
   · 2 days between operations in different departments for move
   · 1 day between operations in different work centers for move
   · 0 days between operations in same work center for move
— 1 day to put away in stores
— 2 days to pick components and move to first work center
— 1 day for release
— Always round hours up to a full day

weekends that are used to resolve a problem of being behind schedule, or to solve a temporary capacity problem in a particular work center—should not be considered in the calendar as scheduled workdays. Since in a company different work centers or departments might work different calendar days, the software needs to support the ability to have separate calendars for each work center. In Figure

Figure 4.7   Manufacturing Calendar

\multicolumn{7}{c}{JUNE}

S	M	T	W	T	F	S
					1 *371*	2
3	4 *372*	5 *373*	6 *374*	7 *375*	8 *376*	9
10	11 *377*	12 *378*	13 *379*	14 *380*	15 *381*	16
17	18 *382*	19 *383*	20 *384*	21 *385*	22 *386*	23
24	25 *387*	26 *388*	27 *389*	28 *390*	29 *391*	30

Calendar Day   M-Day

\multicolumn{7}{c}{JULY}

S	M	T	W	T	F	S
1	2 *392*	3 *393*	4 *Holiday*	5 *394*	6 *395*	7
8	9 *396*	10 *397*	11 *398*	12 *399*	13 *400*	14
15	16 *401*	17 *402*	18 *403*	19 *404*	20 *405*	21
22	23 *406*	24 *407*	25 *408*	26 *409*	27 *410*	28
29	30 *411*	31 *412*				

4.7, weekends are not included as scheduled days, nor are public holidays such as July 4 for the United States.

We can now do the backward scheduling for a planned shop order: 40 pieces of part #163824 (see Figure 4.8).

Figure 4.8   Work Order No. W109 for Part #163824

163824	Adapter		40		W109	
Part Number	Part Description		Quantity		Order No.	
OPN. No.	Dept.	Work Ctr.	Operation Description	Set Up	Run	
			Pick			
			Release			
10	Fab	16	Saw	0.5	.10	
20	Mach	24	Turn	3.0	.20	
30	Mach	22	Drill	2.0	.10	
40	Mach	19	Tap	1.0	.20	
			Store			

This shop order contains the routing information, the order number, the quantity to be completed, and the scheduled order due date. This quantity and due-date information are obtained from the Material Requirements Planning system.

Using the graphic representation in Figure 4.9, we can put in the planned queues from Figure 4.5, which would be 1 day for operation 10, 2 days for operation 20, 1 day for operation 30, and 1 day for operation 40. Looking at the scheduling rules in Figure 4.6, we would include the order-release time of 1 day, pick time of 2 days,

Figure 4.9   Scheduling Diagram: Adding Queue Time

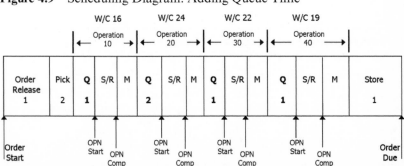

and the time to put away into stores of 1 day. (These numbers are for example only, and are not to be taken as recommendations. Most scheduling systems permit the use of fractional days or hours. We are using full days in order to keep the arithmetic simple.)

Next we calculate the setup and run times (see Figure 4.10).

Figure 4.10   Calculating Setup and Run Times for Work Order No. W109

163824	Adapter		40		W109			Order Due Date: 7/31		
Part Number	Part Description		Quantity		Order No.			Lead Time		
								Hours		Days
OPN. No.	Dept.	Work Ctr.	Operation Description	Set Up	Run			R	S&R	S&R
10	Fab	16	Saw	0.5	.10			4	4.5	1
20	Mach	24	Turn	3.0	.20			8	11.0	1
30	Mach	22	Drill	2.0	.10			4	6.0	1
40	Mach	19	Tap	1.0	.20			8	9.0	2

For operation 10, we multiply the run time to produce one piece by the order quantity of 40 pieces, which results in a total run time of 4 hours. If we add to that the setup time of 0.5 hours, we have a total setup and run time of 4.5 hours. We do the same calculation for each operation, 10 through 40.

In this example the scheduling will be done in days (ERP systems typically use fractions of days or hours) rather than hours; setup and run times must be converted into days for the backward scheduling. To convert to days, we find out how many hours per shift there are and how many shifts per day (see Figure 4.6). In the case of operation 10, we have 8 hours per shift and 2 shifts per day, because work center 16 works 2 shifts, for a total of 16 hours. Since 4.5 hours can be accomplished in 16 hours, we schedule 1 day (see Figure 4.10). Fractional days can either be rounded up or down. In this example, fractional days are rounded up per our scheduling rules. For operation 20 in work center 24, we again work 8 hours per shift and have 2 shifts per day for a total of 16 hours. The 11 hours we require also will fit in one day, so we schedule it as such. Work center 22 is also a 16-hour day. Operation 30 has 6 hours of work required, so we also schedule it as 1 day. However, operation 40 in work center 19 is scheduled for only one shift, so there are only 8 hours available. Since 9 hours of work are required, 2 days will have to be planned.

When we add our setup and run times to our graphic presentation, we have 1 day each for operations 10, 20, and 30, and 2 days for operation 40 (see Figure 4.11).

Figure 4.11 Scheduling Diagram: Adding Setup/Run Times and Move Times

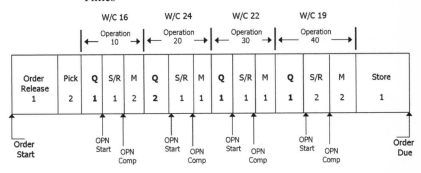

To determine the move time, once again we return to our scheduling rules (see Figure 4.6).

The move time from operation 10 to operation 20 is 2 days, because the work is moving between different departments (see Routing Figure 4.8). For operation 20 to operation 30, the move time is 1 day, because it's moving between work centers, but staying in the same department. The same is true between operations 30 and 40. Between operation 40 and the stockroom, the move time is 2 days because the work moves between different departments (see Figure 4.11). Note that if the move time is only 1 or 2 hours we could say move time was 0 because there is usually enough softness in shop-floor numbers to permit this, and it can get part-completed product to the next queue more reliably.

To calculate the operation start and due dates (see Figure 4.12), we begin with the order due date of July 31, which is the date the order is scheduled by MRP to go to stock. We locate that date on the manufacturing-day (M-day) calendar (see Figure 4.7), which turns out to be M-day 412. We subtract 1 day for stores and 2 days of move time between operation 40 and stores. We have an opera-

Figure 4.12   Scheduling Diagram: Adding M-Dates Using Backward Scheduling Logic

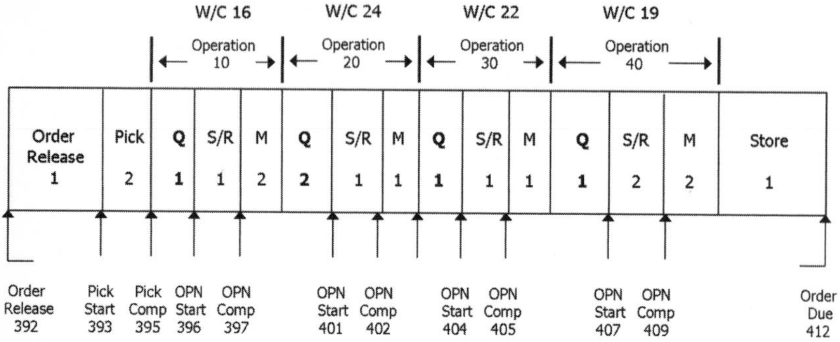

tion due date of M-409. Subtract 2 days of setup and run time, and we have an operation start date of M-407. Subtract 1 day of queue and 1-day move time, and we have a due date for operation 30 of M-405. Subtracting 1 day of setup and run time gives us a start date of M-404. Two days of combined move and queue time between operation 20 and operation 30 provide a due date of M-402. One day of setup and run time means a start date of M-401. Subtracting 4 days of combined move and queue between operation 10 and operation 20 gives a due date of M-397. One day of setup and run time gives us a start date of M-396. Subtract 1 day of queue and the pick complete date is M-395. Subtract 2 days to pick and the pick start date is M-393. Finally, we subtract 1 day to release and the planned order-release start date is M-392.

As Brian read through the backward-scheduling exercise, he nodded his head in understanding. It made perfect sense. It was how he had always scheduled everything else in his life. For example, he would talk to his wife about going to a friend's house for dinner and playing cards. They were expected at 8:00 P.M. Brian knew that it took 35 minutes to drive there. So, in order to be on time, they had to leave their house by 7:25. It took him 10 minutes to dress and 20 minutes to shower and shave. This activity had to begin by 6:55. The drive from Hayes to his home took 15 minutes: 6:40. To allow for traffic delays and bathroom-access delays, he would add 15 minutes buffer time. This meant that if he and his wife were to arrive at 8:00, he had to leave the factory by 6:25. This was backward scheduling.

It became evident to Brian that if the supervisors participated in the development of the information used in backward scheduling (order release, picking, queue, setup, run, move, and store), the schedule dates would have a good deal of credibility. All Brian needed to do was explain the simple logic the computer used to calculate the operation start dates and complete dates. Then, assuming that the order due date from Material Requirements Planning was correct, he could allow his supervisors to participate in setting the queue and move times—they already had a say in setup and run times through their routing-accuracy efforts—and they would then believe the operation-complete dates. Brian knew that both education and participation would be absolutely critical in order to bring his supervisors into the process, so that he could hold them accountable for the accuracy of the data.

Brian's only concern about using backward scheduling at Hayes was that they were always accepting orders inside of lead times. One day, while reviewing the backward-scheduling logic in the training material with Joan, Brian asked her about the problem. She told Brian that there was also another method of calculating operation dates called forward scheduling. She explained the difference between backward and forward scheduling. Backward scheduling starts with the need date that is derived from Material Requirements Planning and, by moving backward in time, calculates the dates by which all the operations need to be completed in order to meet that need date. Forward scheduling begins with the expected start date and calculates the operation dates by moving forward in time. If the available lead time equals the planned lead time, forward and backward scheduling will produce the same results. There are times, however, when a job needs to be completed in less than the full lead time, a situation that Brian had experienced more than once.

Brian realized that if the backward-scheduling logic were used then he had to complete a gear that should have a 5 1/2-week lead time in the middle of week 4 (see Figure 4.13).

Today was the start of week 1, so operations 10 and 20 would be past their due dates before the job was released. If this were done often, the first or second operations would constantly be getting work that was already past its operation due date and the last operations would be given the full amount of lead time. This was not a fair distribution of the total time available to produce the product and could be very discouraging to the work centers at the begin-

Figure 4.13   Backward Scheduling for Orders with Shortened Lead-Time

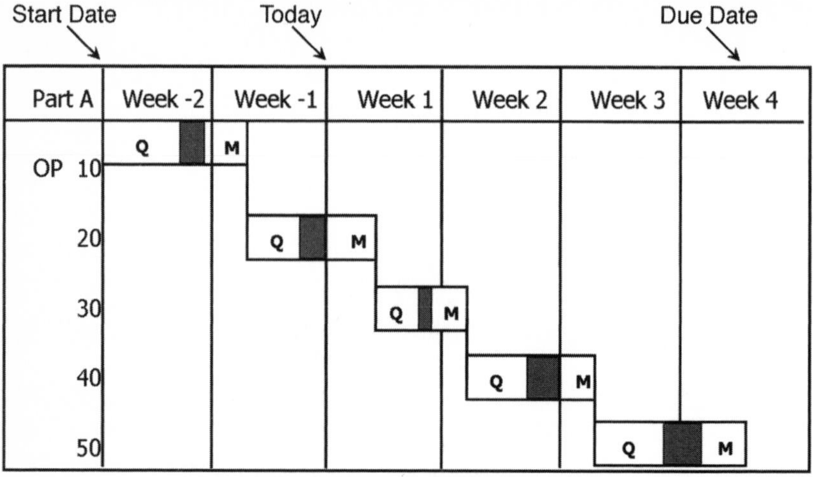

ning of the manufacturing process. Should this happen, those in the beginning would be inclined to give up on the credibility of the schedule and revert to working only on the hot items. Of course, as soon as they reverted back to the hot list, nothing would get done on time and the last operations would suffer.

However, if forward scheduling is used when an order is received 2 weeks inside of lead time (see Figure 4.14), the system would start with today and schedule each operation forward at its planned lead time.

As Joan explained this logic graphically, Brian quickly identified the flaw. The original customer order was promised in the middle of week 4. If the scheduling system "forward schedules," then the operational priorities would show operations 40 and 50 complete dates after the order due date.

Given the two choices, Brian recognized that since forward scheduling could cause the operation due dates to be later than the need dates, it was totally unacceptable. It was also clear to Brian that if the available lead time is greater than the planned lead time, forward scheduling will likely provide completion dates that are earlier than necessary. In doing so, it has established erroneous priorities. Yet, in Joan's example, backward scheduling would produce dates for the first two operations that were past due. It was obvious that he could

Figure 4.14   Forward Scheduling for Orders with Shortened Lead-Time

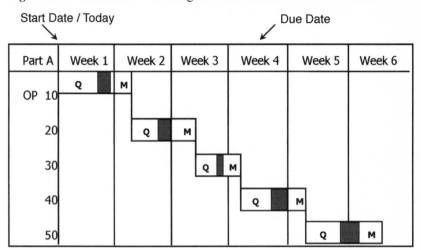

not complete work yesterday. However, Brian also realized that if the scheduling had been done properly, the older dates would indicate that he was behind schedule and would tell him the sequence in which to work (relative priority). Although he couldn't tolerate everything being late, a small number of past-due operations signaled to Brian that he had to do something to get caught up. Backward scheduling would tell him the *absolute* priority, which would not only tell him the priority sequence, but also when the work must be completed. Being able to see absolute priorities would give Brian the information he needed to manage his department properly. However, a lot of scheduled past-due operations are a signal that there is a problem that needs to be addressed.

Brian knew, as does any experienced shop manager, that there are five fundamental techniques that can be employed to schedule products in less than the full lead time. The first is to compress the queue and move times. Hot jobs don't sit around for long periods, because the expeditor is constantly pushing them and can manually override the schedule. This can be accomplished in the computer by determining the difference between the planned lead time and the actual time available, then subtracting that from the move and queue times. For instance, if an order with a normal lead time of 6 weeks had to be done in 4 weeks, and its queue and move times were 3 weeks, we could subtract 2 weeks from that and have 1 week of

Figure 4.15   Short Schedule Techniques: Compressing Queue and Move Times

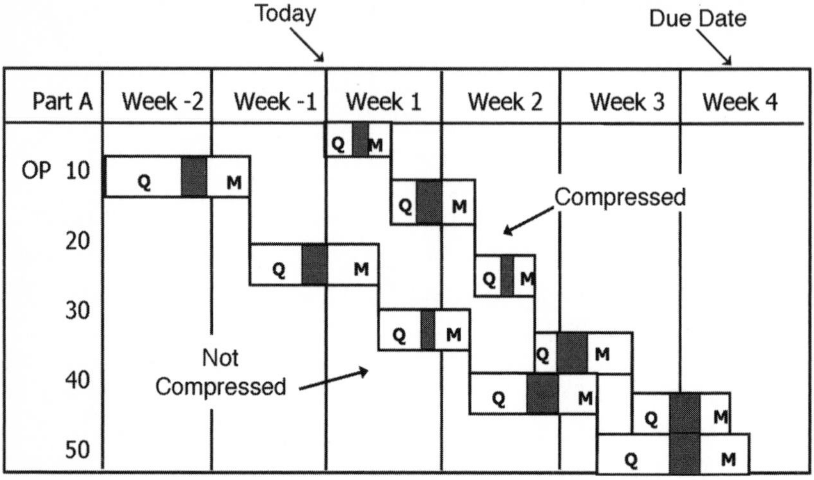

queue and move to be distributed, based on the distribution of the original move and queue times. Figure 4.15 shows how the compression would work.

In this example, we are able to meet the MRP need date without showing the order past due at the first operation. Setup and run times should not be compressed.

Another way to compress queue and move times is for the planner to override the scheduling logic and adjust the scheduled operation start and completion dates to fit the situation. For instance, perhaps one operation needs its entire queue time, but several others don't need any queue time at all. The planner can manually override the operation dates to reflect what is desired. Caution should be exercised when choosing to adjust the dates manually because it is a labor-intensive process. It should only be used when really necessary.

A second technique that can be used to compress lead time is to overlap operations. This involves the moving of pieces ahead to the next operation before the entire run quantity has been completed at the previous operation (see Figure 4.16).

With this technique, lead time can be compressed even more than with the queue/move compression process. The disadvantage of this technique is that multiple moves must be made rather than waiting

Figure 4.16 Short Schedule Techniques: Operation Overlapping

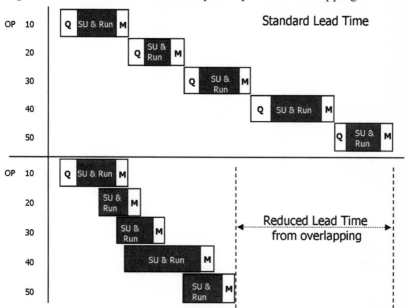

for the whole job to move all together. By overriding the operational start dates calculated by the computer and inserting an earlier start date, even though the previous operation hasn't been completed, we have accurately simulated what needs to happen in order to meet the order due date.

A third way to compress lead times is to split the order into smaller lot sizes (see Figure 4.17).

Figure 4.17 Short Schedule Techniques: Order Splitting

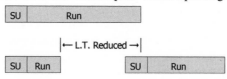

Production can then run fewer parts than normal, thus getting the first pieces through more quickly. The disadvantage of this approach is in the multiple setups that are necessary to complete the original order quantity, as well as the additional handling and transactions.

A fourth approach is to run parts on a multiple number of machines in a work center simultaneously (see Figure 4.18).

Figure 4.18   Short Schedule Techniques: Operation Splitting

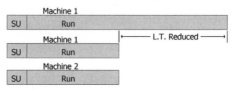

Running a job over two machines that would normally be produced by only one machine obviously cuts the run time by half. Again, the disadvantage is that multiple setups and multiple sets of tooling are necessary.

Finally, additional shifts could be added either as a temporary solution or on a longer-term basis. This reduction in lead time is illustrated in Figure 4.19.

Figure 4.19   Short Schedule Techniques: Additional Shifts

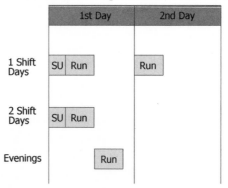

For example, if we are running one shift and have a job that has 3 hours of setup and 13 hours of run time, we would normally set up and run the piece for 5 hours on the first day. The equipment would sit idle until the next day when we would return to complete the job. If a two-shift operation is in place, the first-shift operator would do exactly as we had done in the previous example, but the second-shift operator would complete the job the first day. Once again, there is a disadvantage in that additional costs may be incurred, such as shift premiums and added supervision.

Which technique should be used? It depends upon the individual circumstances. The added costs or inconvenience need to be assessed and weighed against missing the schedule. Brian and his co-managers used a combination of these techniques, depending on the part and the status of the machines and/or operators.

We should note at this point that sometimes circumstances exist that make some or all of these techniques impractical or perhaps impossible. Many companies are running some work centers 24 hours a day, seven days a week, in order to shorten the lead time or to increase equipment utilization. In such cases, the additional shift option is not available. If all machines are being fully utilized, the split operation option is not available. Additional scheduling techniques and the automated scheduling of these techniques will be discussed in Chapter 9.

It is important to realize that controls must be established regarding the release of orders with less-than-full lead times. Material planners should be permitted to compress queues up to a previously agreed upon percentage throughout the process. But if that compression does not alleviate the scheduling problem, they should not release an order inside of lead time without the approval of the supervisor. It is up to the supervisor to tell the planners that they could compress the process more by utilizing the previously described techniques. This is essential to maintaining the accountability necessary to control the factory's operations.

The important factor to remember is that this is not a question of whether or not an order can be completed inside of lead time. The Brians, Dans, and Mickeys of the world have all learned how to do that in order to survive. The real question is how many times it can be done without losing control. To protect themselves against the constant influx of hot parts, companies have traditionally factored lots of cushion into lead times. This, as might be expected, has caused its own share of confusion, since no one is really sure what can be accomplished and what can't. In such an environment, all anyone ever remembers is how quickly a hot part made it through the last time. The unrealistic expectation is that all parts can move that fast.

How much work can a company accept in less-than-full lead time? This varies considerably depending upon how the lead times were set up. More move and queue increases the number of orders inside lead time. Furthermore, we need to realize that the amount of lead-time compression depends on capacity also. If overtime is an option, perhaps as much as 15 to 20% can be accepted. In other situations, experience has shown that anything over 5% causes problems. In some cases, a production order with as little as 50% of standard lead time available can be accommodated, while in other cases, much less lead-time compression can be tolerated before a major impact is felt. If a lot of short-lead orders are accepted and don't seem to cause a lot of problems, the lead times in the system need to be analyzed—they are probably too long. Regardless of the situation, an excessive number of short-lead-time jobs are likely to have a highly unfavorable impact on production schedules.

As Brian will discover when he looks into the process and philosophy of Lean Manufacturing (see Chapter 10), the various techniques for shortening lead times can be a precursor to Lean Manufacturing. When Hayes began compressing queue times, it became obvious that queues were inherently wasteful. It also became obvious that they needed to initiate some major programs to reduce them. The motivation should be to drive queue times down as a matter of course. This was ultimately turned into a significant competitive advantage at Hayes. With a shorter lead time, an order that was formerly inside lead time and had to be thoroughly investigated to see if it could be done, could now be accepted with no investigation and with complete confidence that it could be delivered on time. As lead times are shortened, the previous 5-to-50% guideline will become tighter. Getting people in manufacturing to participate in reducing lead times is contingent upon the adherence to the established lead times. Violating them will cause manufacturing to revert to its old behavior of padding lead times, because they know that the lead times will be violated.

DISPATCH LIST

The work-center schedule ("Dispatch List") that John Hall, General Supervisor at Precision Air Components, showed Brian provided a priority tool for his supervisors that was accurate and allowed them to plan their work. As stated previously, the schedule at Precision Air Components and at Hayes contained the same information that Dennis Jones described in the course (see Figure 4.20).

Figure 4.20   Dispatch List for Work Center 24

WORK CENTER NO.: 24					DESCRIPTION: Lathes				DATE: 7/2	
Order No.	Part No.	Part Description	Qty	OPN No.	OPN Start Date	OPN Due Date	Order Due Date	Setup Hrs	Run Hrs	Next/Prev W/C	OPN Status
		JOBS CURRENTLY AT THIS WORK CENTER									
W123	144398	Shaft	200	20	6/26	6/27	7/19	0	7.0	04	R
W123	144398	Shaft	200	30	6/29	7/2	7/19	1.0	10.0	07	Q
W124	428876	Bolt	3000	30	6/29	7/3	7/24	2.0	30.0	07	Q
W110	330246	Gear	500	20	6/28	7/3	7/18	1.0	15.0	07	Q
W120	407211	Bolt	4000	30	7/2	7/5	7/20	2.0	50.0	07	Q
W112	163726	Hub	40	20	7/3	7/5	7/23	3.0	8.0	07	Q
W128	118132	Gear	400	20	7/5	7/10	7/24	2.0	40.0	07	Q
							TOTAL	11.0	160		
		JOBS COMING TO THIS WORK CENTER									
W129	186846	Shaft	20	20	7/3	7/5	7/12	1.0	4.5	01	Q
W138	258721	Spacer	2000	20	7/9	7/11	7/25	0.5	20.0	05	Q
W140	321406	Hub	50	30	7/10	7/12	7/27	1.0	30.0	01	H
							TOTAL	2.5	54.5		

That information is as follows:

- WORK-CENTER NUMBER: defines the work center. The computer selects all the scheduled orders for operations to be performed in this work center for inclusion on the Dispatch List.
- DATE: the date the computer generated the Dispatch List (used to identify the most current Dispatch List).
- ORDER NUMBER: unique order number assigned to every individual open work order.
- PART NUMBER/ITEM NUMBER: identifies each part or item.
- QUANTITY: the number of remaining parts scheduled to be completed on this order number at this operation.
- OPERATION NUMBER: the specific operation that is scheduled to be performed.
- OPERATION START DATE: the date that the specified operation is to be started (developed by the backward-scheduling logic).
- OPERATION COMPLETE DATE: the date that a specific operation is to be completed (developed by the backward-scheduling logic).
- ORDER DUE DATE: the date the order has been scheduled to be completed by the material planner (i.e., the MRP due date).

- SETUP HOURS: the standard setup hours remaining on this order.
- RUN HOURS: the standard run time remaining (pieces, times standard hours per piece) on this order.
- NEXT OR PREVIOUS WORK CENTER: if the order is currently in this work center, this information indicates where it is to go after this operation is completed. If the order has not yet reached this work center, this information indicates the work center immediately prior to this one on the routing. This information enables the supervisor to contact the other appropriate work centers regarding delays, expediting, and scheduling problems.
- OPERATION STATUS: the latest reported status (running, being set up, or waiting in queue).

In addition to this information, the list of jobs must differentiate between what is currently at the work center and what has not yet arrived. This can be accomplished through either of two options.

First, the jobs can be identified and divided into different sections, as shown in Hayes's Dispatch List. The work in queue or actually being worked on would come under the heading "Jobs Currently at This Work Center." Under operation status, it would show the status at this work center. The bottom section, "Jobs Coming to This Work Center," would list all the jobs that haven't arrived yet. In this section, the operational-status column would indicate the status of the job at its current work center.

The second option would be to put all work in operation complete-date order and indicate through a code whether or not the job was at the work center. This could be as simple as putting an asterisk (*) next to the jobs that are not yet available to be worked on. The status column would remain the same as in the first option.

It is not important which option is chosen as long as the work that hasn't arrived yet is noted on the Dispatch List. There are three reasons for this:

1. It allows the supervisor to see what work is currently available for assignment.
2. It allows the supervisor to see what's due to arrive in order to perform daily scheduling.
3. If the work is past due to its operation start date, it allows the supervisor to find out when it will arrive and why it is late.

The information necessary to determine priority is also contained on the Dispatch List. The order number, the operation start date, the operation completion date, and order due date are displayed for each order. Running only by work-order due date provides no milestones to schedule the time that each order should spend in each operation. If those in the beginning take too much time, the operations at the end have to scramble to catch up. By identifying scheduled priority by operation, priorities can be provided for each work assignment at each work center. If each operation due date is met, the order due date will be met consistently. The supervisor is held accountable for the operation complete date. The order due date is included simply to give the supervisor visibility in case an operation can't meet its operation date. If a supervisor can't meet an operation complete date, then the capacity planner (described in Chapter 5) or supervisor must contact the downstream work centers (later operations) to see if they can make up the lost time. If they can't, and subsequently the order due date will be missed, the material planner must be advised and given the expected new operation completion date. It should be emphasized that the order due date is used for informational purposes only on the shop floor. The operation complete date is what the supervisor is measured against.

Using the same schedule that was used to educate the supervisors on routings, Brian, Tony, and Joan completed the scheduling education. They started a shop schedule-cleanup process. The supervisors, expeditors, and material planners were going to review all the past-due orders to ensure they were needed. Everyone knew the results wouldn't be perfect, but they also knew things would become a lot better than they had been. Working as a team, they all agreed to come in over the weekend to get the work done.

The cleanup over the weekend wasn't perfect but a lot of orders were cleaned up or rescheduled to realistic due dates. It didn't start well, but as soon as the material planners, expeditors, and supervisors figured out that they would be there until they finished, a lot of arguing went by the wayside and a much more realistic plan resulted. Joan and Brian were right in the thick of it, both learning as they went. Roy, Joan's boss, was also there, just to see how it was going and to buy doughnuts and lunch. Nobody wanted dinner either night; they just wanted to get it done.

On Monday morning, Brian was looking over some Dispatch Lists. When he picked up the bar-lathe list, which was the next operation after Dan's bar-sawing operation, he couldn't believe his eyes. The work-coming section showed that there were 48 jobs that were past due at the bar lathe and were sitting in Dan's saw department. They ranged from 1 to 28 days past the operation due date, skewed toward the latter.

In the shortage meeting that morning when they came to the first late gear, Brian spoke up. "That's late because I didn't get it from the saws." Brian pulled out the Dispatch List, looked at Dan, and said, "That's not all. Unless I get these 48 jobs, they'll also be late."

Dan grabbed the Dispatch List and stared down at the sheet. "This is garbage and you know it, Brian."

"I'm afraid it's not. We cleaned the old work out over the weekend, and now it's accurate—I'd bet my bottom dollar on it," Brian said.

"He's right," Joan said, supporting Brian.

After the meeting, Dan went straight to the saw supervisor. "I want you to saw every job around here for Miller. I want his raw-material storage yard chuck full when he arrives in the morning. You understand?"

The supervisor knew enough not to say a word. He nodded his head and called his operators over. Day shift sawed bars. Second shift sawed bars. There was an explicit message for third shift, "Dan wants every bar sawed." The next morning Brian had his bars.

Because Brian had a Dispatch List that showed jobs that were coming to the work center, he was able to pull the work through the previous operations.

After using the Dispatch Lists for a few weeks, Brian found they were surprisingly effective. The number of shortages he had to deal with was decreasing because the supervisors were working to valid dates. The dates were valid because of the work he and people were doing, but also because of the work Roy O'Brian—the Material Manager—and his staff were doing. Unlike Brian's boss, Joan's boss, Roy, saw the vision and was driving hard to get the higher-level processes shown in the Detail Supply Point Model (Figure 2.4) correct. They had visibility of the jobs that were about to come due and could work on them prior to their appearance on a hot list. Joan and Brian agreed that they would give the supervisor only one list and that would be the Dispatch List. If Mickey, in Assembly, identified something as being hot, the material planners would investigate it immediately. If needed, they would change the schedule in Material Requirements Planning to put it on the top of the Dispatch List, even if it meant having to write it in by hand temporarily.

Ralph, however, continued to make his own rounds throughout the factory. Many years after reading Tom Peters and Robert Waterman's book, *In Search of Excellence*[1], he still referred to it by their term "management by walking around."

One evening Ralph walked into the frame-weldment area, supervised by Hank Jones. As soon as Hank saw Ralph, he pulled him over. "I'm afraid this frame isn't going to make it to the assembly line by tomorrow morning, Ralph, and this is the special for Nebraska Implement that Pete promised."

Ralph wasn't pleased with this news and asked why. The problem was that Hank was short of two brackets. The inventory count had been wrong. Realizing he would miss the schedule without the brackets, he had immediately tried to track the parts down. What he found was that there was an open order in the machine shop. "Did you tell them you had to have it?" Ralph asked.

"I sure did. But they told me the brackets weren't due yet, and consequently they were way down on the Dispatch List. They also told me that, unless the material planners changed the operation due date, they were going to work on the jobs that were due ahead of the brackets."

"Well, hell, if you have to have the parts, someone has to get them." Ralph immediately went to Harry, one of the supervisors of the machine shop. "Did Hank call you about those brackets that he needs?" he asked.

"He sure did," Harry replied.

"Did you start working on them yet?" Ralph asked.

Harry said, "No. Brian told us to work the priorities per the operation due dates on the Dispatch List."

"Let me see that thing." Ralph's concern was more than evident.

Harry handed Ralph the Dispatch List. "This doesn't mean a damn thing." Ralph fumed. "What means something is that Hank needs those brackets and he had better get them."

Now, Harry knew who the boss was, and when Ralph spoke he moved or else, even if it was contrary to Brian's instructions. Harry

1. New York: Harper & Row, 1982.

went over to the radial-drill operator and told him to break down the setup. He then hurried to the other end of the shop to talk to Roger, another supervisor. "Ralph wants those brackets right now," he said, "and I'll have one ready for you to start on in about 45 minutes."

"I knew it as soon as I saw him," Roger said. "I just got the milling machine set up and now I have to break it down. A three-hour setup down the tubes. I thought we had something going for us when Brian told us to work to the Dispatch List. I was just caught up, too, and was going to be able to save another three hours on the next job because it was just like the one I have in now. Well, there goes that dream."

"Yeah, I know what you mean," replied Harry. "For the first time, I thought we were actually going to be able to spend our time on something other than chasing hot parts. I knew it was too good to last."

About an hour later, after completing his rounds, Ralph went back to Hank and told him, "You'll get the brackets in a couple of hours." As they stood there talking, the material planner walked in and put two brackets on the table.

"Boy, that was fast," Hank said. "Where did those come from?"

The material planner looked at him oddly. "Didn't the first-shift supervisor leave you a note?" Hank shook his head no. "Well, he called me earlier in the day," the material planner said. "Are you sure he didn't leave you a note?"

Hank checked again. "Oh, yeah, here it is. I didn't see it. I got in a few minutes late. . . ."

The material planner nodded. "He told me he couldn't finish the frame without those brackets. So when I saw that the next order for the brackets was number 25 on the radial-drill Dispatch List, and then it had to go through the mill operation, which already had a heavy load, I knew I had to do something. In order to get them done tonight, the machine shop would have to break a setup on the radial drill and the mill, which would take a considerable amount of time. I figured we'd lose too much productivity that way, so I called up the service-parts warehouse, and they had them. I borrowed these two and promised to return them next week when the open order is done."

As Ralph listened to the conversation, he recognized the problem that he had created by reacting as he had instead of using the tools available to determine the best solution.

The next morning, Joan told Brian about the incident and decided that they needed to act quickly or they never would get Hayes's operations under control. They sat down and came up with some dispatching rules.

RULE 1: Honor only the Dispatch List for priority.

The Dispatch List is intended to reflect the real priorities of the shop schedule. If a scheduled order due date needs to be changed, it's the material planner's job to communicate that to the supervisor either directly or through a shop liaison. The material planner is responsible for maintaining the priorities in the schedule and the supervisor is accountable for meeting the schedule. If anyone else is allowed to change the order due date, the material planner has lost all his or her accountability. If the problem can be resolved by rescheduling some of the operations without changing the order due date, then the capacity planner (discussed in Chapter 5) should do so. There would be no need to communicate with the material planner in that instance. There is no question that management has the authority to change the schedule if they wish to do so. It must be done, however, through a formal procedure that investigates the alternatives first in order to choose the best one. That formal procedure must, of course, be responsive enough to resolve the problem in a timely manner.

RULE 2: If a work center is behind schedule, work on the shop orders in operation due-date sequence.

This rule says, "Get on schedule as soon as you can." To accomplish this, work to the latest Dispatch List priority. There are situations where working out of sequence might get the work center back on schedule more quickly than by working in sequence. That is acceptable only if it won't cause the other jobs to fall behind schedule.

For example, we have seven jobs listed in priority sequence (see Figure 4.21). Jobs 1 and 2 are behind schedule. Job 7 uses the same setup as job 1, but it's not due for four days.

Running job 7 right after job 1 might save two hours by minimizing changeovers, but it would do nothing to get job 2 on schedule. Besides, job 3 would then also be past due, and that would still leave two jobs behind schedule. Job 7 would be ahead of schedule, but that wouldn't benefit anyone. Although this may seem like a good decision locally, from this work center's point of view, it may

Figure 4.21   Dispatch List Showing Operations Behind Schedule

Job #	Operation Comp. Date	Setup	Run Time
1	98	2 hours	4 hours
2	99	3 hours	7 hours
3	100	1 hour	5 hours
4	101	2 hours	7 hours
5	102	4 hours	12 hours
6	103	1 hour	3 hours
7	104	2 hours	6 hours

(Today = Manufacturing Day 100)

have a major impact on many other areas that are expecting all these jobs on time. What this work center must do first is to assess the impact downstream. It must then determine what extra resources need to be applied to get this work center on schedule with the minimum amount of impact on the following work centers. In almost all situations this means performing the jobs in accordance with the Dispatch List and applying the additional resources as needed.

A high level of discipline is needed to make this rule work. The key is to use the operation due dates to make the right decisions for the overall good of the company, even when the temptation is to do what is best in the short term for an individual work center.

RULE 3: If the work center is on schedule or ahead of schedule, work on the shop orders must be done in the most productive sequence that will still maintain the schedule.

Rules Two and Three say that it is more important to meet the schedule than to improve productivity. The notion here is that you can be very "productive" by making the wrong stuff.

This rule gives José, a machine-shop supervisor, the opportunity to improve his work-center productivity. It allows him to use his knowledge and ability when he is on or ahead of schedule. The Dispatch List is a list of priorities, not a dictate of sequence. If today were manufacturing (M) day 97, it would make good sense, because of setups, to run job 7 and then job 4. This rule permits that. If the work center falls behind schedule, the supervisor must assess the downstream impact prior to working jobs out of sequence. Unless the downstream situation allows for jobs to arrive late, the supervisor, in accordance with Rule Two, must return to the top of the Dispatch List and get back on schedule. It is far more cost-effective overall for the company to concentrate on keeping on schedule than to emphasize productivity. One small area operating late can create inefficiencies in many other areas.

RULE 4: Do not release an order with a past-due start date without shop approval.

Launching an order with a past-due start date doesn't do any good if the shop cannot meet the final due-to-stock date. If the order is going to be late, it is best to know it at the time of release, so that a valid date can be established. That will allow everyone to have valid priorities. It also keeps one work center from working to meet a schedule that another work center can't possibly meet.

RULE 5: Do not break setups in response to a newly issued Dispatch List, unless it has been previously agreed upon.

This is common sense. Occasionally, errors are made by the material planner inputting a date or analyzing situations that result in the Dispatch List showing inaccurate information. Since Rule Four is in place, a job should not show up as past due without the supervisor's prior knowledge. Therefore, it is wise for the supervisor to check before breaking a setup. (Had Ralph understood this rule, he would not have been so quick in ordering a setup to be broken.)

RULE 6: Notify the material planner of any shop order that will miss its order due date.

The sooner a problem is reported, the better chance there is to react to it with the least amount of disruption to the process. Once a supervisor realizes that waiting until after the fact to advise the material planner of a delay only puts him further behind, he becomes quite comfortable with this rule.

The tool used to communicate such a problem is called an Anticipated Delay Report. It can be a specific document, as in Figure 4.22, or it can be handled by using the previous day's Dispatch List, noting on it the jobs that are in trouble and all other pertinent information. There are any number of methods, including verbal communication. The important point is that there needs to be a formal process to communicate the information as early as possible.

Initially at Hayes, using the Anticipated Delay Report was something of a joke because so much work was past due. Brian, Tony, and Joan knew there was a lot of cushion in the schedule, so they decided to use the Anticipated Delay Report only if a job would miss the order due date by more than five days. Gradually, they worked to reduce that grace period.

They accomplished this by having Tony go to each work center every day. He would check with the supervisors to see where they stood in relationship to their operation due dates. To reinforce the importance of Tony's task, Brian randomly checked work centers later in the day, after Tony had made his rounds. If anyone else wanted to know, they could look it up on the Enterprise Requirements Planning system on-line Dispatch List screens. The closest managers could of course also do this, but it is important they "show the flag" each day by walking around.

If Tony and the supervisor agreed that a work center was so far behind in regard to its operation due date that the order due date would be missed by more than the prescribed tolerance, Tony would communicate that to the downstream work-center supervisor to see if that time could be made up. If it couldn't, Tony and the supervisor whose work center was behind would work together on the an-

Figure 4.22   Anticipated Delay Report

Anticipated Delay Report: WORK CENTER 04: Date 7/2					
Work Order	Part No.	Comp Date	Cause	New Date	Action
			Signature:		

ticipated delay report. What Tony really needed was the supervisor's commitment on when the order would be completed.

Normally, Tony started this process with the first operations. By the time he reached the downstream operations, the majority of the problems had been found and resolved.

Once the new completion date was determined, Tony would communicate that to the material planner to figure out what needed to be done. Sometimes, it was as simple as having Assembly work around the past-due part. Other times, it meant that an order would have to be split or the schedule compressed at all costs. There were also times when the delay would impact on the delivery of a tractor. These times, however, were now occurring with less frequency. Equally as important, they were getting early warnings when a tractor delivery might be delayed. This gave them the time to take the appropriate action, to ensure the delivery would not be missed. The supervisors also recognized that the closer they stayed to the schedule, the more flexibility they had to react to emergencies.

As time went on, the tolerances on those items that were late continued to tighten. Eventually, the process improved to the point where supervisors were dissatisfied if a job went even one day past the operation due date.

Again, it is important to emphasize that the Dispatch List is not a job sequence mandate: It's a priority list. Although priority is arguably the most significant input to the assignment of work, there are other considerations, and a good production supervisor is aware of these. A good supervisor knows more about how to achieve the highest levels of productivity than a material planner or a computer does. A good supervisor will know which operator and/or equipment is best suited to each particular job. These rules give the supervisor the flexibility to improve productivity and, at the same time, preserve the integrity of the priority process. The most difficult part of this process is to reduce the load to no more than a few past-due jobs. Once that has been accomplished, it is relatively easy to maintain it.

It is no secret that working behind schedule is expensive. Costs begin to mount as soon as overtime work commences or money is spent on alternate operations. The effort should be made to meet the scheduled operation dates initially, rather than reacting after the work is late. The emphasis should be on every work center meeting the schedule rather than worrying about the performance of an individual area. If the schedule is consistently met by all work centers, it will result in each area being productive, that is, producing just what is needed. This allows all areas to operate in a least-cost environment.

Once the dispatching rules were completed, and all the machine-shop personnel understood them, Brian and Joan agreed that it was crucial for Ralph and Pete to sign off on these new rules. It was agreed that Brian would be the best one to approach Ralph, since he worked for him. The backup plan was for Roy to do battle with Ralph. Ralph gave in more easily than Brian anticipated. Maybe it was Brian's well-timed example of productivity losses that softened up Ralph, especially when he used a bracket for an example.

"Okay, okay, Brian," Ralph exclaimed, "I'll sign the thing. But just don't tell me I have to give up my shop tours. I really believe in 'management by walking around.'"

Pete was easy to convince once Ralph had signed and Roy explained the process to him. His only comment was, "I'll do anything to get this place on schedule."

DISPATCH LIST SEQUENCING CONSIDERATIONS

When Brian introduced the Dispatch List, there had been some fear that by adopting a formal scheduling system, supervisors would be reduced to following orders from a computer and would no longer direct their own departments. Implementation of the Dispatch List proved that there was no basis for this fear. Once the work center was on schedule, the supervisor was free to decide the proper sequence in which to do the work. The difference the supervisors found was that their first consideration was now the schedule, and they were to concentrate on it. Productivity was a natural extension of this process.

When a work center finishes a job, the supervisor goes to the Dispatch List to see what is next on the list. Once the priority has been established, the capabilities of the machine have to be taken into consideration. For example, the machine that just opened up could be one of the older machines in the work center, unable to hold the tolerance necessary for the top job on the Dispatch List. It would be foolish to put that job on that machine and produce poor-quality parts. There could also be a problem with an operator who has never before run a specific job—a job with very definite idiosyncrasies. The supervisor must take such matters into consideration and would most likely decide to run a different sequence from that on the Dispatch List.

Other factors that could prompt alternate-sequencing decisions are unscheduled maintenance activities, the late arrival of a job coming from an upstream work center, or a priority need from a downstream work center. This list can go on to include as many different variations as there are companies or people in them. It's always best to leave the supervisor to consider the impact on the ability to meet the schedule. The supervisors must use their experience and good common sense to make their decisions.

What Brian learned through experience was that the Dispatch List provided valid priorities by operation. It allowed him to know where he stood against the schedule, so he could adjust if necessary. It helped him identify potential problems and resolve them before they caused trouble. Whenever an operation couldn't be finished on time, that delay was communicated and the problem highlighted. But, most important, it provided him with vital information in a simple and direct format.

The Dispatch List is not a replacement for supervision, nor does it dictate the sequence for running jobs. It is a tool for the supervisor. It depends upon accurate data and reliable information from Material Requirements Planning, as well as accurate and timely reporting of activity from the shop floor. It does not self-correct when data or reporting is wrong. Therefore, it is important to maintain the integrity of the information properly. Otherwise, if the supervisor has little confidence in the Dispatch List, the local scheduling will regress to the informal system, and all the problems that brings.

Things were beginning to show some improvement at Hayes, and Brian decided he needed to do a little "management by walking around" of his own to make sure everything was all right. He went to José's desk to check on the Dispatch List. He couldn't find the Dispatch Lists anywhere. Brian immediately tracked down José. "Where are all your Dispatch Lists?" Brian asked, fearing that they had been thrown away.

"They're at the machines," José replied. "The operators are figuring out what has to be done next, unless, of course, they have a question. Then they come to Tony or me."

"The operators?" Brian couldn't believe what he was hearing. "You mean you're leaving those decisions up to the operators?"

José smiled. "Calm down, Boss. We don't want you having heart failure just as things are looking up. Let me ask you, Brian, how are we doing in this department?"

Brian considered José's question a moment. "Well, I guess you've probably got the least past due of any of the supervisors."

"There's no guessing about it," José said proudly. "Ask the operators why."

Brian did just that, and what he found surprised him. He was amazed how informed and knowledgeable the operators were about the schedules and their function within the process. More importantly than that, he was astounded by how much more enthusiastic they were about meeting their schedules. Time and again he heard, "When the information's right, it makes my job easier."

GETTING THE INFORMATION RIGHT

One morning at the shortage meeting, Mickey informed Brian: "I've just been told we are short of the four yokes for the last two special loaders. If we don't get those yokes out of the shop and into Assembly, I'm never going to complete those two loaders due on the 8th." This shortage, and Mickey's outburst, caught Brian completely by surprise. There was nothing he hated more than getting yelled at for something he didn't know about.

Within minutes of the end of the meeting, Brian was out on the floor talking to his supervisor. "So, tell me, why are these late?"

"Late?" came the reply. "I just got the order and it was past due when I got it."

Brian looked at the order and headed up to Production Control to talk to Joan. "All right, Brian, calm down. Let's see why this puppy's late." Joan quickly discovered that on the previous order the shop had scrapped four out of the original twenty pieces. "Those four," Joan told him, "are the four needed for those last two loaders. Mickey was supposed to be covered." Joan dug a little further, "Let's see, the scrap system shows these yokes were scrapped out in the first operation, which was about five weeks ago but the date they were scrapped in the Enterprise Requirements Planning system was four days ago when they went into inventory. As soon as that happened the system recognized that four more were needed, so it notified the material planner to release another order immediately with a past-due date.

"Come on, Brian, if your operator had reported them scrap when you scrapped it, the Enterprise Requirements Planning system would have alerted the material planner and she would have gotten you another order for those four parts five weeks ago."

Brian knew he'd just paid the price for his department's lack of good reporting. If they had told Joan the parts were scrapped in a timely manner, they would have gotten the replacement order much sooner. Unfortunately, this wasn't the only bad news he got from Joan. It seemed there was also a good deal of bad reporting going on in a number of Brian's operations. Brian realized it was time for a little more "management by walking around."

Brian picked up a Dispatch List and ran a check. Joan wasn't exaggerating. There were some transactions getting reported properly, but many others were being ignored or reported days later—maybe too late for action.

Brian immediately headed off to talk to one of his supervisors. "I'm sure there's an explanation for the errors in these reports," Brian said, trying to be as diplomatic as possible.

"The truth is, Brian," the supervisor said, "it takes too long. I can't seem to get all the jobs done and do all this reporting too. It just takes up too much of my time."

The rest of the supervisors gave Brian basically the same answer. José, however, said he didn't have any trouble getting his reporting done and done right. "What I want to know," Brian said, "is how come you've got the time and all the other supervisors are too busy?"

"It's really pretty simple," said José, "Every day when I get the reports and I find errors, I take them back to the operators and have *them* fix the problem. All I did was get these guys to understand that this stuff is important and that they had to fix their own errors. After I went back to them a couple of times and made them correct the reports themselves, they learned."

"Don't the other supervisors do that?"

"Are you kidding? They just try to get through the reports as fast as they can. Getting them out is all they're after. Listen; if an operator is consistently making an error on something, and I get it back the next day, I've got two choices. Either I can take it back to the operator and figure out what happened or I can take the shortcut and guess what probably went wrong and try to fix it myself. That's the fastest way. Maybe 60 to 70% of the time I'm actually right. If I'm not, it comes back the next day and I can just take another guess. Of course, that doesn't solve the problem."

The fact that the rest of his supervisors would be making this second choice had never occurred to Brian. "All I do, Brian, is spend a little more time with my guys up front, show them the mistake, and ask why it was made. Once you understand why you're making a mistake, you stop doing it. They also know I'm serious because I'm out there until they get it right."

Brian was no dummy. He got the point. The next day he was on the floor talking to the operators and supervisors, asking questions, and then asking some more questions. "Why was this operation late? What action is it going to take to catch up? If you're not going to make the due date, who did you tell?" Brian now understood the importance of being out on the floor on a daily basis, walking, talking, listening, and asking questions. It was exactly like the supervisor had said, "The truth is that people respond to the consistency and repetition of your actions, not just what crosses your lips in passing."

The key message that Brian had to communicate to his people was accountability. He also had to make them understand the need for accuracy. If they didn't report their information correctly, or in a timely manner, they were going to get bad information out of the system. And, in the end, they would all pay the price for bad reporting.

Brian's lesson and responsibility, however, went a step further. He had to accept that he could be pleased with his shop's progress, but never again would he be able to be content with merely maintaining the status quo of the shop. He now understood that the only way to compete effectively in today's marketplace was to push and strive for continuous improvement.

Once the Dispatch List has been implemented, the typical daily shortage meeting should be replaced by a daily dispatch meeting that should last only 5 to 10 minutes. Although this new meeting is similar to the shortage meeting, the emphasis is put on avoidance of shortages by focusing attention on operations that are lagging behind schedule, rather than waiting until the actual shortage occurs. This is also the opportunity to discuss jobs that need to be released with less-than-normal lead time, as well as any other situations where action is necessary. A set of rules for this meeting should also be established, such as the following:

1. Monitor the number of jobs that are being written onto the Dispatch List. Most software systems provide ample on-line updating capability, and handwriting jobs onto the schedule should not be necessary. If there are more than a few jobs being written in—the number may vary depending on the quantity of jobs that flow through a work center—there is a problem with the planning and scheduling process that must be fixed.
2. Emphasize that the shop supervisors will honor the Dispatch List, with a commitment from management that all jobs will be handled through the formal scheduling system.
3. No chairs, no coffee, and no BS.
4. Adhere strictly to the notion that "silence is approval."

Since the machine shop was the only area using Dispatch Lists, the standard shortage meeting was continued. However, Brian and Joan decided to hold another meeting in the machine shop prior to the official one in Ralph's office. There were some rough times in the beginning, but it didn't last long and the meeting went quickly and smoothly. Brian was pleasantly surprised when these meetings ended up taking significantly less time than his previous conversations with Tony to update the shortage list. In fact, it was taking less than 10 minutes. Not only were the solutions to the problems they encountered in this meeting better, but each week it seemed there were fewer and fewer problems, because the shortages themselves were becoming fewer.

As Chapter 8 will show, other possibilities for dispatching occur in areas other than production, such as order picking, inspection, order release, design engineering, tooling, maintenance, and numerical control programming. There might be times when, part-way through the manufacturing process, a product has to go to an outside supplier for an operation and then return to the factory for further processing. In such instances, the Dispatch List could be used to communicate priorities to the supplier, as if the outside operation were another operation in the shop.

Though the shop schedule and the Dispatch List made life easier for Brian, he noticed that several of his critical work centers were becoming less critical. What he didn't realize was that by working on the wrong priorities he had been wasting capacity. He would have to break setups, make parts that weren't needed at that point in time, and, worse still, make parts that ended up being scrapped or reworked because of an engineering change. That savings in capacity would be enough in several work centers to assure that a job would be completed on time. What he still needed was accurate and reliable capacity plans. To obtain those, he had to understand what his required capacities were, and what he was actually capable of producing to assure the capacity was in place when it was needed. The key was to plan instead of react. This is exactly what he would learn next.

Chapter Five

Understanding Detail Capacity Planning

As Brian stared down at the printout of the most recent capacity plan lying on his desk, his mind shot back to one of his early meetings with Ralph. It was still during the time when Brian felt under the gun to prove him self. He had tried to show that he was willing to stand up for what he believed was right, but he couldn't tell if Ralph appreciated it or not.

Right in the middle of trying to get the routings accurate, but before Brian had started to use the Dispatch List, Ralph had waved Brian into his office and motioned for him to sit down as he finished a call. After placing the phone back on the hook, Ralph turned to him. "Brian, my boy," he said, in a tone Brian had previously heard him use only with Dan and Mickey—it wasn't just that it was friendly. Ralph was smiling. "I just want to tell you, I've noticed the reduction in the shortages from your departments. That's really good. I know it's because you're spending lots of hours in the shop but, more importantly, you're sending the message that I've been trying to send for the last two years—shortages are not acceptable. I think we had adopted a 'shortage culture.'"

Brian nodded his head in agreement. One of the things that Roxanne Barnes, the instructor from Effective Management, had noted in the course flashed through his mind: With good processes you could change the way people behave at work. It is only when the behaviors are adopted by everyone in the company that the culture really changes. That was one of the things Roxanne noted about Class A companies, the culture was "shortage free." He had to agree with Ralph, the culture at Hayes was just the opposite.

But Ralph wasn't going to let a compliment go without adding a "but." He continued, "The only problem is your productivity numbers have been lagging. Now, I want to be clear about this. I don't want people getting hurt out there or making junk. I want your first concerns to be safety and quality. That's a given. But I don't want to see the emphasis put on on-time delivery one month and productivity numbers the next. I want them both every month."

Brian remembered how confused he had been by what Ralph was asking. There had been a pile of work to get out. Brian had worked every operator who would work overtime for two weeks, running every machine available to get it done. What Ralph was saying, however, was that anybody could run lots of machines, use lots of people, and spend lots of money in order to deliver on time. It was also true that just about anybody could use the best people in the shop on the best machines, and improve their productivity. Ralph wanted them both. What neither of them really understood at the time was that they needed better tools and techniques to accomplish both of these objectives. Like the tools to produce valid schedules on the shop floor, they needed additional tools that would provide accurate capacity plans and a means to control the capacity planning process.

Brian's first response to Ralph's demand was to head up to Elliot's office in Manufacturing Engineering. Elliot was in the process of finishing off a glazed doughnut when Brian walked in. "You didn't save a bite for me?" Brian asked. "That's just like you, Elliot. I come up here to talk turkey and you're downing dessert."

"What can I do for you, Miller?"

"You have to help me get Ralph off my back."

"What does he want now?"

Brian explained the situation. "We're busting our butts down there, and he's telling me productivity is lagging. Elliot, good buddy, you could do me a real favor here."

"Why does this sound like trouble?"

"All you have to do, Elliot, is relax your standards a bit. They're really tougher than they need to be, and there's no way I can meet them. They're just killing my productivity numbers."

"You must be kidding, Miller. I mean, you have to understand my position. I get measured around here on keeping the standard cost of the part down. If I increase the standard times, the standard cost goes up. I don't need to pull out the bottom line for you, do I? Besides, I think you can make the standards if you just put your mind to it."

"Can't you relax them just a tad . . . give me a little breathing room?"

"Sorry, Brian. I can't just go out and loosen all the standards. We agreed a few weeks ago that we were after realistic standards and I really believe it's starting to work."

"Well, it doesn't show in the productivity numbers," grumbled Brian.

"Come on, Brian. Give it a chance. We just got started," Elliot said with a smile. "Use some of your Midwest charm to soften up Ralph a little bit."

"I tried that. I tried being as charming as they come, but it didn't work. What you're asking me to operate on right now, Elliot, is blind faith."

The memory of those earlier times was still fresh with Brian. Now, he picked up the printout on his desk and smiled. Within a couple of months of that meeting, they had implemented the Dispatch List, and last month they had started using the Detail Capacity Planning module of their ERP software. What he had discovered was that by using Detail Capacity Planning, he could arrange in advance to get the right number of people and the right amount of equipment that would enable him to get both on-time delivery and productivity. In addition, the scrap and rework that was created by rushing to make the numbers was also being greatly reduced.

In the beginning, however, Brian would walk onto the shop floor, see the full boxes that held the work orders, and know it was already too late to react effectively to his capacity needs. If he was going to get the work out, he was going to have to get more capacity, but forward visibility into his capacity requirements was nonexistent. He had no idea how much of each resource he would need to line up in the future or, if the work order volume declined, whether he had to lay anyone off. It also meant that he couldn't tell the two operators who had asked for a few days off next month for the opening of the trout season whether they could have the time or not.

Then there was the call Brian got from the Maintenance Department to schedule the refurbishing of one of his machines. A number of Brian's machines were old and frequently breaking down. They simply couldn't hold the necessary tolerances demanded of them. Not only were these conditions causing a good deal of scrap and rework, they were also contributing to a loss in productivity. Finally, Maintenance received the parts and had the time to overhaul the Cincinnati Milacron machining center. The problem was that they wanted to do it right away. Brian, however, had a full load of work ahead of the machine. He tried to explain to Ivan, the Maintenance Manager, that there were bound to be times in the future when the load would be lighter. Unfortunately, he couldn't tell him exactly when that might be. Without this information, Brian was reluctantly forced to let Maintenance have their way.

The problem was compounded after Brian finally had the Cincinnati Milacron machining center back on line, and was starting to catch up. Maintenance called him again and told him they were taking his Hobbs off-line to refurbish the bearings. The Hobb was in the same cell as the machining center so all the machines in the cell were down again. Brian had to go through the whole exercise one more time.

Since his discussion (in Chapter 1) regarding "gut feel" with Mac, the former machine-shop supervisor, Brian recognized it was an ineffective approach to planning capacity and they had to find something better. Then it clicked: the Detail Capacity Planning section of the Effective Management Course. "I was so focused on routings and getting good schedules on the floor I just didn't realize the importance of the Detail Capacity Planning," he thought to himself. "I need to review what was said back then."

Brian quickly scheduled a meeting with Tony and Joan to review the capacity plan. As they reviewed the plan, it showed a large overdue load in his work centers and a future load that tapered off to nothing very quickly (see Figure 5.1).

In frustration Brian stated that they all knew he was going to get more work in the future, in spite of what the plan said. "I need a way to predict what these work loads are going to be, so I can deal with conflicts such as maintenance schedules and people asking for time off."

Joan chuckled to herself. "Brian, you don't see the future load because that's the way we set them up. If you want to see the full load,

Figure 5.1   Machine Load Report

Work Center No. 24		Weekly Capacity: 240 Hrs.
Week	Load	Over/Under-load
Past Due	824	+824
Week #1	286	+46
Week #2	150	-90
Week #3	90	-150
Week #4	39	-201

we can just change the parameter to include both released work orders and planned orders in material requirements planning."

"You mean that the planned work is not a part of the data?" Brian asked.

"That is correct," Joan replied.

"What idiot made that decision?" Brian demanded.

"You did," Joan replied and Brian sat back in shock. "Don't you remember the conversation we had when you first took over the Machine Shop and I asked you about it? I told you that Mac wanted it set that way because he didn't trust the planned orders in the future, and you agreed."

The memory crept back into Brian's brain. It was shortly after he took over, and thinking about system setting back then was the furthest thing from his mind. "Oh yeah, I remember now," Brian replied.

"I suggest we do a quick review of the education material before we set off trying to change anything," Tony suggested. They all agreed.

As they reviewed the material they remembered what Roxanne Barnes, the Effective Management instructor, said: "Capacity planning is nothing more than a great deal of common sense that neatly links things together." She told them how most companies determined their required capacity week by week. It was the capacity needed to meet the schedules. This could then be compared to what is called *planned hours,* which is the amount of capacity made available week by week. "The challenge," Roxanne said, "will be to get your management to understand that this capacity plan is like the work-center supervisor's operating budget. In fact, the accounting group should take the hours by work center, apply the labor costs, and that gives the direct labor operating budget by work center. It is then a matter of adding it up by department to get the department operating budgets. Once you know how much capacity you really need in terms of people and equipment, you can put together a plan to make that capacity available, and the supervisor can be held accountable for executing that plan."

TERMINOLOGY

Capacity refers to the ability to move work through a work center in a given time period. There are, however, several aspects of capacity. The capacity planning process begins by establishing a common understanding of the terminology.

The first step in capacity management is taken when the company decides—through the business plan, the supply plan, and the Master Schedule—what they want to make. The *required capacity* is the capacity necessary to support those plans; in other words, if a company wants to produce a given product, this is how much capacity it will take. In calculating required capacity, no consideration is given as to whether or not that much capacity is actually available or can be obtained. Clearly, that issue has to be dealt with, which is the objective of this chapter.

The *demonstrated capacity* reflects what each work center has produced in the recent past. This is a true reflection of what the work center is capable of producing under current conditions and circumstances, such as product mix, work schedule, staff levels, efficiency, and utilization. It is a proven capability, and it represents what the work center can be expected to produce in the near future without intervention.

Actual output capacity, however, is not always fixed. Machines and people can be added or deleted. Machines deteriorate, or are overhauled to increase their productivity. New people with less training are hired and, in some instances, labor efficiency improves. Therefore, it is up to the work-center supervisor to blend anticipated changes (decreases as well as increases) with demonstrated capacity to determine what the work center can be committed to produce in the future.

Planned capacity is the amount of capacity that is expected to be available during a specific future time period. It is based on the demonstrated capacity adjusted by any changes expected by the work-center supervisor. This may mean adding or deleting shifts, people, machines, overtime, or productivity improvements.

The planned capacity is the capacity expected to be available if operating under normal conditions and to the regular schedule shift pattern. The *maximum planned capacity* establishes a higher level of capacity that could be accomplished if a supervisor were to work the maximum overtime, add a shift, or hire people to run all of the machines. It is the maximum amount a work center is able to produce without capital expenditure for equipment or facilities. A company would prefer to operate at the planned capacity level because it is the most cost-effective, but the maximum planned capacity establishes an upper limit to the available capacity that can be employed for short periods of time.

The first place Brian went after reviewing the Detail Capacity Planning material was back to Elliot in Manufacturing Engineering. "We're going to start using the Detail Capacity Planning module of the Enterprise Resource Planning software and I need your help."

"What do you mean?" Elliot asked. "I calculate the available capacity for all the departments, including yours."

"But I don't think it's right," Brian said. "At least, I never seem to be able to produce what you say I should without working overtime. Something is obviously not adding up."

Elliot tried to explain the process of calculating available capacity for Brian. He told him how he used the traditional industrial engineering method of figuring what is called the rated or nominal capacity. "It's simple," he said. "I multiply the number of machines by the number of hours per shift times the number of shifts per day times the number of workdays per week. That's your 'gross capacity' if everybody worked at 100% efficiency and utilization. But since we know that's not going to be the case, I multiply that gross capacity by the target efficiency and utilization factors for the work center to get how much you should be able to produce."

"Okay," Brian said, "theoretically, I should have that much capacity. But my actual output rarely reaches that level without working a lot of overtime. I've got the machines you say I have, but I don't always have the operators to run them, and those I do have on the payroll aren't always there. Where in your calculations do you figure in absenteeism? Besides, Elliot, as I keep telling you, I haven't been reaching the efficiency levels you think are possible, and my utilization is a joke. You know what shape some of my machines are in."

"We've all got problems, Brian, but that's the way we've always figured our capacity."

"Okay, let me ask you another question," Brian said, staying on the attack. "Where do you get the amount of required capacity from?"

"I get it from the business plan—you know that!" Elliot responded, frustrated.

"Of course I do!" Brian replied, "But we both know how often that's updated—once a year or if there is some kind of crisis. That doesn't work for me. My actual capacity requirements change on a regular basis and I need to see the impact on the shop."

"That's what we have always used and I don't see it changing. We've made it work in the past," replied Elliot.

"Right, but only with plenty of overtime and terrible productivity results. I've got Ralph on my case, not only to get my work out on time to the schedule, but he also wants improvements in my productivity. I need some help, Elliot. I just can't seem to do it with the tools I've got. Look, Elliot, we're both young and relatively new at this game. We need to look at things through a different set of glasses than our predecessors. We need to look at what other companies are doing and see what the best practices are."

"Yeah, you're right, Brian. We shouldn't be fighting between ourselves. We made some real progress with the routings so why not work together on this? What do you suggest?"

"I think that you and a couple of your key people should go to the same course on Capacity Management that Joan and I went to. We would all be working from the same page," Brian followed.

"Good idea. I think I will do just that. I need a vacation from this place anyway."

CAPACITY PLANNING OBJECTIVE

The purpose of capacity management is to identify and solve capacity problems in a timely manner. This means before an emergency arrives and the work load becomes unmanageable, or the work load isn't sufficient to support the number of operators. The objective is to maintain a balance between the capacity that is available and what is required. If more capacity is required than is expected to be available, only two things can be done:

1. Get more capacity.
2. Reduce the requirements.

If less capacity than is available is going to be required, management must once again make adjustments to balance the two.

It is essential to plan the level of available capacity by considering the required capacity, which is determined by the planning and scheduling process. If the required capacity exceeds the current planned capacity, that planned capacity must be increased. There is, of course, some practical limit beyond which we cannot conveniently or economically increase capacity. When the required capacity exceeds this maximum level, some decisions have to be made, such as adding capital equipment, building an addition to the plant, or putting a limit on how much business to accept. These are major decisions that require the attention of top management.

Capacity Units of Measure

To manage capacity properly, it is important to establish a consistent unit of measure. Some companies are accustomed to dealing with capacity in terms of product units. At the Effective Management course Brian had attended, a company that made ball bearings, Beartone Manufacturing, planned its capacity in terms of bearings per day. Good Health Vitamins planned its capacity using tablets per day. And Samson Tires planned capacity in units of tons of molded rubber per week.

There are problems with these approaches, however. Beartone Manufacturing, for instance, makes a broad range of bearing sizes and the resources vary with the size. They also produce special bearings, which require more resources per unit than the standard products do. At Good Health, there are different sizes of tablets to contend with and complex multivitamin tablets, as well as simple tablets. And at the Samson Tire factory, similar variations exist. The point is, if it takes different amounts of resources and capacities to produce specific items on a schedule, planning capacities in gross product terms is inadequate. If there are variations in the product mix and resource requirements, another method must be used. Also, the incoming and outgoing work must be expressed in the same units. For example, Good Health would have a difficult time effectively planning input in pounds of tablet mix and output in numbers of tablets.

Planning in units of *standard hours* is recommended. Standard hours can be used as a common denominator for all products. It's measurable. It allows input and output figures to be expressed in the same units. It also eliminates product variables, such as size and complexity. This is particularly important when work centers produce different products and components. Using standard hours also makes it easier to convert required capacity into the quantity of people or machines needed—the ultimate objective.

With Detail Capacity Planning, the Enterprise Resource Planning system calculates capacity requirements for the orders that are already released, as well as for the future planned orders that have not been released. It was these planned orders that enabled Hayes to generate capacity requirement plans beyond what the machine-load plan was showing.

Brian, Joan, and Tony all felt it was important for the supervisors to understand the logic of this approach, so they again put together education sessions for them, using the material from Effective Management. They had a few questions about the material so Brian called Roxanne Barnes, the Effective Management course instructor, who taught that section. She was very helpful but did ask the question if they had yet developed a working Sales & Operation Planning process, which Effective Management suggested as the first step toward Integrated Business Management, and if the necessary Rough-Cut Capacity Planning process was in place.

Brian had to respond that they hadn't. "Roxanne," he said, "I'm happy that my boss is letting me do the shop scheduling and detail capacity planning. I'm not pushing my luck."

"Okay, but eventually you will have a major problem because you haven't done rough-cut," Roxanne responded.

Let's look at an example of using capacity planning. In Chapter 4, the process of backward scheduling was explained using a shop routing (see Figure 5.2).

On that shop order, the supervisor would need to plan an order release for 40 of part number 163824 adapter in the week of 7/2.

Figure 5.2   Backward Scheduling Diagram

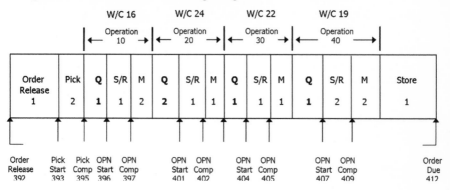

That planned order can now be used to calculate the shop's capacity requirements.

This example returns to work-center 24 and operation 20, which is a turning operation. This particular work center is under José's supervision. The routing shows José that his setup time is 3 hours and his run time is .20 hours per piece. He multiplies the .20 by the 40 needed pieces, adding in the setup time, and he finds that he needs 11 standard hours to produce those 40 pieces in work-center 24 (see Figure 5.3).

What he must now establish is when that capacity is required.

The total lead time for this part is 4 weeks. José knows that it is due in stock on 7/31. The question he needs to answer is when, during those 4 weeks, does operation 20 need to be performed? The answer is obtained via the backward-scheduling logic, as explained in Chapter 4. Beginning with the order due date obtained from MRP, offsetting it by the amount of time it will take to put the parts into stock, the move time, the time for operation 40, and continuing that process on back to operation 20, José can see that operation 20 needs to be performed in week 7/9 (see Figure 5.4).

He knows that it will take 11 hours in week 7/9 to produce those parts.

By going through every released and planned order in the system scheduled for work-center 24, the standard hours required can be loaded into the capacity plan. The planned capacity requirements for work-center 24 are shown in Figure 5.4. By walking through the calculation in the course for the supervisors, José and the other

Figure 5.3   Calculating Required Capacity Hours

(Material Plan X Routing) at Work Center

Part No. 163824	Description: Adapter		On Hand 18	Lead Time 4	Order Qty. 40	
Week Beginning	Past Due	7/2	7/9	7/16	7/23	##
Projected Requirements		12	16	14	8	12
Scheduled Receipts			40			
Projected Available	18	6	30	16	8	36
Planned order Release		40				

X

OPN. No.	Description	Set Up Hrs.	Run Hrs.	Work Center
20	Turn	3.0	.20	24

↓

	Work Center - 24	
OPN.	Hours	Week
20	11.0	?

supervisors understood how the dates were derived. (He was also glad that the computer would do all these calculations for him.)

In the previous example, the required-capacity hours were loaded into the weekly bucket (period of time) that contained the operation due date. There are four ways in which required capacities can be spread across the calendar.

1. Load all hours into weekly buckets containing the operation *complete* date (aka *due* date).
2. Load all hours into weekly buckets containing the operation *start* date.
3. Back load from the operation complete date into daily buckets.
4. Forward load from the operation *start* date into daily buckets.

The first two methods may work for companies that don't have jobs running more than a full day. On the other hand, planning capacities in weekly requirements is inadequate when a job can run multiple days. Situations that require the use of the daily bucket approach (methods three and four) follow:

Figure 5.4   Loading Capacity into Weekly Buckets

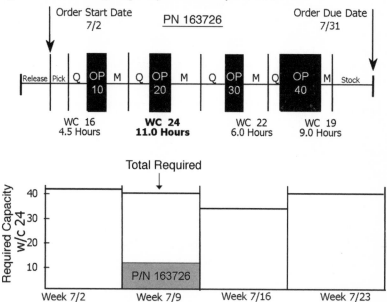

1. When there are long-running jobs, the weekly bucket approach distorts the week-to-week picture. In work centers that have a small number of jobs going through, this picture could be distorted by as little as a 2-day run time.

2. As companies move along the Lean Manufacturing journey (see Chapter 10), the shortening of lead times and reduction of order quantities will mean that weekly capacity buckets won't be sufficient to guarantee daily delivery schedules.

Figure 5.5 shows the results of loading the required capacity into daily buckets. Let us suppose that Operation 20 requires 50 hours in work-center 24 and must be completed on Monday, 7/23. José knows that he can schedule only 8 hours per day. For simplicity of calculation we will not use Load Factor as a consideration in this calculation. This should be taken into consideration, however, when scheduling your facility. Back loading from the due date, José would put 8 hours into Monday, 7/23; 8 hours per day into 7/16 through 7/20; and the last 2 hours would be loaded into Friday, 7/13. The final result is that 2 hours will be required in the week 7/9, 40 hours in week 7/16, and 8 hours in week 7/23.

Figure 5.5   Loading Capacity into Daily Buckets (no Load Factor)

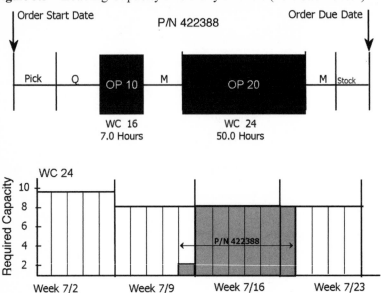

The choice of which alternative to use depends upon the requirements of the individual company. Whichever method is used, however, it is important that the users—the capacity planner and shop supervisor—understand the logic of the process.

Available Capacity

The objective of planning is to balance the available capacity with the required capacity. But how much capacity is really available? Several ways to look at available capacity have already been defined. There is the nominal capacity, as determined by Elliot's calculation explained previously. There is the demonstrated capacity, representing recent actual performance, and so what can be expected to be available in the future if nothing changes. And there is the planned capacity and the maximum planned capacity. Which one should be used? Actually, all of them play a role in managing capacity.

To begin with, there are some fundamental decisions that senior management will have to make regarding how they typically want to run the facility. At Hayes, Pete—the General Manager—and his

Figure 5.6   Hayes Capacity Guidelines

Desired Capacity:

2   Shifts per day

8   Hours per day

5   Days per week

Maximum Capacity:

2   Shifts per day

10   Hours per shift

6   Days per week

staff have decided to schedule the plant to work 2 shifts per day, 8 hours per shift, 5 days a week (see Figure 5.6).

They have also chosen to place an upper limit on the scheduled working hours of two shifts per day and 10 hours per shift, thus authorizing 2 hours of overtime per shift. They have decided against scheduling the factory to operate more than 6 days a week on an ongoing basis. These are the guidelines that Pete gave to the staff. The supervisors were expected to do whatever was needed, within these guidelines, to get the work done. This is not to say that in a real emergency a Sunday can't be worked as well, but it will not be scheduled on an ongoing basis.

It is then the responsibility of Brian, Dan, and Mickey, working with their supervisors, to translate these guidelines into specific operating schedules for each work center. If the guidelines have to be exceeded in a work center, it needs to be brought to Pete's attention so that he can consider the necessary short- and long-term solutions. If, on the other hand, the guideline level is not required in other work centers, only the amount of time needed to fulfill the requirements should be scheduled.

Basically, the guidelines represent Pete's overall management strategy for the way the factory will be run. The individual work-center planning provides the details by which Brian, Dan, and Mickey can plan their different resources.

Calculating Capacity Requirements

Brian, Dan, Mickey, and their supervisors were accustomed to monitoring their efficiency and utilization quite closely. To learn how to balance these, they needed a good understanding of what each is. Utilization is a measure of the use of available resources, usually machinery and people, in a productive capacity. It determines the percentage of the hours when a person or machine was available (attendance hours) that were actually spent producing parts (charged hours). Efficiency is a measure of performance against the standards. In other words, during the time a person or machine was being used, how efficient (or effective) was that use. Efficiency is the earned hours (at standard) divided by the charged hours. When combined together, utilization and efficiency provide the commonly used measure of productivity. The calculation of these factors is explained in Figure 5.7.

For example, the Hayes milling department has 320 labor hours per week available (gross available hours). On average, absenteeism has reduced that to 300 attendance hours per week. If the average total time that the operators spend on productive work is 270 hours

Figure 5.7   Performance Calculations

Base Data:-

Gross Available hours	= 320	
Total Attendance Hours	= 300	
Actual Production hours	= 270	(demonstrated productive hours)
Actual Gross Production Hours	= 280	(clock time, including downtime)
Standard Hours Gross Output*	= 240	(for total units produced)

(* Actual Output quantity. Yield loss, is taken into account in the master data used in mrp calculations)

Calculations:-

Efficiency   = Standard Hours Gross Output ÷ Actual Production Hours
= 240/270 =   89%

Utilization   = Actual Production Hours ÷ Total Attendance Hours
= 270/300 =   90%

Productivity   = Standard Hours Gross Output ÷ Total Attendance Hours
= 240/300 =   80%

Load Factor   = Standard Hours Gross Output ÷ Gross Available Hours
= 240/320 =   75%

per week, the utilization is 90% (270 divided by 300). If the standard hours of output are 240 per week, the average efficiency is 89% (240 divided by 270). To calculate productivity, the supervisor can either multiply the efficiency times utilization, or divide the standard hours of output by total attendance hours, giving us 80% (240 divided by 300).

Load Factor

Load Factor combines the effect of efficiency, utilization, and absenteeism. Unlike productivity, which does not account for absenteeism, Load Factors are equal to the ratio of the output of a work center in standard hours to the gross available clock hours of a resource. This allows the supervisor and capacity planner to translate standard hours of required capacity into resources required at a work center. It also provides a convenient means of converting available people or machines into expected standard hours of output (i.e., available capacity).

To calculate the Load Factor, the gross available hours of machine time and/or manpower that exist in a given work center must first be calculated (see Figure 5.8).

In this case, Brian has decided to run this work center only one shift per day, because that is sufficient to complete the work that is required to be done. The next step is to determine how many operators and machines there are. In this example, Brian has four operators and four machines available at 8 hours per shift. One shift × four operators × 8 hours equals 32 available hours. He multiplies that by 5 days per week and he gets 160 hours available per week. That is the gross available hours. Brian knows, however, that the work center actually produced an average of only 120 standard hours of work per week during the past 4 weeks. That has been the work center's demonstrated capacity. Therefore, the demonstrated Load Factor is equal to 120 (the actual output in standard hours) divided by 160 (the available hours), or 75%. In other words, out of the total time this work center has budgeted every day, Brian can only expect to produce 75% of that amount in actual standard hours of output. This means each operator can be expected to produce 6 standard hours of output for each 8-hour day that person is on the payroll. Each work center, of course, will have its own Load Factor.

Figure 5.8   Calculating Load Factor

<u>**Work Center 24**</u>

1	Shifts Per Day
x 4	Op. Or Machines Per Shift
x 8	Hours Per Shift
= 32	= Hours Per Day
x 5	Days Per Week
= 160	**= Total Available Hours Per Week**

<u>Demonstrated Capacity</u>

120	Actual Output (Std. Hours) per week

<u>Load Factor</u>

120	Actual Output Hours
÷ 160	Available Hours
= 0.75	= **Load Factor**

$$\textbf{Load Factor} = \frac{\textbf{Standard Hours Output}}{\textbf{Gross Available Hours}}$$

Using a Load Factor in planning capacity can help supervisors get a better handle on what output to expect from their work centers under given circumstances. Demonstrated capacity represents what the supervisor can expect to produce in the future unless something changes. If any element affecting the Load Factor is expected to change, it is important that the Load Factor be adjusted to reflect that change (as *planned Load Factor*). The adjustment should be the result of the supervisor's commitment to certain improvements in efficiency, utilization, or absenteeism—not merely the result of management edict or arbitrary adjustments. It is important to get the supervisor to take ownership of the new number. Other more detailed measures, such as efficiency, utilization, or absenteeism, can be helpful in determining where problems are, but in planning capacity they should all be considered collectively, which is what the Load Factor does.

OVERALL EQUIPMENT EFFECTIVENESS

Overall Equipment Effectiveness (OEE) is an increasingly popular measure of work-center performance as it combines the effects of process availability, performance, and quality. This is useful for analysis where OEE falls below goal. OEE is a tracking measure; however it is susceptible to fudging. By contrast, Load Factor is a simple measure and the most effective for Capacity Planning—and it works for both machine-paced and labor-paced operations. The use of Load Factor for Capacity Planning and Overall Equipment Effectiveness to track machine performance is recommended.

PLANNING AVAILABLE CAPACITY

When the Master Schedule changes, either up or down, it is obviously going to have an impact on how much capacity will be needed. Demonstrated capacity reflects how much capacity was used to meet the earlier schedule. The question now becomes "How much capacity will be available to meet the future schedule?" Brian must have a way to figure out how many machines or people will be needed to produce the required output.

What happens when José is informed, via Detail Capacity Planning, that 300 standard hours of capacity are required in workcenter 24? He needs to translate the gross available hours into the expected output in standard hours, which is the planned capacity (see Figure 5.9).

According to the operating guidelines, José is authorized to run two shifts per day. Four machines and four operators are available on each of the two 8-hour shifts, which means there would be 64 gross labor hours available per day. Since the work center works 5 days a week, the gross available hours per week equals 320. Will

Figure 5.9 Calculating Planned Hours

Work Center 24

	2	Shifts Per Day
x	4	Op. Or Machines Per Shift
x	8	Hours Per Shift
=	64	= Hours Per Day
x	5	Days Per Week
=	320	= Total Hours Per Week
x	75%	Planned Load Factor
=	240	= Planned Capacity Standard Hours

320 hours satisfy the schedule that Pete has approved? No, because some of those hours will be lost to absenteeism, lower utilization, and inefficiency. Once the Load Factor of 75% is applied, José knows that only 240 standard hours of output can be expected. He'll need to gain some capacity, by either extending his operating hours or changing some of the elements affecting his Load Factor, such as improving utilization, efficiency, or reducing absenteeism. The Load Factor that the supervisor uses to calculate future available (planned) capacity is called the Planned Load Factor.

The same process can be used to calculate maximum capacity (see Figure 5.10).

Using the figures from the work-center guideline established earlier—2 shifts per day × 5 available machines, × 10 hours per shift, × 6 days per week—indicates to José that his maximum gross available hours would be 600. Multiplying that by the 75% Load Factor would tell him that his maximum planned capacity in standard hours is 400.

Both Brian and José were well aware that during times of extended overtime, such as 10-hour days or 6-day weeks, productivity was likely to slip because of increased fatigue, absenteeism, or machine downtime. They adjusted the planned Load Factor during these periods down to 70%, thus making the maximum planned capacity 336 standard hours.

Ultimately, supervisors like José must make the commitment for output by the work center: It is imperative that he has the proper information available to him to manage his resources.

Reserving Capacity

Brian was going through the example of work-center 24 in the course when he noticed José with his hand up.

"What's wrong, José?" asked Brian. "You understand all the calculations, don't you?"

"Yeah," replied José. "But I'm worried that if we set our staffing levels to required capacity, we won't have enough capacity when the inevitable emergency hits. You know, the hot job that Sales wants us to push, the replacements for the parts scrapped at Assembly, or when the service organization has a tractor down in the field. Even though our planning has improved a lot, we still get a fair share of unplanned emergency work. I think I should plan a

Figure 5.10   Calculating Maximum Planned Hours

<u>**Work Center 24**</u>

[2]	Shifts Per Day
x [5]	Op. Or Machines Per Shift
x [10]	Hours Per Shift
= [100]	= Hours Per Day
x [6]	Days Per Week
= [600]	= Total Hours Per Week
x [75%]	Planned Load Factor*
= [400]	= Planned Capacity Standard Hours

* Note: Planned Load Factor should be adjusted to reflect expected
changes in productivity and absenteeism

little more available capacity so that I'll be able to handle it without overtime."

Brian admitted that José had a good point. Even though they had made progress reducing shortages using the Dispatch List they were nowhere near Effective Management's Class A level. It was obvious that they probably never would totally eliminate the need for that little extra capacity for the emergencies. Brian knew that Ralph wanted him to keep a little in reserve as well. But what was the best way to do that?

Brian knew that he could simply understate his available capacity on the Detail Capacity Plans and keep a little in his back pocket, so to speak. But he also knew that giving false data was playing the game the way Dan used to with his padded lead times, and others would soon figure out that he could do more than what he was stating. That would destroy all the hard work that had been done to build integrity into the information.

José piped up. "Why don't we just lower the Load Factor a little? That would permit me to put on a few more people to meet the planned requirements, and then I could cover the emergencies."

Brian thought about José's suggestion for a minute before he realized that it was just another way of understating his true available capacity. What he needed to do was to reserve some capacity, but make it visible. Then everyone would know how much capacity he had for the emergencies, and when the workload exceeded that as well, he would feel justified in asking Ralph for more people.

Brian knew there had to be a way.

Joan spoke up. "Why don't I have the material planners put some work orders in the system for reserved capacity? We could set up some dummy part numbers and create routings that would place planned capacity requirements on the work centers that he would designate. We have enough history to be able to figure out where the emergencies are most likely to hit and how much capacity is usually required. The information wouldn't have to be exact, just good enough to cover the average emergency work. It would be extra work for her planners because they would have to manage these special orders very carefully, but I think it would be well worth the effort."

With that comment a buzz went around the room. Finally Brian got control back.

José had his hand up again. "You know, Brian, that seems like a great way to reserve the capacity and make it visible to anyone who wanted to know. These dummy orders will show up in the material plans as well as in our capacity plans. Then, as the actual emergency work hits us, the material planner can simply replace one of the dummy orders with a real order."

Brian told Dan and Mickey about the new idea. As expected, Dan rejected the notion and said he would continue to do the emergency work his way. "I don't want those guys in Production Control getting any more control over me than they already have. I've been managing production shops for over 20 years and I don't need anyone else telling me how to do things. I like to keep a little in reserve through my own means."

Mickey, on the other hand, thought it was a great idea. He felt that if Joan just put a couple of these orders a week into the Master Schedule that would cover him.

Brian called Joan and told her that he would help her gather the data for the machine shop, and that Mickey had promised to do the same for the Assembly Department.

It should be noted that the notion of reserving capacity, though a common practice, should be treated with caution. It is easy to fall into the just-in-case trap and use reserved capacity rather than addressing the real problems.

Creating the Capacity Plan

What follows is an example designed to illustrate how the computer generates the capacity requirements. Since this example pushes a lot of numbers around, a work sheet has been set up to help understand the process (see Figure 5.11).

Figure 5.11   Loading Capacity into Weeks

Work Center: 02

Wk End. W/O #	6/28 391	7/5 395	7/12 400	7/19 405	7/26 410	8/2 415
W125	8		5	8		
W133			10		16	
W116				9		
W152					9	
W134				1	16	
W108						17
Total	8	0	15	18	41	17

Each column represents a 1-week period ending on the dates indicated. By looking at the calendar (see Figure 5.12), we can see that each of the numbered days (M-391, M-395, M-400, . . .) corresponds to the Friday of each given week.

For this example, we will use the timing alternative 3, explained previously, which loads all hours into daily buckets starting from the operation complete date. This example (see Figure 5.13) uses six shop orders—again not using Load Factor in the back-scheduling logic to keep the math simple.

Let's look at work-center 02. Beginning with work order 125, we check to see if that work order goes through work-center 02. It does in operation 20 and 40. It requires 8 hours of setup and run time at operation 20 and 13 hours at operation 40. From the backward-scheduling rules (see Figure 5.14), we see that work-center 02 is capable of producing 8 hours of work per day (one shift).

We must now put the 8 and 13 hours into the appropriate buckets on the work sheet. Using timing rule 3, we identify the operation complete dates—in this case M-391 and M-401, respectively. If the operation is already past due, it will be placed in the first weekly

Figure 5.12   Loading Capacity into Weeks

Calendar

			JUNE			
S	M	T	W	T	F	S
					1 *371*	2
3	4 *372*	5 *373*	6 *374*	7 *375*	8 *376*	9
10	11 *377*	12 *378*	13 *379*	14 *380*	15 *381*	16
17	18 *382*	19 *383*	20 *384*	21 *385*	22 *386*	23
24	25 *387*	26 *388*	27 *389*	28 *390*	29 *391*	30

Julian Day   M Day

			JULY			
S	M	T	W	T	F	S
1	2 *392*	3 *393*	4 *Holiday*	5 *394*	6 *395*	7
8	9 *396*	10 *397*	11 *398*	12 *399*	13 *400*	14
15	16 *401*	17 *402*	18 *403*	19 *404*	20 *405*	21
22	23 *406*	24 *407*	25 *408*	26 *409*	27 *410*	28
29	30 *411*	31 *412*				

bucket. Since operation 20 is due on M-391, it will fall into the week ending 391 bucket. Operation 40 is due M-401, which by referring to the manufacturing calendar is a Monday. Since our scheduling rules (see Figure 5.14) say this work center (02) works on one shift and each shift is only 8 hours, we cannot schedule any more than 8 hours in that day. Consequently, the other 5 hours will have to go into the previous day, M-day 400, a Friday, which is in the week ending 400 bucket (see Figure 5.11). Work order 133 also goes through work-center 02, and it requires 10 hours due on M-day 398 and 16 hours on M-day 408. Since 398 is a Wednesday, 8 hours can be put into Wednesday and 2 hours into Tuesday, so all 10 hours can go into the week ending 400 for operation 20. Operation 40 is due on M-day 408, which is also a Wednesday, so 8 hours can be worked on Wednesday and 8 hours on Tuesday. This way, all 16 hours can go into the week ending 410 bucket. Operation 40 on work order 116 is scheduled on M-day 403 and takes 9 hours. Since 403 is a Wednesday, 8 hours can be done then and 1 hour on Tuesday. Thus, all 9 hours can be placed in bucket 405. Work order 152 has operation

Figure 5.13   Using Work Orders for Detail Capacity Planning

Work Center 02: Shop Orders

PN		264		
WO#		125	Rel. Date	382
OPN.	WC.	Total Hrs.	Start Date	Comp. Date
10	01	5	386	387
20	02	8	390	391
30	03	5	395	396
40	02	13	399	401

Due Date   404

PN		173		
WO#		116	Rel. Date	385
OPN.	WC.	Total Hrs.	Start Date	Comp. Date
10	01	4.5	389	390
20	04	11	393	394
30	07	6	397	394
40	02	9	401	403

Due Date   406

PN		268		
WO#		134	Rel. Date	382
OPN.	WC.	Total Hrs.	Start Date	Comp. Date
10	01	8.5	386	387
20	05	18	390	392
30	06	9	394	396
40	03	9	400	401
50	02	17	404	407

Due Date   410

PN		264		
WO#		133	Rel. Date	388
OPN.	WC.	Total Hrs.	Start Date	Comp. Date
10	01	6	392	393
20	02	10	396	398
30	03	6	402	403
40	02	16	406	408

Due Date   411

PN		173		
WO#		152	Rel. Date	391
OPN.	WC.	Total Hrs.	Start Date	Comp. Date
10	01	4.5	395	396
20	04	11	399	400
30	07	6	403	404
40	02	9	407	409

Due Date   412

PN		268		
WO#		108	Rel. Date	388
OPN.	WC.	Total Hrs.	Start Date	Comp. Date
10	01	8.5	392	393
20	05	18	396	398
30	06	9	400	402
40	03	9	406	407
50	02	17	410	413

Due Date   416

Figure 5.14   Example: Scheduling Rules for Work Center 02

- **Allow:**
  - 8 hours / shift
  - Work center 06 & 02 : 1 shift
  - All other work centers: 2 shifts
  - 2 days between operations in different departments for move
  - 1 day between operations in different work centers for move
  - 0 days between operations in same work center for move
  - 1 day to put away in stores
  - 2 days to pick components & move to first work center
  - 1 day for release

40 due on day 409, which is a Thursday. Therefore, 8 hours can go in Thursday and 1 hour on Wednesday. All 9 hours can be placed in the week ending 410 bucket. Work order 134 takes 17 hours for operation 50, with an operation due date of 407. This is a Tuesday, so we can place 8 hours in that day and 8 hours in Monday, which leaves us 1 hour short. This hour would have to be done on the previous Friday, M-day 405. One hour would then be placed in the week

ending 405 bucket and 16 hours in the week ending 410 bucket. And, finally, work order 108 takes 17 hours in work-center 02 with a due date of 413. That would make 8 hours on Wednesday, 8 hours on Tuesday, and 1 hour on Monday. All 17 hours can go into the week ending 415 bucket. We then total the hours in each week: 8 in week 391, 0 in week 395, 15 in week 400, 18 in week 405, 41 in week 410, and 17 in week 415.

Once the software has processed all the information for all the released and planned orders going through a work center, it generates a Detail Capacity Plan (see Figure 5.15).

Figure 5.15   Detail Capacity Plan for Work Center 24

WORK CENTER NO.: 24						Date: 8/06				
Description: Lathes						Demo. Cap'y.: 120				
Department No.: M						Max. Plan Cap'y.: 400				
Week	Order No.	Part No.	Part Description	Qty.	Opn. No.	Opn. Due Date	Order Due Date	Setup Hrs.	Run Hrs.	Stat.
8/5	W123	144398	Shaft	200	30	7/1	7/18	1.0	10.0	R
	W124	428876	Bolt	3000	30	7/2	7/23	2.0	30.0	R
	W110	330246	Gear	500	20	7/3	7/17	1.0	15.0	R
	W120	407211	Bolt	4000	30	7/3	7/19	2.0	50.0	R
	W112	163726	Hub	400	20	7/4	7/22	3.0	8.0	R
	W129	186846	Shaft	200	20	7/4	7/11	1.0	4.5	R
							TOTALS	10.0	117.5	
8/12	W128	118132	Gear	400	20	7/9	7/23	3.0	36.0	R
	W138	258721	Spacer	2000	20	7/10	7/24	0.5	20.0	R
	W140	321406	Hub	500	30	7/11	7/26	1.0	30.0	R
		163726	Hub	400	20	7/12	7/29	3.0	8.0	P
		330246	Gear	500	20	7/12	7/30	1.0	15.0	P
							TOTALS	8.5	109.0	

This plan displays all work orders scheduled to go through work center 24 for the weeks 8/6 and 8/13. The header record shows the work-center number, a description of that work center, a department number, the date of the plan, the demonstrated capacity of the work center, and the maximum planned capacity.

Each line of the detail plan contains the following information for each work order in each weekly period:

• the work-order number
• the part number
• the part description

- the quantity of product remaining to be produced at this operation in this work center
- the operation number to be performed
- the date this operation is scheduled to be completed
- the date this work order is scheduled to be completed (to the stockroom or to shipping)
- the setup hours remaining to be completed on this work order at this operation
- the run hours remaining to be completed on this work order at this operation
- the status code of the planned or released work order

This detailed plan can give each supervisor a comprehensive picture of all the work that is expected to be produced by this work center over the Material Requirements Planning horizon, as set in the Enterprise Resource Planning system. That could be 12 months of data. As one can imagine such a plan would be very lengthy and full of detail, much of which would change over time, and a typical shop-floor supervisor would pay no attention to it. What the supervisor really wants to know is the total hours required out of a work center in each week over a shorter horizon, normally 13 weeks (3 months). Then, working as a team, the capacity planner and shop supervisor can quickly determine whether that figure is more or less than the shop has planned. If that figure reasonably matches the supervisor's planned available capacity, it is acceptable. However, if it's greater or smaller, the supervisor will have to initiate some corrective actions. This information is available from the Summary Capacity Plan.

Summary Capacity Plan

The software should generate a view that is easy to read, like Figure 5.16, which is a summation of the detailed plan.

In this plan, only the total hours of load for each week are shown, rather than the individual order detail. It also offers a week's information on one line, so a supervisor can see the shop capacity needs for the time horizon required.

The summary plan header record contains the following information:

- the date of the plan
- the work-center number
- a description of that work center
- the number of machines in that work center
- the number of operators available for that work center
- the ratio of machines to operator (in this case, one operator can run two machines simultaneously)
- the scheduled days per week for that work center
- the scheduled shifts per day for that work center
- the scheduled hours per shift for that work center
- the demonstrated capacity for that work center
- the maximum planned capacity for that work center
- the Planned Load Factor for that work center

Figure 5.16   Summary Capacity Plan for Work Center 24

Summary Capacity Plan

Date	8/06	No. Machines	5	Hours / Shift	8
Work Center	24	No. Operators	2	Shifts / Day	1
Description	Lathes	Mach / Oper	2	Days / Week	5
Demo. Cap'y.	120	Max. Cap'y.	400	Load Factor	75%

			MACHINE CAPACITY						LABOR CAPACITY		
Week	Reqd. Cap'y (Hrs)	Plan Cap'y (Hrs)	Load vs. Capacity(%)				Reqd. Cap'y (Hrs)	Plan Cap'y (Hrs)	Load vs. Capacity(%)		
			50	100	150				50	100	150
8/06	128	150	xxxxxxx				64	60	xxxxxxxxxxx		
8/13	118	150	xxxxxx				59	60	xxxxxxxxxx		
8/20	116	150	xxxxx				58	60	xxxxxxxxx		
8/27	126	150	xxxxxxx				63	60	xxxxxxxxxxx		
9/03	130	150	xxxxxxx				65	60	xxxxxxxxxxx		
9/10	144	150	xxxxxxxxx				72	60	xxxxxxxxxxxxxx		
9/17	140	150	xxxxxxxxx				70	60	xxxxxxxxxxxxxx		
9/24	150	150	xxxxxxxxxx				75	90	xxxxxxx		
10/01	166	150	xxxxxxxxxxxx				83	90	xxxxxxxx		
10/08	160	150	xxxxxxxxxxx				80	90	xxxxxxxx		
7/28											

This information is required to do a good job of analyzing the capacity plan without having to switch between multiple screens.

In a work center that contains equipment resources and labor resources that need to be capacity planned, supervisors must plan capacities for both. The systems display the capacity plans for both resources on one plan as in Figure 5.16. Others have separate plans for each. Having both resources on one page makes it easier for the capacity planner and supervisor to use, but it is not particularly important which approach we use. Other aspects of planning multiple resources are discussed later in this chapter.

Each side of the plan has the same data requirements but, as shown in Figure 5.16, the data itself is not necessarily the same. Let's look at the machine side of the plan first. The required capacity is the standard hours of machine output required to support the schedule. This number was generated from the Detail Capacity Planning system. The person accountable for the required capacity is the capacity planner.

Referring back to Figure 5.15, we can see the breakdown of the 128 hours required in week beginning 8/6. It is made up of 10.0 hours of setup time and 117.5 hours of run time. The total has been rounded up to 128. Further breakdown of the total hours into the individual jobs is also obvious.

The planned capacity represents how much capacity, in standard hours, is expected to be available to apply against the scheduled jobs. The planned machine capacity of 150 hours per week is determined as follows: 5 machines $\times$ 8 hours per shift, $\times$ 1 shift per day, $\times$ 5 days per week, $\times$ a 75% planned Load Factor. This is the work-center supervisor's number. The supervisor is the one who is responsible for knowing how much work can be generated from his or her work center. If the supervisor recognizes that more capacity will be needed to meet the required capacity, it's up to the supervisor to initiate action to get it. The updated planned capacity must also be recorded in the database.

Note that the work center in Figure 5.16 has five machines available and two operators who run two machines at a time. This means that the work center can only run four machines at any one time. It may seem that the maximum capacity should be calculated on the basis of only four machines, since that is all we can run. But capacity is defined as the maximum sustainable output for the scheduled working hours. We want to know how much *machine* capacity we have assuming there would be enough operators to run all the machines available and enough work to keep them all busy. The maximum capacity of 450 hours is calculated on the basis of how many total machines we have. The operator question will be addressed separately.

Let's look at it another way. Suppose that an operator was added to the first shift. Now the work center can run all five machines, although one of the operators would be, nominally, "inefficient" since the shop would be working at only half capacity (running one machine rather than two). However, the real *machine* or maximum capacity is based on all five machines.

The load-versus-capacity section graphically tells the supervisor at a glance the relationship between the required capacity and the planned capacity. It is the ratio of the required capacity to the planned capacity expressed as a percentage and displayed in bar-chart form. Although a welcome supplement, it is not a prerequisite to successful capacity planning. The ability to see the relationship between required and planned capacity out into the future means that decisions can be made as to whether or not to work overtime, to add machines, to move people in from other work centers, to split an order, or whether the schedule itself has to change.

On the labor side of the plan, this work center has one operator running two machines simultaneously. The required labor hours, therefore, are one half the machine hours. The planned labor capacity of 60 hours is derived as follows: 2 operators $\times$ 8 hours per shift, $\times$ 5 days per week, $\times$ the 75% planned Load Factor. Notice that beginning with week 9/24, however, the planned labor capacity has been increased to 90 hours. This reflects the supervisor's intent to bring another operator on board at that time.

This plan is telling José that he has sufficient machine capacity to meet the plan until the week of 10/01. He does not, however, have enough labor capacity with a straight 40-hour week. He will have to get more labor capacity to meet the schedule. He'll also have to make a commitment to move the work through the work center as efficiently as possible.

The required capacity is not level. It ranges from a low of 58 labor hours to a high of 83. José also knows that the work will not arrive at the work center exactly as planned. To determine his base requirement for people, he averaged the hours over the next 4 weeks and arrived at a little over 60 labor hours. Since the variation from week to week wasn't excessive, he could average the output over the next month and plan his staffing levels accordingly. The amount of variation permissible is dependent on the amount of queue at the lathes and at the downstream work centers.

In this case, José has decided to work overtime for the weeks 9/3 through 9/17. In the week of 9/24, the labor overload is 15 hours (75 required, 60 available). This is more than can be made up with reasonable overtime, so José has decided to bring a new operator on board that week. Since this is only a one-shift operation, José can see from the summary plan that he doesn't have enough machine capacity after 10/10. He'll need to put the new operator on the second shift.

As indicated by the required capacity data, José is not going to have enough work to keep this operator busy running two machines. By subtracting the 60 hours for the two first-shift operators from the required capacity, we can see that he only needs 15 additional labor hours in week 9/24, 23 hours in week 10/1, and 20 hours in week 10/8. Since the operator is capable of providing 30 standard hours of output per week, it is obvious that the new operator will be under-utilized. What should José do? He can't hire part of an operator. In this case, José is aware that there is an overload situation in the de-burr work center. He has decided that he will take some hand-de-burr work from that work center and bring it to the lathe work center, where the operator can do that work when the lathe is on automatic cycle. When there is no scheduled work for the operator, José plans to send him to the de-burr work center to help out there. That way he will get full utilization of the operator and, at the same time, solve the de-burr overload problem.

Planning Multiple Resources

There are several instances in which a supervisor needs to plan multiple resources in a single work center. The previous situation, where both machine and operator capacity must be planned, is the simplest case. Other situations involve multiple labor skills, labor pools, tooling, fixtures, and test equipment.

There are fundamentally three ways to handle these situations. First, if the second resource capacity is directly proportional to the machine capacity, as in the previous example, the required capacity is calculated by multiplying the required machine capacity by a factor that defines the ratio between machine hours and the second resource hours. This factor is stored on the Work Center Master file in the database. In the case where the second resource is labor, it is sometimes called a crew factor. It represents the number of operators required per machine. In the previous example, the factor is 0.5, or one operator per two machines. In other cases, the number may be greater than one, as with Mickey's paint line. In this case, Mickey had two people loading the line and three people unloading it. The machine (line) capacity would be calculated, and then multiplied by five to arrive at the number of operator hours required.

The second situation is where different amounts of a resource are required to perform the operation rather than just multiples or fractions of the machine resource. For instance, operators of different skills may be required; such is the case when an operator, technician, and an inspector are required simultaneously. Another common situation in this category is the planning of tooling capacity in addition to the basic machine capacity. To plan these multiple resources requires that data for each required resource be included on the routing for the operation in question. Each resource would be given its own identifying resource number (i.e., work center). The software can then calculate the required amount of each resource needed and the schedule for when it is needed, just as we did earlier for the machine capacity. The difference is that separate calculations are necessary for each resource. A separate capacity planning plan is also necessary for each resource.

Brian had several fixtures that consumed a considerable amount of capacity. It was an ability he liked to have, so he went to the system analyst, Laura Sanderford, to see what could be done. "Listen, Laura, I'd like to know if the software will allow me to add a second resource to the routing so I can plan my fixtures?" Brian asked.

"Just let me take a look first, and I'll let you know in a couple of days," she replied.

True to her word, Laura gave Brian a call two days later. "It's not in the software, but something we can add," she said, "but there's a problem. It's going to take a lot of programming. Are you sure this is something you really need to get the job done?" she asked.

Brian had been down this road before. There were always lots of things the computer could do, and they all required programming.

This was another case when he had to make a decision regarding his priorities. He knew this one was far from being on the top of his list, especially after Laura explained to him what it would cost. As it would turn out, he could duplicate the tooling for less than the programming would cost.

The third multiple-resource situation involves those circumstances where operators are capable of running a variety of equipment, such as the use of labor pools or crews. The machine capacity must be calculated separately from the labor capacity since each needs to be planned independently. This involves the work-center identification issue that was discussed in Chapter 3.

Brian saw an example of this when he went on the visit to Good Health Vitamins. Hal Beckman, Materials Manager, took him to the packaging department, where he had five packaging lines, each capable of handling different package sizes and configurations. He only ran four of them at a time, because one line was usually being changed over to the next product by a separate setup crew. This meant he only needed four operating crews. However, he wanted to plan the line capacity separately from the operating crew and setup crew capacities to be sure that he didn't overload either the crews or any single line. Hal did this by assigning each packaging line its own work-center number, tying all of them into an operating crew resource-center number at the same time. He also assigned an operation number to the setup and assigned that to a setup resource center. Then he modified his software to add up the operating capacity requirements from each line, to get the total capacity requirements for the operating crew. He had separate capacity planning plans printed for the operating crew, the setup crew, and for each line.

This was actually a simple modification, and Brian found it could be very useful at Hayes. By having the system add up the standard hours by supervisor, the supervisor could see the total people required. This, in turn, would ensure that if several work centers only needed a partial operator, the supervisor wouldn't plan a full operator for them and thereby over-plan the number of people required. We saw this in the example of José sharing a lathe operator with the de-burr bench. This does mean, however, that people need to be crosstrained. The capacity plan can be beneficial in determining where people will need to be shifted from and where cross-training would be required. By adding another summary, then, Brian could see the total people requirements for his department.

Infinite and Finite Loading

To backtrack a bit, when we first generated the required capacity on the capacity plan, we never took into consideration how much capacity we actually had. What we were doing is a process called infinite loading. The concept of infinite loading is to take everything that is scheduled and load it into the work center to an infinite level, without regard for available capacity. The potential problem with this approach is that work centers do not have infinite capacity.

While this is called Infinite Loading, it is a misnomer when operating with Class A behaviors. The capacity at the Sales & Operations Planning and Master Schedule levels would have already been reviewed and be in the ball park before the Detail Capacity Planning process would begin (see Figure 2.4). This process will be discussed in detail in Chapter 7.

An alternate concept is finite loading. (Note that *finite loading* is similar to, but in some critical aspects different from, *finite capacity scheduling,* which will be explained in Chapter 9.) Finite loading is based upon the notion that we should put no more into the work center than it can be expected to produce. Although this may be exactly what we want to achieve, employing the finite-loading process requires some understanding and caution. The finite-loading process loads the work center in priority sequence up to a preestablished limit. If the scheduled load exceeds the limit in a given period, the computer automatically reschedules the operation to reduce the load.

The results of these two approaches are shown in Figure 5.17.

In the top graph (infinite loading), the load is very erratic and exceeds the available capacity in several periods. Obviously, some action should to be taken to level this load and avoid the overload periods. The bottom graph represents what the load would look like after applying the finite-loading technique. The load is level and doesn't exceed the available capacity in any period.

Although the finite-loading concept is valid, and the result appears excellent, there are some significant concerns with the approach. First, it assumes that capacities are fixed, which is often not the case. Additional capacity can be gained by working overtime, adding people, adding a shift, or any number of other methods that the managers of that area have learned to employ over the years.

Figure 5.17   Infinite vs. Finite Loading

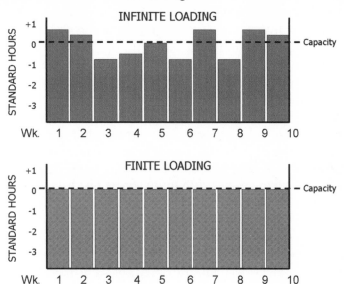

Machines that run 24 hours per day, 7 days per week, don't have that flexibility and therefore are candidates for the finite logic.

Second, with finite loading the computer automatically reschedules the operation due dates, either in or out, whenever the stated load limit is exceeded. Moving the dates out results in the rescheduling of all downstream operation dates. This will invariably cause some of the other downstream work centers to become overloaded, and they, in turn, will need to be rescheduled. This massive rescheduling will result in the order due date being rescheduled to a future date. As this chain of events moves up through the bill of material, part number by part number being rescheduled out to a future date, the Master Schedule will ultimately be impacted, causing customer deliveries to be missed. This could be devastating to a company.

Automatically rescheduling operations to earlier dates has the opposite effect of moving them out. Instead of going up through the bill of material, the rescheduling goes down. This results in many expedite messages in the Purchasing Department. Since suppliers are often manufacturing companies themselves, constantly asking them to expedite is not always practical and is always expensive. Even if they were able to do it, trying to react to all the expedite messages would be virtually impossible. If rescheduling is to be done, we should have human involvement and not have this duty assumed automatically by the computer.

Later we'll talk about more modern, but much more demanding, systems that can exploit prescribed flexibility; but at this point Hayes's process reliability, data precision, and performance are not good enough to employ such Advanced Planning systems (see Chapter 11).

One of the biggest issues with finite loading is that, since it automatically reschedules capacity requirements, the supervisor is not able to see the actual future capacity required in order for a work center to support the needs of the Master Schedule. It only loads the shop to the bottleneck work center's capacity, leaving other work centers underloaded. To many, this may not seem like a problem. In reality, however, it is a problem since the nonbottleneck resources are not being effectively utilized and that drives up operating costs. By temporarily getting more capacity for a bottleneck work center, the other work centers can operate at near full capacity. This not only reduces the cost of operating the facility, but it also allows more product to be shipped.

The greatest problem with the finite-loading technique, however, is that we allow the computer to make the decisions. Its ultimate "decision" may be to reschedule the customer! When the computer makes the decisions, there is no accountability, but accountability is the key to successful management.

The alternative to these approaches is Detail Capacity Planning. The concept behind Detail Capacity Planning, like finite loading, is to put no more into the work center than it can be expected to produce. The first step begins the same way as does infinite and finite loading; that is, to load the work center in priority sequence. However, rather than the computer automatically rescheduling overloads as in finite loading, management balances the planned capacity with the required capacity by flexing the equipment availability, the work force, the tooling, working overtime, and so on. It can also be accomplished by changing the required capacity via alternate routings, subcontracting, or make-versus-buy decisions. Usually, rescheduling is only done as a last resort because the existing schedule reflects what is needed to meet the Master Schedule. Given a large number of capacity problems, the analysis required to level the load can be overpowering. Therefore, a technique is needed to assure that the capacity is in the ballpark prior to running Detail Capacity Planning. As Roxanne pointed out to Brian both in the course and during their call at the beginning of the chapter, Detail Capacity Planning needs the up-front leveling to be successful. We will see in Chapter 7 why this is true and learn how to do Rough-Cut Capacity Planning.

The difference between finite loading and Detail Capacity Planning is people—planners and schedulers. These people can consider all the various situations that might arise, such as the skill sets of the available operators, how the machines are running, or the quality of the material, and apply their knowledge and judgment to the situation. What happens when the overload is only slight? Can the order be split? Are there some ways to work around the problem? If there is no resolution and the Master Schedule must be changed, which item on the Master Schedule would have the least impact? It is best to have people make these decisions since people can be held accountable for making them and computers cannot. Whatever solution is finally chosen, someone must be accountable to assure it is executed.

Infinite loading is a bad name, because it implies infinite capacity. Obviously, that doesn't exist. Detail Capacity Planning is a process of using the infinite-load concept and using people to adjust the overloads and underloads so that it makes good sense for the company.

Detail Capacity Planning is a very effective tool when capacity can be flexed (overtime, shift length, additional or fewer resources, etc.). However, in some situations, capacity cannot be flexed. The finite-scheduling technique is valid in those situations. The process of finite capacity scheduling will be discussed in Chapter 9.

Hayes had started using the Dispatch List from their software package in July. Two months later in September, they also started using the Detail Capacity Planning capability. During the course, Brian explained to the supervisors that they would review each of their work centers with Tony and check the capacity plan for any possible overloads. If there were no problems evident in a particular work center, they should skip over it. If they found a problem they could solve without the approval of Brian or Joan, they should go ahead and make the adjustments and advise them of what they had done. It would be José's responsibility to review the information with the second- and third-shift supervisors for their concurrence.

They would meet every Tuesday at 2:00 P.M. to review the plans. If there was a problem that they did not have the authority to resolve, they should bring it up at the meeting for discussion. Brian and Joan then documented those things that José and Tony were not authorized to do: add a new employee, work overtime, start a new shift, subcontract work, or purchase capital equipment.

The supervisors and Tony went to work with the plans. When Jose and Tony did their review, they immediately found there was a three-week period where the operator capacity for the large Hobbs was overloaded. They had plenty of machine capacity but not enough people to run the equipment. José knew that he had some people in the Shaper work center that had been crosstrained in the Hobbs work center as well. They looked at the Shapers and the load there was fairly light. José figured they could safely move two of the operators from the Shapers to the Hobbs and the problem would be solved. Fortunately, because of the operators' crosstraining, moving from one work center to another did not present a problem.

Next they looked at the multiple-spindle drill and found there was only a slight overload for one week. As they scanned the plan, they couldn't see any way to relieve the overload other than working overtime on a Saturday. They made a note of it for their meeting with Brian and Joan.

When Tony and José came to the Vertical Broach, they found there was a large overload, which they referred to as a "bow wave." What that meant was that the Broach was constantly behind schedule, because by the time it would finish one job the next would already be late. They called it a "bow wave" because the stack of work resembled the wave pushed up in front of a large ship. Although the future load did not exceed its machine capacity, it did exceed the labor capacity. This work center had been working two shifts with considerable overtime. It was apparent they would never get caught up just by working overtime. They concluded that they needed to add a third shift to maintain the load that was coming at them and also continue to work the overtime until the "bow wave" was gone. A quick calculation showed that would be in three weeks if they could get another operator for third shift immediately. This was something else that would have to be discussed with Brian and Joan at their meeting.

Moving on, they saw that a heavy load was going to hit the large CNC Lathes in six weeks. They looked at the detailed capacity plan and found that they could actually split the job and reschedule part of it out into the future.

Their next decision would not be as easy. When they checked the capacity of the Surface Grinder, they found a huge overload 12 weeks out that extended through the full year's horizon. There was no possible way they could reschedule it. After some further consultation, it was decided that they were going to have to subcontract that work out. When they reviewed the CNC Drills, they found the same situation as with the Surface Grinder—an overload through the full horizon with subcontracting appearing to be the only feasible solution.

Subcontracting, however, was only a temporary solution because it was expensive and significantly increased the lead time. Beyond those considerations, José and Tony knew that Brian would want to control his own destiny on these parts. The question was "What could they do?" As José and Tony were mulling over this predicament, they flipped through the Detail Capacity Plans. The answer dawned on them. What about the machines where there was excess capacity? Hayes management had learned that making parts just to keep machines busy was bad business. Not only were inventory carrying costs incurred, but also that practice resulted in valuable space being used to store parts that weren't needed. Perhaps even more wasteful when making parts that weren't needed right away was the risk of obsolescence due to engineering changes. As Tony and José scanned through the Detail Capacity Plans, they found five machines in various work centers for which there was absolutely no foreseeable need. Why did this extra capacity exist? When Hayes had purchased some newer, faster machines, the old machines were kept around just in case they were needed, but they had not been used in months and, in some cases, in years. Tony and José figured the best solution would be to trade the five excess machines for a used CNC drill and Surface Grinder. Tony and José made note of the problem and their suggested solution for their meeting with Brian and Joan.

On Tuesday at the conclusion of the capacity planning meeting, Brian and Joan were amazed at how fast Tony and José picked up on the process. In fact, they agreed with all of their recommendations. They quickly concluded that they needed to expand the process to the rest of the supervisors who work for Brian. The only problem Brian and Joan had with Tony and José's recommendations was their idea to trade the excess equipment for a used CNC drill and Surface Grinder. This was not something Brian or Joan had the authority to approve. That would take Ralph's approval.

When Brian approached Ralph, he was flabbergasted by the idea. "You can't do that!" he said, shaking his head from side to side.

"Why?" Brian asked, holding his ground.

"You just can't," Ralph said, not too convincingly. "I mean, it's never been done before."

Brian smiled as Ralph walked right into the position Brian had planned. "Don't you remember what you told me, Ralph? 'Cause it to happen.' If I get Elliot to go along with it, will you work on Sharon in Finance?"

"How do you talk me into these things, Miller?" Ralph complained.

"Because you know I'm right or you're beginning to like me," Brian suggested with a grin.

"All right. You got your way," Ralph said with a laugh. "Now, get out of here."

It wasn't easy, but Brian pulled it off: five redundant machines for two used but nonetheless good ones. "Not bad," Brian thought to himself, "and moving those five machines out has left me some open space. Maybe now's the time to get Elliot going on that rearrangement of equipment that he's been talking about." Brian laughed as he thought about Ralph. He decided it would probably be wise to hold off telling Ralph about that idea for the time being.

The point is that the Detail Capacity Planning information itself didn't make the problems go away. Rather, it pointed directly to them and let management know, in advance, that there were problems that needed to be fixed.

After a capacity planning meeting, Tony, José, Joan, and Brian were talking in Brian's office. "You know," Tony said, "planning may be a lot more effective than expediting, but sometimes I miss the thrill of chasing a part through the shop and the satisfaction of getting it to Assembly. Now that we're working all these problems out early, expediting just isn't required. My job as expeditor has changed."

"You probably want a title like Capacity Planner that the Effective Management group uses," Brian said.

Tony shrugged. "That might not be a bad idea. It just might send the right message to people."

Joan agreed. "Tony, I think you got something there. We may not be Class A but there is no reason not to adopt as much of the practices as we can. We probably should change the pay range, too," Joan said, giving Tony a wink.

"Thanks," growled Brian. Changing Tony's title was no problem. Getting a pay-range change was always a problem.

As we will see in Chapter 7, if Rough-Cut Capacity Planning has been done properly by senior management during the Sales and Operations Planning process and at the Master Schedule level, major capacity constraints should have been dealt with already. When done properly, Rough-Cut Capacity Planning will level the capacity to the point that the majority of the capacity problems can be relatively easy to solve by the supervisor and the capacity planner.

MEETING THE CHALLENGE

At Hayes, after several months of diligently working with his supervisors and the capacity planners on capacity planning, Brian got a call from Ralph. Brian went up to Ralph's office as requested.

"I have to tell you, Brian," Ralph said, taking a drink of coffee from his double-sized, "I'm-the-Boss" coffee mug, "I didn't think all this capacity planning you've been doing would work. I really didn't. But the information has been a great help in getting the right capacity at the right place at the right time. Your shortages are down and you're starting to show some real productivity improvements. Even Sharon and the rest of her cohorts in Finance are pleased that a production manager seems concerned about costs. You were absolutely right about capacity planning." Brian couldn't help but smile. All his efforts were beginning to pay off. "Now all we have to do," Ralph added, turning his back on Brian to check a schedule on his desk, "is go to work on Dan and get him to do the same. And I want you to help him do that."

Brian was amazed at how fast his good feeling could evaporate. Getting his shop running well seemed like child's play compared with the assignment he'd just been handed. Then Ralph laughed. "Don't worry, Brian. I'll get Dan to listen. You just show him how to use the new process to plan his capacity."

A couple of days later, Brian had the perfect opportunity. Dan tracked him down and told Brian that they were going to install a new CNC Laser Burner, a project that would basically shut that area down for about five weeks. The capital request finally had been approved for the purchase of this new burner to replace the three old ones that were crammed into the shop.

"We have to take two of the old burners out first and then install the new burners," Dan said, outlining the plan, "but I can leave the small single-torch burner down in the corner for emergencies. This means we'll only be able to do a small amount of burning for five weeks. We don't want to subcontract the work because it will be a lot more expensive. So, I'm going to need you to help me figure out how we can meet the schedule without subcontracting."

As it turned out, this wasn't such a difficult task. Brian, Dan, Joan, and the capacity and material planners all got together. They looked at the Detailed Capacity Plans for the weeks when the changeover would take place. Taking the total hours for those five weeks, they found the work could be spread over the preceding three-month period by adding people to the second shift, adding a temporary third shift now, working overtime, and rescheduling some jobs. They could build up stock in advance and just shut the burners down for five weeks.

Joan's material planners rescheduled the planned orders forward into evenly loaded time periods and firmed them. They made sure the material would be available by checking what was needed and rescheduling it to be delivered earlier. They checked the summary capacity plan and made sure the adjusted required capacity would be reasonably level in the periods prior to the planned shutdown of the burners. Of course, the capacity requirements during the five weeks of the shutdown were now zero and were reflected as such in the capacity plan. With that accomplished, all that had to be done was for Dan to execute the plan.

When Dan saw how the capacity planning process helped him resolve this apparent dilemma, he was ready to begin in earnest to maintain the information required to support it. He now realized he could use these new tools to manage his department better. He even pledged to use the technique for reserving capacity that he had summarily rejected earlier.

RESPONSIBILITIES

Capacity management is not merely a computer exercise. It's true that in most environments capacity planning cannot be accomplished without a computer, but neither can it be done without good people who understand what it's all about and how to deal with the information produced by the computer. Also, capacity management cannot be performed by one isolated group. It takes teamwork and commitment.

The first consideration in analyzing a Detail Capacity Plan is to ask the supervisor if the shop can meet the capacity plan. If the shop can, there's nothing further to do. If it can't, alternatives must be found. Can capacity be increased? Can alternate work centers be used? An option may be to subcontract that operation. The last option to be considered is to reschedule some of the workload. This does not mean all jobs are rescheduled, but only those selected jobs that will impact least on the Master Schedule. This is not handled automatically through the computer, but rather the production supervisor, capacity planner, and material planner select the jobs to be rescheduled, using the detailed capacity plan from Detail Capacity Planning and the material plans from the Material Requirements Planning system. The key to success is for the supervisors and the capacity planners to work together, bringing both their expertise and knowledge of their jobs to bear. No matter how helpful a computer can be, it cannot solve problems that require human judgment. It can supply information, but people need to make the decisions based on that information.

If the area supervisor and capacity planner can't get the capacity required, it's the capacity planner's responsibility to notify the material planner. The capacity planner and the material planner must then work together to try and reschedule the components. If they can't, it's the material planner's responsibility to notify the Master Scheduler of the capacity constraint and the inability to reschedule the components to satisfy the Master Schedule requirements. A customer reschedule may be required, which should involve the Sales Department. If the problem is of such magnitude that the Production Plan can't be supported, top management is going to have to review the Supply Plan. Obviously, middle-management people will also be involved in this process every step of the way. Fortunately, if the entire capacity planning process is followed, the need to change the Master Schedule is very infrequent, and changing the Supply Plan is almost unheard of.

A capacity planning meeting should be held every week to review the capacity plans and to begin any corrective actions that may be required. This meeting should include the production supervisors and capacity planners. Attendance by the material planners may also be helpful in some situations. A common mistake made by some companies is to focus attention only on the near term. It is important to review the entire planning horizon at least monthly and recognize potential problems in advance. This will give people plenty of time to resolve any constraint.

Brian was pleased with the job they had done implementing capacity planning. It provided him with the ability to see the capacity required to meet the latest Supply Plan, Master Schedule, and Material Requirements Plans by work center and time period for a full year. With this future vision, he no longer had to check work-order boxes to know he needed more capacity. Nor did he have to wait until the work in a work center dried up to know he needed less capacity. Brian had the information he needed to take corrective action, to balance the planned capacity with the required capacity. He knew that capacity planning required accountability, and he saw to it that he stepped up to his responsibility—the planned capacity. The capacity planner was also required to meet his responsibility—the required capacity. If a major change took place that would alter his capacity requirements, Brian could always have the capacity planner run the capacity plan in the middle of the week. It didn't take Brian long to realize that with the right processes and tools, and the right management behaviors, it is indeed possible to get the right job done on time and still be very productive.

Chapter Six

Controlling the Flow of Work

Brian could see that things were getting better at Hayes. With Dispatch Lists communicating valid priorities and Summary Capacity Plans letting him know what his capacity needs were going to be, the shop had never run better. That didn't mean that things were great, but they were definitely improved. Brian could actually afford the luxury of finishing a morning cup of coffee in his office before hitting the floor. It was a small sign, but there was a time when it would have been impossible for him to have even considered it. However, there were still problems that needed to be addressed.

Brian's coworkers, Dan and Mickey, had to agree that some of this "new stuff" had made their lives easier. Dan was starting to come around, fully embracing the use of the Dispatch List and the Summary Capacity Plan. In fact, he now swore by it. Of course, Dan tended to swear about everything. The one thing that Dan did resist was when Ralph, the Production Manager, tried to get him to use Input/Output/Queue Plans.

Dennis Jones, the Effective Management instructor, had spent considerable time in the course emphasizing the importance of the Input/Output/Queue Plan.

When Brian realized that the Input/Output/Queue Plan was a part of the shop floor control process, and that the software that Hayes had purchased provided it, he started using the Input/Output/Queue Plan at the same time he started using the Summary Capacity Plan.

The shop floor is complex, dynamic, and stochastic and so needs to be controlled, lest unexpected happenings cause chaos. The Input/Output/Queue Plan monitors the total amount of work that moves into a particular work center and how much output is produced by that work center. The plan is comprised of information regarding Planned and Actual Input, Planned and Actual Output, and Planned and Actual Queue levels. All the data are expressed in standard hours. The focus of this plan is on the performance of the work center against the capacity plan day by day and week by week. It also provides a convenient means of monitoring the actual queue against the plan.

The ideal situation would be to have a smooth workflow into a work center and a similarly steady output. Input/Output/Queue Control is the process of balancing "supply in" against "supply out" at each work center or cell in the real world of the shop floor to control throughput time. The Input/Output/Queue Plan gives a snapshot of how effective the loading and execution processes are against planned performance. In Chapter 10 we'll see just how much more important the Input/Output/Queue Plan is when going to Lean or Flow. However, things are rarely ideal. In the typical job shop or "batch" environment, rather than continually moving a few pieces at a time, work usually moves from work center to work center in larger batches because of lot sizing practices. Breakdowns and delays in the feeding work centers often interrupt the input process. Similar delays and interruptions in the producing work center make the output anything but smooth.

Production areas usually establish queues in their work centers as a buffer against such interruptions and variances. Some supervisors believe that having lots of work in queue will enable them to increase the productivity of their work center. The assumption is, at this point, that it is expected and, in fact, desirable to have some queue in the work center. (The reduction of queues and the impact on Input/Output/Queue control will be discussed later in this chapter.)

A common misunderstanding regarding Input/Output/Queue control is that the output should always be kept equal to the input. Although the intent is to keep the incoming and outgoing work in sync, there are circumstances where they will not be equal. Normal day-to-day fluctuations mean that sometimes the input is higher than the output and sometimes it is lower. Of course, we do not expect such fluctuations to be greater than the specified queue can buffer. There are other circumstances that call for the input to be different from the output by design. For instance, if the work center has gotten behind schedule, and the queue has built up, it needs to be brought back in line with the objective level. Or if the queue level has fallen below an acceptable level, it needs to be brought back up. In either case, the only way to bring about an adjustment in queue level is to make the input different from the output, either more or less as the case may be. The objective of Input/Output/Queue control is to keep Actual Input, Output, and Queue hours equal to their respective planned levels. This is the essence of control. It is when we deviate from the plan that we get into trouble.

The Input/Output/Queue Plan contains the information to support this control (see Figure 6.1).

Figure 6.1 Input/Output/Queue Plan

WORK CENTER NO.: 24 Description: Lathes					Date: 9/03 Department: M			
Week	8/5	8/12	8/19	8/26	9/2	9/9	9/16	9/23
INPUT								
Planned In	128	118	116	126	130	144	140	150
Actual In	108	98	124	142				
Cum. Dev.	-20	-40	-32	-16				
OUTPUT								
Planned In	120	120	120	120	132	132	132	180
Actual In	110	120	100	90				
Cum. Dev.	-10	-10	-30	-60				
QUEUE								
Planned Q	50	48	44	50	48	60	68	38
Actual Q	40	18	42	94				
Dev.	-10	-30	-2	44				

Cumulative Tolerance: ± 25 Hours   Desired Queue: 50 Hours

The plan should display the recent-past performance against the previous plan. At least the latest four-week period is recommended. The plan should also display the planned input, output, and queue levels for the short-term future. Some companies prefer to show only four weeks each way, while others want as much as twelve weeks each way. The right amount varies by work center, but it must give enough visibility to indicate a trend without becoming overburdened with data.

Figure 6.2   Summary Capacity Plan

Date	8/06	No. Machines	5	Hours / Shift	8
Work Center	24	No. Operators	2	Shifts / Day	1
Description	Lathes	Mach / Oper	2	Days / Week	5
Demo. Cap'y.	120	Max. Cap'y.	400	Load Factor	75%

	MACHINE CAPACITY					LABOR CAPACITY			
Week	Reqd. Cap'y (Hrs)	Plan Cap'y (Hrs)	Load vs. Capacity(%)			Reqd. Cap'y (Hrs)	Plan Cap'y (Hrs)	Load vs. Capacity(%)	
			50	100	150			50 100 150	
8/06	128	150	xxxxxxx			64	60	xxxxxxxxxxx	
8/13	118	150	xxxxxx			59	60	xxxxxxxxxx	
8/20	116	150	xxxxx			58	60	xxxxxxxxx	
8/27	126	150	xxxxxxx			63	60	xxxxxxxxxx	
9/03	130	150	xxxxxxx			65	60	xxxxxxxxxxxx	
9/10	144	150	xxxxxxxxx			72	60	xxxxxxxxxxxxxx	
9/17	140	150	xxxxxxxxx			70	60	xxxxxxxxxxxxxx	
9/24	150	150	xxxxxxxxxx			75	90	xxxxxxx	
10/01	166	150	xxxxxxxxxxxx			83	90	xxxxxxxx	
10/08	160	150	xxxxxxxxxxx			80	90	xxxxxxxx	
↓									
7/28									

Planned Input is the input into a work center that is required to meet the material requirement plan (which is derived from the Master Schedule) and maintain the planned queue within a predetermined tolerance. The data for the Planned Input comes directly from the detail capacity plan and are the same as the Required Capacity for the work center as found in the Summary Capacity Plan (see Figure 6.2).

The rationale is that, if the work center is to be able to meet the capacity plan, work must be fed to each work center in accordance with its scheduled output (Planned Hours) unless an adjustment in the queue level is desired. If the actual queue is lower than necessary to support efficient work-center operation, the input would have to be temporarily increased beyond the scheduled output or the scheduled output decreased to build the queue to its desired level. Conversely, if we want to reduce the queue, the input would be decreased or the output increased. If no adjustment of input is necessary to increase or decrease the queue, the required capacity numbers from the Summary Capacity Plan can be loaded directly into the Input/ Output/Queue Plan. Unless essential, resist the temptation to smooth the Planned Input by averaging the data from the Summary Capacity Plan over a 4- to 8-week period. A further note of caution is in order here. Such smoothing of input is not acceptable in companies where the philosophies of Lean Manufacturing are bringing about significant reduction in queues (see Chapter 10).

As the queues get smaller, so does the cushion for meeting the schedule. If the supervisor is going to meet the schedule, the shop is going to have to produce what the schedule calls for every day of every week. Averaging capacity requirements might actually shift some load to a following week, a result that is totally unacceptable from a scheduling perspective. As a company moves closer to the ultimate goal of zero queues, daily capacities must be planned and monitored. (For further reference, see the capacity bucketing rules in Chapter 5.)

Actual Input is the work that has physically been received by the work center. It is equal to the pieces moved multiplied by the standard hours per piece for the operations to be performed. The Actual Input is then compared with the Planned Input. The cumulative deviation (CUM. DEV.) line on the Input/Output/Queue Plan monitors the variance between what was planned and what actually arrived in the work center. Since the actual will seldom be exactly equal to the plan because of normal fluctuations in work flow, a tolerance should be established to trigger any corrective action that is necessary to maintain the Planned Input. The input line measures the performance of the feeding work centers. In the case of a late job release or a material shortage, the input line measures the performance of another department, not this one. It is the Capacity Planner's responsibility to determine the cause and initiate corrective action.

There is no single right answer as to what the tolerance should be. Some companies use a portion of a day's worth of work, such as 75%. Others use a percentage of the Planned Queue level. The way to establish tolerance is to get the supervisor and capacity planner together and work it out; then work on reducing it. A number will need to be negotiated that is mutually acceptable. The number may also change over time as circumstances change.

The second part of the Input/Output/Queue Plan is also divided into planned and actual data. The Planned Output is what the supervisor has agreed to produce in order to meet the capacity plan and maintain the Planned Queue within the previously agreed upon tolerance (see Figure 6.1). Again, this tolerance is used to trigger any necessary corrective action. The Planned Output should be equal to the Planned Capacity from Summary Capacity Plan. Short-term adjustments in output may be required to change the Actual Queue or to accommodate week-to-week fluctuations. When this is the case, the Planned Output on the Summary Capacity Plan should be altered to reflect what the expected output is going to be.

The Actual Output is the work that has actually been completed by the work center. In capacity terms, the Actual Output is the demonstrated capability. It is calculated by multiplying the pieces completed by the standard hours per piece. Again, it is measured against the established tolerances of the Planned Output. Monitoring output in this manner is a measurement of the work center's performance against the previous commitment by the production supervisor during the capacity planning meeting.

The third section of the Input/Output/Queue Plan monitors the queue level. The Planned Queue is the result of the Planned Input and Planned Output. It is computed by taking the beginning Actual Queue and adding the Planned Input, then subtracting the Planned Output period by period. The Actual Queue is calculated in similar fashion by starting with the beginning Actual Queue, adding the Actual Input, and subtracting the Actual Output period by period.

Figure 6.1 shows the Input/Output/Queue Plan used at Hayes. During the week of 8/6, José, the work-center supervisor and Tony, the capacity planner, got together to review the Summary Capacity Plan and the Input/Output/Queue Plan. Since this was their first review, there was no past history displayed. The Planned Input data on the plan came directly from the Machine-required-capacity column of the Summary Capacity Plan. The Planned Output line came from José after looking at the Planned Capacity from the labor side of the Summary Capacity Plan, which told him the amount of hours the machine would have operators present. He then multiplied that by two (because one operator was running two machines) to give him the total standard machine hours work center 24 was expected to produce. The resulting 120 hours was José's commitment. The Input/Output/Queue Plan was simply a reflection of the summary capacity plan.

Next they reviewed the queue levels.

Work center 24's Planned Queue was 2 days (see Figure 3.5 in Chapter 3). Since the Planned Output is approximately 25 hours per day, the Desired Queue was 50 hours (see "desired Q" in the lower-right corner of Figure 6.1). The actual beginning queue from the previous Friday was 42 hours.

José and Tony understood that normal, everyday occurrences would cause variations in the Actual Input and Output. They agreed that there was no cause for concern unless the cumulative deviation from the plan exceeded plus or minus 25 hours. By doing so, they set their tolerance at plus or minus 25 hours.

They computed the Planned Queue across the 8-week horizon and compared it against the Desired Queue. They found that the queue would end up way out of tolerance if they didn't make a correction in the first weeks of September. José agreed to work one shift on each Saturday for the weeks of 9/3, 9/10, and 9/17. This raised the output to 132 standard hours for each of those weeks. Since this adjustment would bring the queue back in tolerance, they approved the plan.

The following week, 8/13, Tony and José again sat down to review the Input/Output/Queue Plan. The Planned Input for the week of 8/6 was 128 standard hours. The Actual Input was 108 standard hours, which produced a cumulative deviation of minus 20. Since this was within tolerance, no action was necessary. The Actual Output of 110 for 8/6 was only 10 hours short of the plan, so no corrective action was required on the output side either. The next week, 8/13, however, the Planned Input was for 118 standard hours, but only 98 actually arrived. This pushed the cumulative deviation to minus 40 standard hours, exceeding the tolerance. This triggered action by Tony. José added emphasis by saying that, although he didn't run out of work, he was worried about the future because the Actual Queue was now only 18 hours.

By examining the previous operation's Input/Output/Queue Plan, Tony found out that the saws had not met their Planned Output. When Tony spoke with Dan's supervisor in the saw department, he learned that the reason that the input fell below the tolerance was a quality problem with the raw material. He called the material planner. She told him that Purchasing was having some new material shipped in right away. Dan had already instructed the saw department to work overtime when the material came in and to get it to the lathes as soon as possible.

The next week when they reviewed the Input/Output/Queue Plan the Actual Input to the lathes for week 8/20 was 124 hours versus a plan of 116. This was a result of the action taken by Tony, Dan, and

Purchasing. Eight of the delinquent 40 hours were made up. It was still below tolerance, however, and Tony told José he would stay on top of things until the input got back within tolerance.

Tony, meanwhile, produced 100 hours in the week of 8/20—20 hours below plan and 30 hours cumulative deviation. José and Tony didn't get too excited about it, even though it was outside of the tolerance. They thought that as long as the actual queue for that week—42 hours—was within tolerance, they had things under control. In the week of 8/27, true to his word, Tony had kept on top of the input problem and the Actual Input was 142 hours, bringing it back within tolerance. Things were different for José. One of José's operators was out sick for 2 days, and he didn't have anyone to fill in. By the end of the week, he was 30 hours short of his plan for the week and minus 60 hours cumulative deviation. The Actual Queue was a whopping 94 hours. Tony had been doing a good job getting the input within tolerance. Now José was going to have to pull out all the stops to get his output caught up.

José had also become painfully aware that the Dispatch List was showing the same problem. He was falling behind schedule. When he was running about 25 hours behind in output, the Dispatch List was showing some of that, but the downstream work centers were making up the difference by not allowing the work to sit in queue. With this large amount of past-due work, they were unable to make up the time. It was then up to Tony and José to figure out when the work would actually be completed, so they could communicate that to the material planner.

José suddenly recognized the importance of keeping his output close to the plan, regardless of what the input did. He knew he had to do his part and rely on others to do theirs. He was also thankful that he had the Input/Output/Queue Plan. It showed him exactly what his status was and gave him some good data to help him plan his corrective action. He also knew that the plan had been a big help to Tony in his endeavors to get the incoming work on schedule.

Now, why would Dan have any objections to using a plan like this? When Ralph asked him why, he replied, "Because it's garbage, that's why. These plans," Dan said, pointing down at the pile of sheets before him, "are reporting movement of material that never arrives. What good is that to me?"

Ralph pointed out to Dan that the shop movement transactions that fed the Input/Output/Queue Plan were also used to update his

Dispatch List and Summary Capacity Plan. If the data on the Input/Output/Queue Plan were unreliable, so was the Dispatch List. If Dan had really been using his Dispatch List properly, he would have seen that there was work indicated as being in the work centers that wasn't really there, and he should have questioned it. As it turned out, the source of the problem was in Dan's own department. It was his people's move transactions that had created the inaccurate data. It was later brought to Dan's attention that an inspection operation was missing from several of the routings. When the previous operation was reported as completed, the software system indicated that the work had been moved to Dan's work centers as indicated on the routing. The material handlers had in fact moved the jobs to inspection as required, even though the routing didn't show the need. So when the Input/Output/Queue Plan said the work was in Dan's department, it was really in inspection. Had Dan's supervisors used the Input/Output/Queue Plans properly, they could have immediately tracked down the problem and eliminated it. It was also clear that these work centers were not using the Dispatch List as they should have been. Had they been using it correctly, the problems would have been seen, because the status column on the Dispatch Lists would have been incorrect. Instead, Dan ignored it, and tried to pass it off as a Production Control problem.

When this was pointed out to Dan, he threw up his arms. Not known for his even temper, he blurted out what would now surface as the real reason behind his dislike of the Input/Output/Queue Plan. "You know, there's another thing about that plan. It's like I've got a bunch of spies hanging around my department." Suddenly, it dawned on Ralph what the problem was: Dan didn't like being held accountable for the work he had committed to produce, so he reverted back to the old behavior of shifting the blame onto Production Control and discrediting the plan.

Good capacity management processes, when operated in a Class A manner, clearly identify the problems and people who are accountable for them. The Input/Output/Queue Plan is a tool that provides data so people can be held accountable to do what they say they will do. It also provides a valuable control on the process; it is the performance measure for capacity planning. Brian had heard from Hal at Good Health Vitamins about an episode that had taken place in his factory. Like Hayes, Hal's factory had just gone through the process of implementing an Enterprise Resource Planning system and they were generating Dispatch Lists and Summary Capacity Plans. One day, Hal got a call from the packaging department supervisor about a problem that had surfaced.

The supervisor was using the capacity plan to plan her people levels, but she had to work overtime to get the work out. "Something isn't right," she said. She showed Hal the Input/Output/Queue Plan, pointing out that a lot more work was coming into the work center than was planned. The incoming work was also more than what was required according to the capacity plan.

Upon further investigation, they found that, because they were keeping extra material for emergencies and the lead time for packaging was relatively short, the Master Scheduler was taking emergency orders from customers within the same week that the product had to be shipped. Material Requirements Planning created new material orders, and the material planner was just releasing the orders for scheduling on top of what was already scheduled. The capacity plan, which was run only once a week, never showed the additional work, because it was in and out so fast. The supervisor, however, saw the orders on the Dispatch List. Consequently, to get everything done, she ended up working Saturdays on an ongoing basis. The good news was that everything was getting done. The bad news was that the supervisor had to work her crew every Saturday, but didn't have the information in time to plan for it in advance.

The Input/Output/Queue Plan helped them to identify the problem quickly. They realized they had two options. They could say "no" to the customers, which was not something they wanted to do. Their second choice was to anticipate that customers would order inside of lead time and plan for it in the Master Schedule. This would increase the required capacity via Summary Capacity Plan and allow the supervisor to plan to have the additional capacity available. This is the reserved capacity issue discussed in Chapter 5. The risk was that the supervisor would have people with nothing to do if the orders did not come in.

The message here is that with an Input/Output/Queue plan, a supervisor can be held accountable for meeting the committed output that was agreed upon via capacity planning. It gives the supervisor the ability to monitor performance against the plan. If what was supposed to arrive in the work center is either greater or less than what was expected, the capacity planner is accountable for finding the root cause and initiating corrective action.

Unfortunately for Brian and his colleagues at Hayes, this was a lesson they had to learn the hard way. The problem arose shortly after they replaced the three old burners. As mentioned in Chapter 5, Hayes was going to need five weeks to finish the job of installing the new burner. Not without a great deal of trouble, Dan, Joan, and Brian, together with the material and capacity planners, had worked out a plan to cover their future capacity requirements for the weeks that the burners would be out of service.

Everything went according to plan. When it was time to shut down the old burners, Dan and his crew had met their schedule. Maintenance had asked for one week to tear out the old burners, two weeks to install the new one, and a two-week learning curve to bring the new one up to full production. It all started smoothly. In fact, they started using the new burner earlier than they had anticipated.

Then problems started to surface. The machine wasn't coming up to the expected output level because of problems with the CNC programming. Two weeks after it was installed, the cumulative Actual Output was below the agreed-upon level and outside the tolerance. Three weeks later it was further outside the tolerance. Roy, the Materials Manager, scheduled a meeting in Ralph's office. Dan was there, as was Joan. The discussion centered on the Input/Output/Queue Plan, which showed the low output and a large queue. Joan was the first to speak. "Roy, we're going to have to subcontract this work until they figure out how to get the programming right, or we're going to be in real trouble."

"I don't want to subcontract," Roy said. "The cost difference will be too much, and since the subcontractor won't use our material, it's going to cause our inventories to rise. If that happens, Pete will have us strung up. Dan, you and Elliot have to get out there and get that blasted burner working."

Everyone agreed not to subcontract the work. Roy, Pete, and Joan felt good about the plan of action, but Dan and Elliot were concerned because they weren't sure that they could fix the problem.

The following week, Ralph, Dan, and Pete descended on Roy's office. Joan happened to see them going in and could tell by the red color of both Pete and Ralph's bald heads that they weren't happy campers. Dan was surprisingly laid back.

"Gentlemen," Roy said, the calm before the storm, "what seems to be the problem?"

Ralph, with his customary brashness, said, "There's no work for the welders. You haven't released any work orders for them and now we're going to have to send people home."

Pete, the General Manager, stepped forward, trying his best to maintain his calm, only to be betrayed by his beet-red face. "Why aren't you releasing the work orders?" Roy, of course, had no idea, but suggested they go check it out with Carl, the planner. As they went by Joan's office, she decided to tag along and see what all the ruckus was about.

As they arrived at Carl's desk, Roy asked, "Carl, are you not releasing work orders to the weld shop?" Roy was afraid of the answer to follow.

"That's right."

"Why, Carl?" Roy was feeling the back of his neck begin to burn from the trio of fire-breathing dragons behind him.

"Well, I'm supposed to review each work order to see if the components are in inventory before I release it, and if the components aren't there, I shouldn't release the work orders, right?"

Roy nodded. "That's right, isn't it, Dan?"

"Absolutely!" came Dan's reply. "I don't want you sending me jobs without all the parts." Dan's voice echoed off the walls of the room, and the other material planners in the room cringed.

Joan stepped in. "Why aren't there any components, Carl?"

Carl pulled up an order on his computer screen. "Well, this first job is missing part numbers 136469, 192423, and 182630, and this job is missing part number 173268, and this job is missing. . . ."

"Hold it. Hold it. Where are those parts?" Joan asked.

Carl switched to the open order status screen and looked up part number 136469. "It's at the burner," Carl said, showing Joan the location. Then, looking up all the other numbers, he summarized, "They're all at the burner."

Pete just about went through the ceiling. He immediately called Ralph, Dan, and Elliot into his office. The meeting was not quiet.

When they exited Pete's office, Ralph was immediately on the phone to get a technician flown in from the manufacturer to show Hayes's numerical-control programmers how to correct the problem.

Joan, Dan, and the production supervisors had been monitoring activity with the Input/Output/Queue Plan, and they had seen this problem developing. The plan showed that the output from the burner was lagging behind the agreed-upon levels, and there was a steady buildup of queue in the work center. At the same time, the Input/Output/Queue Plan for the welding work center showed that the input was below plan and their queue was approaching a dangerously low level. Seeing the evidence of a problem and taking action to fix it are two different things. By observing these trends, they should have been able to do something before the situation reached the critical stage. Since they hadn't initiated the corrective action in a timely manner, they ended up sending most of the welders home on Thursday and Friday. Then they had to call them back on Saturday and Sunday because the technician had easily solved the problem and had the burner running at near full capacity in a matter of hours. The moral of this situation is that you can't just plan and measure, you must also take the appropriate action.

ESTABLISHING QUEUES

One important factor in the proper use of the Input/Output/Queue Plan is establishing realistic queue levels. The queue level is the total amount of work, expressed in standard hours, that is physically in the work center, waiting to be worked on at any given time. Although there may be some pieces still running on the machine, most software leaves these pieces in queue until they are reported completed. The other jobs that have not been started are also in queue.

Since queues have a significant impact on throughput time in the work center and the work-in-process inventory levels, the queue levels should be as small as possible, and a plan should be in place to reduce them continuously. This raises a couple of questions. How much queue is appropriate? Which work centers should have queue and which shouldn't? The reality is that it's going to be difficult to come to a complete agreement on these questions.

Invariably, production people want a lot of queue. It gives them flexibility. It also relieves the Mother Hubbard's cupboard syndrome. No supervisor wants to go to the cupboard and find the cupboard bare. Queue acts as a cushion just in case something goes wrong, but it also hides the source of the problem.

On the other hand, the smaller the queue in the work centers, the faster the throughput and the lower the work-in-process inventory. Short throughput time gives the company the flexibility to respond quickly to customer demands. The practice of having large work-in-process inventories in the hopes of maintaining maximum flexibility is outdated: The most flexible companies are those that can produce products in extremely short lead times. There is really no standard answer as to where and how much queue a work center or department needs. It varies from work center to work center and from plant environment to plant environment, but it should be repeated that the ultimate goal is to get queues down as low as possible. This topic will be discussed further in Chapter 10.

To settle the issue, it must be understood why there are queues in the first place. The purpose of queue is to uncouple operations from one another, so that the work centers aren't negatively impacted by variations in the rate of incoming work. In determining how much queue is desirable, several things must be considered. Capacity is like time; it can't be stored. If it's not used, it's lost. If a machine typically has a full load, such as a bottleneck, it is not desirable for it to run out of work. So in order to prevent interruptions of production due to delays in incoming work, there should be queue in front of it. Common practice is to have queues in front of bottleneck equipment to avoid shutting it down.

Another area that typically has queues is equipment that has little or no rescheduling capability. If there are constraints on the ability to offload work to alternate work centers—including outside subcontracting—queues are put in place to avoid losing capacity. Equipment, however, isn't the only consideration. If high labor skills are involved, there is a good chance a capacity constraint exists. Operations such as these would be candidates for queue.

These are some of the considerations for establishing queues, but who decides how much queue? The people involved in this decision are the production supervisors, capacity planners, and material planners. Production is involved because of the objectives that they must meet on the shop floor, including productivity and schedule attainment. The material planners have to have input because of the impact that queue has on lead time and work-in-process inventories. Each of these parties has their own objectives regarding the amount of desirable queue. The capacity planner's role is to view the issue from both sides and to achieve consensus on what is best for the company as a whole.

When Brian, Dan, and Joan sat down to establish the desired queue levels with their supervisors and planners, Brian and his production partners had a lot of good reasons why they wanted more queue. They all felt it improved their productivity. Dan was particularly adamant about having queue because it helped avoid delays when suppliers or feeding work centers didn't deliver on time. He also wanted queue because of potential tooling delays and material shortages. They all believed that queues were motivational for the labor staff, offering a sense of job security. Queue protected them against the loss of capacity that resulted from machine breakdowns upstream and against part shortages. It gave them the flexibility to combine setups, thus reducing changeover time. It offered a buffer against variation in the work flow. There seemed to be no end to the list.

What they didn't want to accept was that queues are a cover-up for the real problems that face production. An argument in favor of queue says, "I believe the input will be interrupted, so instead of fixing the problem, I'll have some extra work here just in case." For each and every one of the reasons this group offered for needing queues, there was a solution to the problem that would eliminate the need for queue. This is not to imply that these alternative approaches are easier to accomplish than adding more queue, but they will be more productive and better for the company in the long run.

It would be helpful to take a closer look at the reasons that the Hayes staff gave for needing queue and some alternate approaches.

1. Queues equal job security.

The effect that a light workload has on productivity is that things just slow down (Parkinson's Law: Work expands to fill the time available). One way to handle this is to share the information on the Dispatch Lists and capacity plans routinely with the work force. If they understand it, they will know how much work is ahead of them without needing to see it there in queue. Of course, they must develop confidence in the information and that the work will really be there as scheduled.

2. Queue is valuable to fall back on when suppliers or feeding work centers don't deliver on time.

Wouldn't solving the problems that cause these delays be a better solution? If the feeding work centers use Summary Capacity Plans, Dispatch Lists, and Input/Output Plans effectively, and if they solve their quality and machine breakdown problems, their on-time completion to schedule is going to improve dramatically. The technique of Supplier Scheduling has also proven helpful in getting suppliers to deliver on time. When the feeding work centers and suppliers deliver on time, the need for the queue "buffer" is diminished.

3. Queue protects against delays from tooling availability problems.

Using better planning and scheduling techniques for the tooling can avoid these delays. Many companies put tooling on their bills of material and routings, thus enabling them to schedule tooling availability in concert with the shop orders on which they will be used (see Chapter 8).

4. Queues protect against upstream equipment breakdown.

Implementing good preventive maintenance programs in all work centers can minimize interruption of incoming work flow because of breakdowns in equipment upstream.

5. Queues offer protection from parts shortages.

We all recognize the problem of parts shortages. One of the primary goals of Class A is the elimination of parts shortages because of better scheduling and planning. If we are able to do a good job with Master Scheduling, Material Requirements Planning, Capacity Planning, Input/Output/Queue control, and the rest of the tools, we won't experience parts shortages.

6. Queues allow for combining setups.

Practically every production supervisor in the world tries to save setup time by combining jobs with similar setups. But rather than just accept setup times as they are and juggle the schedule around, it is better to reduce the setup times so they are not a problem. There are techniques that can radically reduce setup times. One such technique is the Single Minute Exchange of Die (SMED)[1] approach. Such reductions eliminate the need to resequence work to combine setups. Grouping parts in the schedule with similar setups will reduce the need for queue. The material and capacity planners should

1. Referred to by Shigeo Shingo (Toyota) 1969. In use in Toyota at least 10 years earlier.

do this, but it is a cumbersome process whenever multiple operations are involved.

7. Queues allow time for maintenance to be performed in the feeding work centers without interrupting production downstream.

Maintenance operations can be scheduled using the Material Requirements Planning system to schedule the work in the same manner as a production part. That work will also be loaded into the capacity planning system where it can be analyzed and rescheduled if necessary because of a capacity constraint. The Dispatch List will reflect the preventive maintenance work, as in any other job. In fact, instead of Brian trying to push maintenance work into the future because it always seems to be scheduled in an overload period, Brian would now be insisting that Maintenance do the work in the scheduled period because the capacity has been reserved (see Chapter 5).

The point is that, rather than accepting the need for queue, it is entirely possible to eliminate it. The money saved from the lower work-in-process inventories and faster throughput times can be used to solve the problems that create the need for queue.

ADVANTAGES OF QUEUE REDUCTION

The reality is that there are far more significant advantages to reducing queues than there are to sustaining them!

One of the greatest advantages in reducing queues is the reduction in lead times. When the need for queue in a work center is reduced, the planned queue for the work center should be reduced in the database. When that happens, the back scheduling logic will reschedule the operation start and due dates out into the future by the amount of time that the queue was reduced. If we look at the two examples in Figure 6.3, we can see that by reducing the queue at operation 10 by 4 days, and reducing the queue at operation 5 by 4 days, the order release date will be moved from M-day 82 to M-day 90.

The impact is that no work will be released for 8 M-days. If the work center were 8 days behind schedule, reducing the queue by 8 days would stop the release of work for 8 days, allowing the work center to get back on schedule. Caution needs to be exercised here

Figure 6.3   Effect of Queue Reduction on Lead-Time

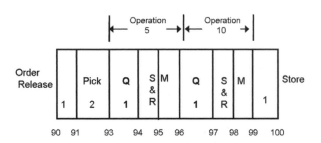

to make sure that any queue that is removed is really excess. Everyone must realize that the cushion has been removed, the dates are realistic and they have to be met. Reducing queue also reduces work-in-process inventory and factory space requirements, because there is less material out on the floor. We can reduce the rework quantity resulting from defective upstream operations since there is less defective material in the pipeline. And we reduce damage to work-in-process because there is less inventory sitting around the shop floor to be bumped into, knocked over, rusted, or spoiled. We also need less material handling and storage equipment.

In spite of all these advantages, it is still difficult for production supervisors and material planners to find agreement on establishing planned queues. And typically there is no concentrated effort to reduce queues.

The goal is to get the actual queue as small as possible, without losing capacity or productivity or missing schedule. A queue-reduction program starts by collecting information. We need to know what the current actual queue is. How much material is actually out on the floor? That information can be obtained from the Input/Output/Queue Plan or from the Dispatch List. We also must know what the current planned queue is. This is the figure that has been loaded into the computer by the capacity planners that we used in the back-scheduling exercise. We also need to generate a list of problems that people believe are the reasons that the queue is necessary.

For Brian, this meant talking to each of his supervisors and asking, "Why do you need this much queue here?" and recording the answers.

The next step of the queue reduction process is to get the Actual Queue in line with the Planned Queue. If in looking at the Input/Output/Queue Plan, we see that the planned queue is 70, but the actual queue is 100, we know there's 30 hours more work in the work center than there should be. This excess workload will also be evident on the Dispatch List and will likely be past-due work. That queue needs to be worked off unless an immediate reduction in the planned queue is reasonable. If it is, simply reducing the planned queue is all that is required. If not, the queue must be worked off. That means overtime, subcontracting, using alternate machines— anything and everything the supervisor can do to reduce the work-load.

Once the Actual Queue is brought down to the Planned Queue level, the production supervisor and planner should review the list of reasons for queue and prioritize them. We suggest working on the problems in order of their simplicity when trying to solve them. Don't tackle the toughest one first. It is often possible to get as much reduction in queue from solving a lot of little problems as it is from solving one big one, and it usually won't take as long. It is important to show some quick benefits from the process to build enthusiasm and commitment to the process.

Brian's department decided that since a preventive maintenance program was already underway at Hayes, they would focus their attention on that issue in each work center. A short while later José came into his office. "We've got the preventive maintenance program set up on the automatic chucking lathes and since they feed the hobbs I'm willing to part with one day of queue in front of the hobbs."

"Good work. Just think of eliminating that queue as an old friend who's moved away," Brian said, with his tongue planted in his cheek.

"Right, like quitting smoking," José said, "only without the weight gain."

Brian called Joan and asked her to have the planners remove a day of planned queue from the database for the hobbs. This has to be done carefully. When a day of planned queue is removed, it means that the lead time has also been reduced by a day. Therefore, all the orders that are supposed to go through that work center will be rescheduled. The software, utilizing its backward-scheduling logic, will reschedule the orders to be released one day later than before.

Oliver Wight, known for his ability to explain complex concepts in simplified terms, compared work flowing through a work center to water flowing through a funnel. Using Ollie's analogy, the release of work has been continuous, like water running out of a valve (see Figure 6.4).

Figure 6.4   Oliver Wight's "Funnel" Analogy

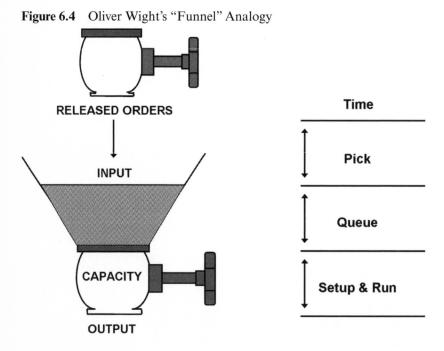

The work flows into the work center where it is stored in queue, like water in the funnel, until it is worked on and moved out of the work center. Now, for one day, we are shutting off that valve for all orders that are routed to that work center. That won't create a problem if we have more than one day of queue in the work center. At the end of the day, the work center will have produced one day's worth of output, while receiving no input. This reduces the actual queue by one day. Then, the input of work is resumed, which allows the work center to maintain the actual queue at the lower level.

The key to resolving and avoiding these queue problems is communication between all participants. We need to recognize that when we change the planned queue time for a particular work center in the database, all jobs yet to go through that work center will be rescheduled. When we change the planned queue time, the backward-scheduling program will recalculate the operation dates. The calculated lead time should be compared to the lead time on the item master file in Material Requirements Planning, and should cause the Material Requirements Planning lead time to be adjusted by the amount of queue reduced. Then, when we rerun Material Requirements Planning, the order start dates are recalculated, in turn causing the order due dates for lower-level parts to be adjusted. This cascading effect causes further adjustments to the operation dates. In a really successful company, it is essential to reduce queue levels. This must be done with care. Making large reductions in queue without solving the problems first can result in a delay in the incoming work to the work centers and this can cause the work center to run out of work.

After all the heat he took for delays and excess work-in-process in the welding shop, Dan told Joan to have the Material Planner just go in and take three days of planned queue time out of the weld area. Joan figured Dan knew what he was doing, so she did it. After the schedules were rerun, Brian didn't get any new work for the milling machines for three days.

"Joan," Brian said, "we have a problem out here. My milling machines haven't received a thing to work on in three days."

Joan went to the terminal and looked up the schedule of work to be released. She explained to Brian that numerous jobs had been scheduled to be released earlier, but they had been rescheduled for a later release because she had reduced the planned queue time in the weld area.

"Why did you do that?" Brian asked.

"I just did what Dan told me to do," Joan replied. "I assumed you two had talked this out and understood the impact."

At that moment Dan passed by.

"Hey, Dan, come here a minute." Brian called to him, "Can you explain to me why you didn't talk to me when you were planning on making a large change to your queue? Didn't you understand that you couldn't just remove queue without talking to everyone concerned? It not only affected the burning machines, but a lot of my machines also." Brian was the victim of a breakdown in communication. The real reason there was no communication was that Dan didn't understand the impact that changing queue levels would have on the other work centers. Education was the solution to the problem. People need to understand the *what* and *why* of a proposal before jumping into action.

Input/Output/Queue control allows companies to reduce queues in a controlled fashion. The plan displays what the queue levels are currently and what they were intended to be. It also predicts what the future queue levels will be. The plans can then be changed by either increasing or decreasing the input or output to bring the queue in line with the desired queue levels.

We have shown how the Input/Output/Queue Plan is used to monitor input, output, and queues by work center and time period. Corrective action is initiated when the variance between the actual and the plan exceeds the preestablished tolerance. When Input/Output/Queue control is used in conjunction with capacity planning, the work throughput can be kept under control.

An integral part of this monitoring process is to make queue reduction a conscious effort in each work center. As queues are reduced, they become much more easily managed, making their control easier as well.

Effective use of Input/Output/Queue control requires good teamwork. The capacity planner is responsible for monitoring the input plan and verifying the integrity of the input data; the production supervisor is accountable for creating the output plan and the integrity of the output data. In the weekly capacity planning meeting, they review the Input/Output/Queue Plan at the same time as the Summary Capacity Plan. Working the two together is critical to successful capacity management.

Step-by-step, the planning and scheduling process led Brian and his colleagues into a better quality of factory life. Step-by-proven-step, they found planning becoming less of a burden and more of a tool with which they could fine-tune their ability to deliver to their customers' needs, while operating more efficiently. Step-by-step, they gained the necessary knowledge and applied it, making everyone's job, from the bottom to the top, easier and more productive.

Chapter Seven

Applying Rough-Cut Capacity Planning

Several weeks later, Brian had just returned from a four-day weekend, an anniversary present he'd promised his wife. Four days off—Friday through Monday! Brian was somewhat surprised that Ralph had approved his request. Things definitely must be getting better at the plant. Why else would Ralph have given him those days off?

Brian had barely eased himself back into his chair with the smell of the fresh mountain air still lingering in his memory when he saw Tony's note expressing concern over the gear shaver attached to the new capacity planning information. His capacity plan had effectively been allowing him the visibility to plan ahead successfully. While it was not as good as he would have liked it to be because the plan bounced around, it provided visibility. He had asked Joan why the capacity plans weren't more stable and she said this was because of the Master Schedule and Material Requirement Planning. Those plans were not as good as they could be. Roy, her boss, was pushing it but wasn't getting a lot of help from Ralph or Pete Smith, the General Manager. They both agreed it should be done, but Roy just couldn't get them to put any emphasis on it.

He clicked quickly through the screen shots of the Detail Capacity Plan for each work center until he came to the gear shaver. He couldn't believe his eyes! The workload for the gear shaver that showed up on the plan for October and November was well above anything they had seen before and above maximum capacity. The work hadn't been on the plan last week! It would be impossible to turn out that much work, even if he worked his people all the overtime he could. Brian also knew that the work couldn't be subcontracted.

Working back through the information in the system that was creating the overload, he found that the Master Schedule had been changed over the weekend. Knowing that any change to the Master Schedule during that time frame had to have Ralph's approval, he immediately called Ralph to find out what had happened.

Sure enough, Ralph had changed the Supply Plan mix from small tractors to medium tractors to satisfy a shift in demands from Iowa Tractor, one of Hayes's best customers, and had instructed the master scheduler to make the corresponding changes to the Master Schedule.

"Why did you make those changes without considering whether or not we had the capacity to do it?" Brian asked as politely as he could. "I thought we had gotten away from just shoving stuff into the Master Schedule without running through the material and capacity planning processes to be sure we could do it."

"You know how Lenny gets when he has a hot customer," Ralph said, referring to the vice president of Sales and Marketing. "And Pete insisted on an answer right then. Roy said we could run a simulation in the Master Schedule, Material Requirements Planning, and then Detail Capacity Planning but it would take a couple of days. In the heat of the opportunity, we agreed to move out the forecast for small tractors to make room for the additional medium tractors. Since the number of total tractors was the same, we figured that we would have the capacity to handle it."

What Ralph didn't realize was that the medium tractors had gears that required a shaving operation, but the small tractors did not, and the gear-shaver work center was already scheduled near its maximum capacity. Brian had brought that to Pete's and Elliot's attention, but neither wanted to do anything about it. Pete just couldn't be bothered with it because it wasn't causing him any pain, and Elliot, like a good Manufacturing Engineering manager, said he would put it in the capital budget for next year.

When Ralph changed the product mix, he was not aware of the additional load that it would put on the gear shavers. After making the change to the Master Schedule, those changes were exploded down through material requirements planning into Detail Capacity Planning, where, for the first time, the impact was visible.

After Brian showed him the Summary Capacity Plan, Ralph shrugged his shoulders and said, "Sure, now I can see the impact, but when you're in a meeting with all that pressure on you, who's got the time to go through all that? We needed to give Lenny an answer right away. You can 'make it happen,' can't you, Brian?"

Ralph could see from the look on Brian's face this was not the right thing to say. Even though he was the boss, he knew when he was wrong, so he quickly answered his own question. "Okay, so take me through this in detail so I can understand it before we go around spreading the bad news."

Brian knew this was a huge breakthrough for Ralph. He really wanted to understand what Brian was doing. Brian took full advantage of the opportunity to get Ralph up to speed as well as he could.

Knowing the news they brought was not good, Ralph and Brian went back to Lenny and Pete and told them they couldn't meet the new plan. Pete's immediate reaction was to tell Ralph that they had made a commitment to the customer and that he and Brian would have to "do the best you can."

Ralph reminded them of an earlier situation when one of Brian's supervisors had gotten the Dispatch List for one of his work centers and immediately saw that the work center was overloaded. Remembering similar occasions when management had told him to "do the best he could," the supervisor arbitrarily decided to work on a small-tractor part as opposed to a medium-tractor part. At the same time, one of Dan's supervisors looked at the Dispatch List for one of his work centers, which was also overloaded, and, "doing the best he could," he decided to work on a part for a medium tractor instead of a small one. As a result of their actions, the Assembly Department ended up with some of the parts for both the medium and small tractors, but not all of the parts required for either size tractor. The result was that neither the large tractors nor the small tractors shipped on time and inventories went up.

Ralph asked Pete and Lenny if they wanted the production supervisor to decide which parts to work on at the gear-shavers and thus decide which customers would get their tractors. Of course, Pete and Lenny did not want that to happen. Brian explained that when an overload situation exists, it makes sense to address the issue up front and adjust the Master Schedule, so that at least some product will be assured to ship on time.

Both Pete and Lenny knew, in spite of what they wished could happen, that when Ralph said he couldn't do something, it meant he really couldn't do it. They also figured it was better to call their customer now than to wait until later. Reluctantly, Lenny agreed to go through the ordeal of apologizing to one of their best customers for having promised something they couldn't deliver. He knew the customer would not be pleased with the news, but Lenny, from long years of experience, knew it better to call now than wait until the tractors didn't show up on time.

"When will we be able to get more small tractors?" Lenny asked, "because my indications right now are that the mix will change toward small tractors for all of our customers. In addition, we are starting to see the demand for small tractors go up, which is in alignment with our forecasting indicators that the total volume of tractors is going up."

The whole conversation caused Brian to realize that if the Hayes senior-management team had known the impact of their decision prior to making the commitment to the customer, they could have avoided making this embarrassing and potentially costly mistake and having to redo the plans. Lenny's last statement made it clear that this was part of an ongoing conversation with sales and marketing. Lenny constantly wanted to react to the market place. Brian realized he needed a way to enable them to evaluate the impact of such decisions on capacity quickly before the commitment was made. Ralph needed the ability to make a quick assessment of the capacity requirements, regardless of what Pete and Lenny threw at him. Also, Roy needed the ability to see what the suppliers were doing. In his short time as Machine Shop manager, he knew the impact of not having material even if he had the capacity.

Suddenly, Brian remembered a discussion about planning capacity at the higher levels in the material-planning process during the Effective Management course that they attended. He recalled that Roxanne Barnes, the instructor, kept emphasizing the importance of Integrated Business Management (Chapter 2, Figure 2.1) and the role played by a rough-cut approach to capacity planning at that level. Again and again she said that to get real control of your capacities you need to test it prior to dumping the plans into Detail Capacity Planning. Brian decided to take a chance and give Roxanne a call. He remembered her saying if they have a problem not to hesitate to call. "We're not lawyers," she had said. "We don't charge for phone calls."

As soon as the meeting was over, Brian raced back to his office, dug out his notebook from the course, which had her phone number in it, and called Roxanne. He was a little shocked when she picked up the phone because he assumed she would be off teaching a course or consulting. He was equally shocked when she remembered who he was.

"Of course I remember you," she said. "I always remember students who really take an interest in what I'm saying and act like they are really going to go back to their companies and take some action. What can I do for you?"

Brian gave her a history of what he had done with the routing, Dispatch Lists, Detail Capacity Planning, and Input/Output/Queue Planning. He then explained the current situation.

"Wow," Roxanne said, "you have really accomplished a lot. Why don't you just keep going with rough-cut capacity planning?"

"Because I don't think I have the clout or understanding of the Integrated Business Management process to deal with the senior management. Joan and I have done the shop-floor stuff with the support of Roy, the Materials Manager, and the blessing of Ralph, my boss, the Production Manager. What I remember you saying is that, for the Resource Requirements Planning level of rough-cut to work (see Figure 2.4), we need the commitment of senior management. I'll never forget what Dennis Jones, your cohort, told us regarding the difference between commitment and involvement. 'It's like a ham-and-egg breakfast. The chicken is involved, the pig is *committed*.' I also agree with you that in order for the Resource Requirements Planning processes to work it will require the Integrated Business Management process, and that will really take the *commitment* of our top management."

"Dennis does love to tell that analogy," Roxanne chuckled, "but it is true. You need to get management committed."

"I just don't know how to do that. Yeah, Ralph and Roy let us do our thing with the shop, but Joan and I changing their behaviors— well, that is just another story. Do you have any suggestions?"

Roxanne paused a moment and then cautiously said, "Well, what we have found successful is to do a one- or two-day visit to run a diagnostic for the senior managers about Integrated Business Management, and especially their role in Resource Requirements Planning. This way they would recognize for themselves that they have an essential role in this. In the same visit we would then facilitate a workshop for them on defining the role actions and values for senior management. That would give us the opportunity to size up the situation and make some high-level recommendations. It doesn't always work but we have a better than 50% track record of getting the company on the right track. By that I mean they agree to put a plan in place to resolve their business issue."

Brian was thinking rapidly as Roxanne spoke. "I could never get you in here to do Integrated Business Management. They just wouldn't go for it."

"What about saying we are going to review approaches to capacity planning? Might they go for that?"

It was now Brian's turn to pause and consider her question. "Well after what happened today, they might just consider that. I'm not sure though, because to my knowledge they have never used a consultant before. I would have to go test it."

"That's fine," Roxanne replied. "But let's take a few minutes to talk about how you might go about it. I've found that with a little coaching you will be more successful."

Brian and Roxanne spent the next half-hour discussing the situation. Brian tried to give Roxanne as much information on Hayes as he could so Roxanne could help Brian formulate a plan.

First step in the plan was for Brian to talk with Joan and get her input. They then both talked to Roxanne for more coaching. Next step was Roy. He quickly agreed to take a leadership role, but identified Ralph as the major obstacle. He said they had used consultants before, but Ralph always seemed to have had a bad experience. Willingness to change popped immediately into Brian's head as the reason. Roy went on to confide to Joan and Brian that he was not the best one to approach Ralph.

"If I suggest something," Roy explained, "Ralph is immediately against it. Brian, you are the one who has the best opportunity to sell it."

"Me?" Brian questioned. "Why me?"

"Because Ralph has come to respect your ability to figure out new and better ways to operate. We have had lots of people come up with good ideas, but your ability to plan and execute as well is where you have excelled. That's why he likes Mickey so much. Ralph is recognizing that the problem with Mickey is that he has the 'not invented here' syndrome, and therefore doesn't come up with breakthrough ideas."

Brian was staggered with Roy's response but agreed to approach Ralph. The key was to get Ralph to suggest it to Roy. Roy would then agree. As a team they could then take it to Pete, the General Manager, and Roy was confident that he would go along with it.

"That was easy," Brian thought to himself as he left Roy's office, "Except the sell-to-Ralph part."

Brian carefully planned what he would say, and made sure the timing was right. He checked with Ralph's administrative assistant to see if Ralph had time available right after his lunch-time bridge game with his cronies. He was in luck; there was a half an hour free. The next step was to be sure he was in a good mood, which meant Ralph doing well with cards.

"Brian," Ralph welcomed him, "sit down and take a load off your feet. What's up?" he asked, as Brian sat down.

"How'd you do at cards?" Brian asked casually.

"Roger and I kicked butt today. So what kind of special favor do you want? You don't ask that kind of question unless you're trying to see what kind of mood I'm in, Miller. I know that means you're up to something. You want some more vacation or just a couple of days off? Either is okay. That it?"

"Oh boy," thought Brian, "Do I just take the time off or do I go for it?"

"Well, I'll take the time off but that isn't why I really came here. I was thinking about how to do a better job of long-range capacity planning." Brian started out with his well thought-out case.

It was all going perfectly until Brian put the last part about the consultant coming in to make some recommendations. That's when Ralph hit the ceiling and started ranting about consultants. Brian just sat back and listened until Ralph was through.

"Can't you just trust me on this one, Ralph?" Brian asked. "I haven't let you down before. Anyway the consultant I want is really good. She knows what she's talking about."

"Can't you and Joan just do it like before?" Ralph asked.

"I don't think so. It will take some involvement of Lenny, Pete, and Roy to make this work. We will really need the consultant to help sell this. The consultant I want to use is Roxanne Barnes from Effective Management. It's the same company and person that taught the course. She is really good."

Ralph just sat and thought for a while. Then he said "You think she's that good?"

"You bet," Brian replied,

"She's not going to come in here and undermine everything we have done is she?"

"No, she's the one who taught us all this stuff anyway. After discussing this with her, she's really telling me that we have our act together. It's Roy and the other departments that are the problem."

The last part is what made the final sale. "Okay, I'll go talk to Roy. Anything else you want?"

"How about the time off?"

"After what you just threw at me?" Ralph said with a big frown, which turned to a smile. "Of course."

Roy played his role just right, at first resisting then finally agreeing. Pete quickly bought in. As far as he was concerned, anything that would provide them with better information to run the business was at least worth examining.

Roxanne made the visit and worked her magic. After spending most of the day looking at some of their key processes she did a wrap-up session with Pete and his staff, which both Brian and Joan attended. How Roxanne did it Brian didn't know, but by the end of the presentation, Roxanne gained the interest of most of the top management, not only with an approach for capacity planning, but with the Effective Management's process to implement Integrated Business Management. Pete in particular picked up on the huge advantage. She suggested a 90-day program to get them up and running quickly, which included an inexpensive piece of software to provide the Sales and Operation Planning information, a financial view, and the Resource Requirements Planning capability.

As they left the meeting, Ralph came over to Brian. "Well Miller, you were right. For once the consultant gave us some good press. I think that Lenny isn't a happy camper right now. When Roxanne said he had to forecast, I thought he was going to blow a fuse! It's about time someone took on Sales and Marketing."

"Thanks," Brian mumbled. He had gotten another offhand compliment from Ralph, but was hoping that Ralph wouldn't find out that he had been in cahoots with Roy.

Roxanne returned in two weeks to conduct an assessment. The report of the assessment, which included a cost-benefit analysis, pointed out how lacking they were in the top-level planning processes. Pete quickly grasped the opportunity for Hayes Tractor. He named himself the champion for the process. He also liked the concept of Class A, and decreed that Hayes would achieve Class A processes regarding Integrated Business Management, which was Effective Management's improved version of the Sales and Operation Planning process that was currently in place.

Jennifer Westlund was named the Demand Manager and was responsible for pulling together all the demand information. Joan was named the Supply Manager and was responsible for pulling together all the supply information; and she was named the overall project manager. Brian got the responsibility for Resource Requirements Planning. The plan started with education of all areas. Roxanne worked on the demand side. She brought with her Dennis Jones to help the supply side develop Resource Requirements Planning.

Dennis and Brian laid out a detailed project plan to get Resource Requirements Planning up and running quickly. They started with education of all the key managers who would be using Resource Requirements Planning. They then designed a roll-down education plan for the whole organization for awareness and the specifics for functions that had operational requirements to support the effort.

The education started with a basic understanding of terms. Resource Requirements Planning and Rough-Cut Capacity Planning (see Figure 2.4) are used to describe different levels of the planning process, even though the processes are similar. The process of rough-cut capacity planning differs from Detail Capacity Planning in that it uses a load profile for times, which will be described later, against the schedule, as opposed to using the output from Material Requirements Planning that was explained in Chapter 5.

The first level is using the output from the Integrated Business Management process, which is the Supply Plan. This is most often referred to as Resource Requirements Planning. The second level is the Master Schedule, which is referred to as Rough-Cut Capacity Planning. The terms aren't important; what is important is that a common set of terms is used to describe the process for accurate communication.

The focus of both forms of rough-cut is to estimate resource and capacity requirements before a commitment to any changes in their overall plans. First, Resource Requirements Planning is run against the aggregate Supply Plan. If the resultant resource requirements are considered feasible, the Supply Plan is approved. The approved Supply Plan is then sent to Master Scheduling, which breaks the aggregate family-level numbers down into the next level; these are usually specific, finished items or options. Then Rough-Cut Capacity Planning is run, against the proposed Master Schedule, to see if it is feasible. Again, if the resultant capacity requirements are feasible, the Master Schedule is approved and the Material Requirements Planning system is run. This now provides the data to drive the Detail Capacity Plans and the Dispatch Lists.

Whenever a significant proposal to change the Supply Plan or the Master Schedule is made, the rough-cut processes must first be used to assure capacity is available. Resource Requirements Planning would be used when Lenny asked for significant changes in the Supply Plan: Those longer-term large changes are covered in the Integrated Business Management process. It permits senior management to establish an overall game plan for the company. The idea is not to determine detailed capacity requirements at this stage, but to get a rough-cut sense of the plant's capabilities. We're simply asking, "Are we in the ball park?" By following this procedure before decisions are made regarding the Supply Plan, senior management can get a good idea of whether or not they can accomplish what they want to. If the plan that senior management wants to execute is not valid, they need to examine the alternatives and make adjustments accordingly. Resource Requirements Planning allows them to do this, and to address critical decisions promptly. It gives them the opportunity to see the impact of future plans and to initiate capacity changes well before they become crises.

When a short-term change is requested at the Master Schedule level, as was the case with the move from the medium tractor to small tractor, Rough-Cut Capacity Planning is used to test the feasibility of the plan before customer commitments are made. Rough-Cut Capacity Planning tests the validity of the Master Schedule from the perspective of capacity requirements prior to committing to the changes and running Material Requirements Planning and Detail Capacity Planning. This allows the master scheduler the opportunity to initiate action early in the process to make midrange capacity adjustments or to avoid making commitments beyond the company's capabilities. This is important because once Material Requirements Planning is run, the shop and suppliers start executing the new plan that has been generated. Then, if only one resource, whether it is an internal or external one, can't accomplish the required work, the plan has to be changed and people will have to undo what they have just started. It is better to know that the Master Schedule is at least feasible before doing all of that. A little effort up front with Rough-Cut Capacity Planning can alleviate a lot of nervousness in Material Requirements Planning, as well as the frustrations felt by the users when trying to keep pace with a fast-changing schedule.

It is necessary to do the rough-capacity calculations at both the Supply Plan and Master Schedule levels. The Resource Requirements Planning process uses a Resource Profile based on the most likely mix of products in the family. But actual product mix variability can be quite significant in regard to the amount of capacity required for each end item. This means that the mix of product in the Master Schedule could cause the capacity requirements to vary considerably, even though the total units in the Master Schedule are within the Supply Plan guidelines.

All too often management is under the impression that the rough-cut process is only used when the plans are increasing. That is not the case. It is just as important when the volume is decreasing. When the workload is decreasing, it means the company won't be fully utilizing its equipment or people. Decisions must be made regarding what to do with the excess workforce or equipment. The alternative would be to keep the people and build inventory, take in some subcontract work, or implement any other creative idea that management comes up with to utilize the resources. These are decisions that senior management must make in a timely manner, and the Resource Requirements Planning process helps them to do so.

The first step in implementing the Resource Requirements Planning process is to identify the key resources. Since the process is to be used to get a quick, rough estimate of the impact of high-level decisions on capacity, there is no need to look at every work center. The key resources are the critical resources that are involved in the manufacturing process—those that are most likely to be a constraint. Potential candidates for Resource Requirements Planning are bottleneck work centers and work centers that can't be offloaded, such as unique processes or a unique piece of equipment. Other candidates are work centers with long lead times to change capacity, such as a work center with highly skilled labor content. Work centers with a scrap/yield problem or low utilization/high downtime should also be considered, as should critical suppliers. If a company is an engineer-to-order manufacturer, design engineering should be another important candidate for consideration as a key resource. Other resources to consider are quality control, suppliers, floor space, and tooling.

For Hayes, the first step was to identify the resources that were most likely to constrain their process. Dennis Jones, the Effective Management coach, emphasized that the best people to decide what resources to include in this process were the managers of the resources themselves, because they were likely to know the constraints better than anyone else would. Brian and Dennis scheduled a workshop and invited Ralph, the Production Manager; Joan, now the Supply Manager; Elliot, the Manufacturing Engineering Manager; Carol, the Quality Control Manager; Harold Bloom, the Purchasing Manager; and Dan and Mickey.

The workshop started with education. Dennis gave a detailed explanation of what the Resource Requirements Planning process was all about, emphasizing that it would give senior management some key information to help them develop the Supply Plan for the future while minimizing the risk of overloading the factory.

Ralph leaned forward in his chair and gave Brian a hard stare. "This was supposed to be about the other departments, not ours. Is this shifting, and are we are going to be the scapegoats again?"

Brian swallowed hard. A confrontation with Ralph in front of this whole group was the last thing he wanted. But before he could answer, Dennis stepped in and said, "Trust me; Roxanne is pulling the other organizations through a knot hole right now. They have a long list of processes to improve. What we are doing is developing a process so that when they come up with a plan we can test it to be sure we can support it. This tool will be enable you to identify the problems in enough time to do something about it."

"So what happens if they ignore our input, like Lenny always wants to do?" Ralph shot back.

"That's a very good question," Dennis replied. "I think by Pete committing to the Class A process, that kind of behavior will be exposed. When the question of capacity comes up, the Class A practice is to ask two questions. The first is 'Can you do it?' If you can't, that's the end of the discussion. The second is, if you can do it,

'What will it cost?' Class A behaviors insist that management know what the cost of making a decision is before you make it. Class A processes don't decide, they turn it into a business decision. Before I get off that topic I want to be sure that everyone recognizes that capacity is almost infinite."

Ralph started to fly out of his seat, but Dennis held up his hand to Ralph and said, "Given the time and money, could you produce anything that Sales and Marketing asked for, Ralph?"

Ralph settled back in his seat. "No problem. Give me the visibility and get the behaviors of the rest of top management to change, so that we have the time and money, and I'm all ears."

"Well, if Pete is serious about Class A, Roxanne will get the behavior change. What we need to do is get the visibility."

Dennis proceeded with the establishment of key resources. He suggested that they limit the list of key resources to the 10 most critical. He reasoned that was a good place to start. They could always add more resources as time went on. The Resource Requirements Planning system could handle as many as they needed and reviewing them was an easy process that he would explain in the future.

They decided to start with the machine shop. Brian led that discussion and quickly came to an agreement that the most critical resources in Brian's area were the shaver, the CNC Lathes, the CNC Mills, and the Vertical Broach. It was a place to start.

Resource Requirements Planning is done by product family, using the same families that are used for the Integrated Business Management process. They know from the work that Roxanne had done so far that the Hayes Tractor Company had agreed on three product families: large, medium, and small tractors.

Another key piece of data that the Rough-Cut Team needed was a Resource Profile, sometimes referred to as a bill-of-resources. This is the tool used to determine what the resource requirements are going to be. The Resource Profile is an estimate of the capacity required in each key resource to produce a single finished unit (end item or finished goods) in each of the product families (see Figure 7.1).

The capacity requirements numbers can be obtained either directly from the existing databases or from estimates. If the bill-of-material and routing files exist and are reasonably accurate, a computer program can be written that will access the bill of material to extract the manufactured parts for each product. If the data from the bill-

Figure 7.1   Resource Profile

Key Resource		Product Family		
W/C No.	Description	Small	Medium	Large
24	CNC Lathes	.70	1.00	1.40
35	CNC Mills	.50	.60	.80
40	Gear Shaver	.00	.60	.80
90	Vertical Broach	.15	.18	.20

of-material and routing files are not available or not reliable, or if the computer support to calculate the numbers is not available, the data for the Resource Profile should be estimated from information gathered from Production and Manufacturing Engineering. It is not difficult to get useable data in this manner. These people are knowledgeable because they work with the information day in and day out. It is not necessary for these numbers to be precise, since the data will be used only for rough-cut estimates of capacity requirements.

As an action item from the workshop, Brian needed to develop the Resource Profile for the equipment the Rough-Cut Team had settled on. The Information System analyst said getting an answer as to whether the Enterprise Requirements Planning software would provide the times for the Resource Profile would take a while. Rather than delay the process while the Information Systems analyst figured it out, Brian decided just to develop it himself. He started by pulling up the multilevel bill of material for one of the medium tractors. (See Figure 7.2.)

By looking at the routings for those parts, Brian could determine which of those parts were processed through the critical resources. He could then extract the necessary data for those key work centers.

Brian found that the gears for the medium tractor needed to go through the shaving work center. Looking these parts up on the routing file, he saw that for a three-speed transmission gear set, it took 0.13 hours to shave the first gear, 0.15 hours to shave the second and third gears, and 0.13 hours to shave the reverse gear. If he took the normal lot size and setup time—in this case 100 pieces and 1 hour, respectively—he could amortize the setup time for each

Figure 7.2   Multiple Level Bill of Material

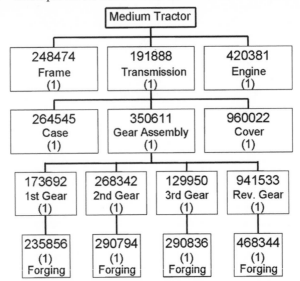

gear manufactured. In this case, it was 0.01 hours (1 hour divided by 100 pieces). By adding together the run time for the gears with the amortized setup time, he had the total time to produce one gear set. Then, he multiplied that by the quantity in the bill of material. In this example, that number is one, because only one of each gear set is used per tractor.

When Brian added the gear numbers together, he found he needed 0.6 hours of shave time to produce the three-speed gears for a medium tractor (see Figure 7.3).

He put the 0.6 into the Resource Profile under Gear Shaver/medium tractor. He then took the same steps for every key resource and product family. The result for Brian's machine shop looked like Figure 7.1.

RESOURCE REQUIREMENTS PLANNING CALCULATIONS

To calculate Resource Requirements Planning, the Supply Plan quantity for each product family is multiplied by the hours in the Resource Profile corresponding to that key resource/family combi-

Figure 7.3   Amortized Resource Profile Time

P/N* Time in Hours

1st Gear Time $= (.13 + .01) \times (1)$ $= .14$
2nd Gear Time $= (.15 + .01) \times (1)$ $= .16$
3rd Gear Time $= (.15 + .01) \times (1)$ $= .16$
Rev. Gear Time $= (.13 + .01) \times (1)$ $= .14$

Total Σ of P/N Times $= .60$

*Times per P/N = [(run time per piece) + (SU ÷ order Quantity)] × BOM Qty]

nation. The capacity required to support the Production Plan for each family is then added together to provide the total capacity that is required for each key resource. This process is then duplicated for each month in the planning horizon.

At Hayes, to produce the parts on the CNC Lathes for the 300 small tractors planned for October, the Resource Profile hours of 0.7 hours per tractor in work center 24 (see Figure 7.1) is multiplied by the planned production quantity of 300 tractors. The result is 210 hours of capacity required (see Figure 7.4). The medium tractor Resource Profile of 1.0 hours per tractor times the 200 planned tractors equals 200 required hours. The large tractor takes 1.40 hours per tractor. Multiplied by the 20 tractors planned, a total of 28 hours is required. By adding the 210, 200, and 28 hours together, the required capacity for the CNC lathe is 438 hours. This process is continued through all the key resources resulting in a Resource Profile for the month (see Figure 7.4). The Resource Profile is then created for each of the next 18 to 24 months depending on how far the forecast goes. Then, comparing the required capacity with the planned capacity for those work centers for each time period shows the capacity status of the critical resources.

Brian didn't have to do the calculations. He simply needed to enter the critical work centers and the Resource Profile into Effec-

Figure 7.4   Resource Capacity Plan by Month

Key Resource	Product Family & Volume			Required	Planned
W/C No. Description	Small 300	Medium 200	Large 20	Capacity	Capacity
24 CNC Lathes	210	200	28	438	500
35 CNC Milling	150	120	16	286	300
40 Gear Shaver	0	120	16	136	130
90 Vertical Broach	45	36	4	85	120

tive Management's software and the Resource Capacity Plans were generated.

The Resource Requirements Plan for the CNC Lathes looked like Figure 7.5. If the required capacity is reasonably close to the planned capacity, management can approve the plans and proceed with the development of the Master Schedule. However, this does not preclude having to make adjustments to planned capacities once Detail Capacity Planning has been run. Remember that at this stage this is only rough cut.

As a rule of thumb, if the difference between the required and planned capacities in the rough-cut mode is greater than about 5%,

Figure 7.5   Resource Requirements Plan—"Do Nothing" Scenario

Resource Plan Work Center 24: CNC Lathes				
Month	Required Capacity	Planned Capacity	Variance	Maximum Capacity
Oct	435	500	62	560
Nov	512	500	-12	560
Dec	512	500	-12	560
Jan	512	500	-12	560
Feb	512	500	-12	560
Mar	575	500	-75	560
Apr	600	500	-100	560
May	624	500	-124	560
Jun	624	500	-124	560
Jul	624	500	-124	560
Aug	624	500	-124	560
Sep	624	500	-124	560
Oct	650	500	-150	560
Nov	700	500	-200	560
Dec	700	500	-200	560

some corrective action should be taken to balance available capacity with the projected requirements. This breakpoint—5%—is somewhat arbitrary. It depends upon the individual work center.

Looking at the plan for CNC Lathes (see Figure 7.5), Brian saw that October was under loaded by 62 hours. Brian figured that he could use that time to do some maintenance and to do some further education and training of his crew. For November through February, the plan indicated that the work center would be overloaded by 12 hours. Considering that the plan was only a rough estimate of the required capacity, Brian wasn't concerned about it. However, the increase in the Supply Plan starting in March was going to cause problems. Not only were the estimated resource requirements greater than Brian's current plan, they were significantly greater than what Brian considered his maximum capacity. He was going to have to show this as an issue in the Supply Review step of the Integrated Business Management process (see Figure 2.2). This Resource Requirements Planning approach was giving him a five-month advance warning of a rather serious problem.

Alternate plans at the Integrated Business Management level can be quickly evaluated by looking at the Resource Requirements Plan. We can easily see what product families are impacting on which work centers. By altering the capacity in these work centers and/or the Supply Plan, we can vary the results of that impact.

There are several ways to get more capacity if necessary. Actions such as overtime, hiring more people, cross-training, using alternate work centers, and subcontracting are likely to impact the cost of the product. Increasing capacity to meet the requirements of the unconstrained Demand Plan may require capital investment in equipment or facilities. Another shift may need to be added, requiring additional supervision and training. Major make-or-buy decisions may also be considered.

Similarly, reductions in capacity requirements may increase costs as a result of underutilized equipment or labor. On the down side, potential labor reductions may be identified. Senior management will be made aware monthly of these potential cost/service issues in the Integrated Business Management process.

All of these senior-level management decisions need to be made as a part of the Integrated Business Management process so the

Supply Plan will reflect what the company is really going to execute from the supply side. Since the factory Supply Plan belongs to senior management, they should be informed of the consequences of their decisions and actions before they approve it. By using Resource Requirements Planning, they can look ahead at the future capacity requirements and test the validity of the Supply Plan during the Integrated Business Management process, thereby improving the chances of being able to meet the plan within reasonable costs.

The Integrated Business Management software was installed on a laptop computer. In addition to being the Demand Manager, Jennifer Westlund was established as the Integrated Business Management coordinator and as such she collated the input data and operated the software. With the forecast, a supply plan and the machine shop load profile data loaded, they were ready for a demonstration. Jennifer hooked the laptop to a projector in the executive conference room. Jennifer walked them through the process. She had put in the original forecast and supply plan. Lots of discussion ensued, even though it was only demonstration.

Joan then turned it over to Brian to demonstrate the Resource Requirements Planning function. Using the original Supply Plan (see Figure 7.4), they agreed that Brian could probably have worked around the tight situation in the gear-shaver work center (136 hours required versus 130 hours planned). However, when they ran a second scenario changing the mix between small and medium tractors (decreasing the small tractors from 300 to 200 and increasing the medium tractors from 200 to 300), they could see that the required capacity would be 196 hours required versus the 130 planned (see Figure 7.6).

Brian calculated the maximum capacity for the shavers running 3 shifts, 7 days a week to be 150 hours if they could maintain the

Figure 7.6   Resource Requirements Plan by Month—New Plan

Key Resource		Product Family & Volume			Required Capacity	Planned Capacity
W/C No.	Description	Small 200	Medium 300	Large 20		
24	CNC Lathes	140	300	28	468	500
35	CNC Milling	100	180	16	296	300
40	Gear Shaver	0	180	16	196	130
90	Vertical Broach	30	54	4	88	120

Figure 7.7   CNC Lathes—Resource Requirements Plan

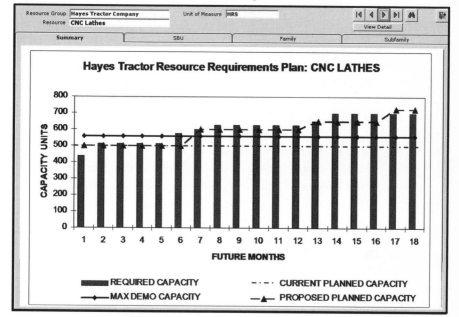

current 90% load factor, which was unlikely. It was clear that the revised mix in the Supply Plan created a major problem.

Brian then moved to the CNC Lathes. To make the plan easier for management to see, Brian switched to the graph format (see Figure 7.7).

This graph clearly showed the capacity constraint in 6 months and the additional constraint in month 14. Brian knew he would have to come up with some solutions to all the constraints the Resource Requirements Plan had pointed out. Brian had also included in the display a possible solution, as a "proposed capacity plan." This was based on: first, a process upgrade to reduce throughput time medium-term; then investment in an additional lathe that would create future headroom longer-term. Ralph glared at him, because he knew Brian was flying a kite! Brian tried to look innocent. "It's only as an example," he said.

Ralph, Pete, and Lenny recognized that, with this information, they could easily have avoided the hassle they had encountered earlier. They complimented the team for the work that they had done. They agreed that they would use the Resource Requirements

Planning process as an integral part of the Integrated Business Management process. They also agreed that they would use it to evaluate any emergency situations like the one with Iowa Tractor, one of their best customers.

With the help of the Effective Management coaches, Hayes had the Integrated Business Management process up and running in less than 90 days. That didn't mean it was Class A yet, there were still a lot of old imbedded behaviors that needed to be eliminated. Pete insisted that Roxanne continue to coach them through the process until they reached Class A.

To a much lesser extent Dennis worked with Brian and the other areas to get the Resource Profiles established and to learn how to use the resulting charts to manage the business better. He also started putting pressure on the implementation team to start working on the Master Schedule level.

Joan took the leadership role and followed up with their Enterprise Requirements Planning system experts. During the next implementation team meeting she reported what she had learned.

"Our software does have the capability to do Rough-Cut Capacity Planning. We just never considered using it since we had Detail Capacity available to us. We need to create a plan to implement it, just like we did Resource Requirements Planning." They all agreed and proceeded to develop the plan.

ROUGH-CUT CAPACITY PLANNING CALCULATIONS

Whereas Resource Requirements Planning uses the Supply Plan as input, Rough-Cut Capacity Planning uses the Master Schedule. The purpose is to test the validity of the Master Schedule before firming it up and running the Material Requirements Planning and Detail Capacity Planning. The same key resources that were used with Resource Requirements Planning must be used but can be expanded significantly.

The differences between Resource Requirements Planning and Rough-Cut Capacity Planning are:

1. The profiles for Rough-Cut Capacity Planning are developed for each master scheduled part number rather than product family, and are called Load Profiles to distinguish them from Resource Profiles used in Resource Requirement Planning (see Figure 2.4). In Hayes' case, part numbers 36492, 32846, and so on represent specific op-

tions of the small tractors (see Figure 7.8). Some software packages provide the capability to generate the Load Profile for master scheduled items by searching the database for the parts and operations involved and doing the calculations based on the current bills of material and routings.

Figure 7.8   Load Profile—Small Tractors Family

Key Resource		Part Number					
W/C	Description	36492	32846	25173	31962	26874	21349
24	CNC Lathes	0.65	0.75	0.70	0.60	0.70	0.80
35	CNC Milling	0.55	0.60	0.50	0.45	0.40	0.50
40	Gear Shaver	0	0	0	0	0	0
90	Vertical Broach	0.12	0.18	0.15	0.10	0.20	0.15

2. The Rough-Cut Capacity Planning Load Profile data are multiplied by the master scheduled quantities rather than the Supply-Plan quantities (the Master Schedule must be adjusted to meet the new Supply Plan prior to this time).

3. Additional resources may be added for the Rough-Cut Capacity Planning process. The accuracy of the plans is better because it recognizes mix change at the Master Schedule. Therefore, checking more work centers makes sense, and there is really no limit as long as the Load Profiles are established and are accurate.

Figures 7.8 and 7.9 are the Load Profile and the calculation of the hours required for the members of the small tractor family only. For example, in the case of Master Schedule part number 36492, the Load Profile time of 0.65 (see Figure 7.8) would be multiplied by the quantity for that MPS part number, which is 50 (see Figure 7.9), resulting in 32.5 standard hours of capacity required. This would be

Figure 7.9   Rough-Cut Capacity Plan Calculation

Key Resource		Part No.						
W/C No.	Part No.	36492	32846	25173	31962	26874	21349	Total
Description	Quantity	50.0	40.0	100.0	20.0	80.0	10.0	300
24	CNC Lathes	32.5	30.0	70.0	12.0	56.0	8.0	209
35	CNC Milling	27.5	24.0	50.0	9.0	32.0	5.0	148
40	Gear Shaver	0.0	0.0	0.0	0.0	0.0	0.0	0
90	Vertical Broach	6.0	7.2	15.0	2.0	16.0	1.5	48

repeated for each item and work center to get the total capacity requirements.

The same process is repeated separately for the medium- and large-tractor families, and then the three numbers for each key resource are totaled (see Figure 7.10).

Figure 7.10   Rough-Cut Capacity Plan—By Resource

Key Resource		MPS Summary			Required Capacity	Planned Capacity
		Small	Medium	Large		
No.	Description	300	200	20		
24	CNC Lathes	209	197	29	435	500
35	CNC Milling	148	138	18	304	300
40	Gear Shaver	0	114	12	126	130
90	Vertical Broach	48	35	6	89	120

Doing Rough-Cut Capacity Planning at this level provides an opportunity to see the impact of product mix changes in the Master Schedule. For example, referring to Figure 7.9, if the master scheduled quantities are changed, the changes in the capacity requirements for the key resources can be seen immediately. The total capacity requirements calculated in this manner (see the "Required Capacity" column of Figure 7.10) are slightly different from the capacity requirements calculated for the small-tractor family from the Supply Plan (see Figure 7.4) using the Resource Requirements Planning process. That is because the Supply Plan calculation uses the "representative-item" approach to get its Resource Profile; whereas the Master Schedule calculation uses the Load Profile data for each Master Schedule part number. Therefore, a mix shift in the Master Schedule can cause the required capacity to change.

Since the Master Schedule is in weekly or daily increments, Rough-Cut Capacity Planning should be displayed in weekly buckets rather than the monthly buckets commonly associated with the Resource Requirements Planning process.

OPERATIONAL REQUIREMENTS

Varying levels of computer support are used for Resource Requirements Planning and Rough-Cut Capacity Planning. Some companies have complete modules as part of their Enterprise Resource

Planning software. Others use "bolt-ons" like the Effective Management software. What is important is that the calculations are correct and the display of the information is usable, which is of particular concern to top management. They only see the information once a month, and easily understood graphs—like the ones in the Effective Management's software—are important if top management is really going to use the information. Trying to create spreadsheet programs on a personal computer requires loading some data manually, which just takes too long.

Assuring that the data are available and that Resource Requirements Planning and Rough-Cut Capacity Planning are done in a timely manner is the responsibility of the Supply Manager. In companies where that position does not exist, the organization needs to be reviewed and the position created, or allocated to the master scheduler if that person is senior enough in the company.

The owners of the manufacturing resources are responsible for the numbers in rough-cut. They must accept responsibility for the identification of the key resources and the development of the Resource Profiles and Load Profiles. They are also the ones who must take action based on the output from each of the rough-cut processes.

Resource Requirements Planning should cover a minimum of 18 months. Some companies go out five years or more. The resource requirements should be expressed in monthly increments for the first 12 months. After that, those periods can be lengthened to a quarterly view if preferred. At the end of each month, that month is dropped, and another month needs to be added to the end of the horizon. The Resource Requirements Plan needs to be reviewed every month as a part of the Integrated Business Management process. Although changes may not be made, reconfirmation is important. Resource Requirements Planning can also be used to evaluate any major change scenario at any time.

Rough-Cut Capacity Planning should be run after Resource Requirements Planning to be sure no capacity problems arise because of product mix or actual scheduled quantities. If additional key resources are planned in Rough-Cut Capacity Planning that are not considered in Resource Requirements Planning, this is the opportunity to evaluate the validity of the Master Schedule with regard to those resources. The Rough-Cut Capacity Planning horizon should be equal to the Master Schedule horizon (typically 52 weeks or more). The Rough-Cut Capacity Plan should be expressed in monthly or weekly increments and reviewed at least monthly. In addition, if changes to the Master Schedule are suggested, a quick Rough-Cut Capacity Planning check can be made at any time, to be certain there are no capacity problems before releasing the changes to Material Requirements Planning.

Keep in mind that even though neither Resource Requirements Planning nor Rough-Cut Capacity Planning may indicate a problem, that does not mean that a capacity problem will not be subsequently revealed via Detail Capacity Planning. Neither Resource Requirements Planning nor Rough-Cut Capacity Planning provide enough detailed information to assure a viable plan in the daily short-term. These techniques only serve as a warning that there is some risk involved in proceeding with the planning process in the light of the capacity situation. The decision to approve the plans or to require further analysis is a judgment call by the managers involved in the process.

ADVANTAGES OF RESOURCE REQUIREMENTS PLANNING AND ROUGH-CUT CAPACITY PLANNING

It is important to keep in mind that these processes are a rough estimate of the company's capacity needs. This, as might be expected, has both its advantages and some limitations when compared to calculating Detailed Capacity Planning. Let us first take a look at the advantages.

As we have mentioned, Resource Requirements Planning tests the validity of the Supply Plan, and Rough-Cut Capacity Planning tests the Master Schedule. They are done at least once a month or whenever there is a major change to be sure that the Supply Plan and Master Schedule have been developed within the realm of reason with the planned available capacity. They should cover the full planning horizon for the Supply Plan and Master Schedule. By doing so, Resource Requirements Planning and Rough-Cut Capacity Planning provide early visibility of whether anything has to be done to alter planned capacity or the Supply Plan or Master Schedule.

As opposed to Detail Capacity Planning, Resource Requirements Planning and Rough-Cut Capacity Planning do not require the use of a routing for every item being built. These processes can use a Resource Profile developed from a so-called typical product, one that is representative of the other products in that family. Both Resource Requirements Planning and Rough-Cut Capacity Planning are simple processes where precision is not critical. Resource Requirements Planning examines only those key resources in the process. Neither process takes long to implement with the proper focus. In many cases, the implementation can be accomplished in less than a week. To do so may require that the number of key resources included at first be limited to only a few.

Resource Requirements Planning takes very little computer time. Therefore, a simulation at the Supply Plan level should only take seconds. This allows senior management to ask "what if" questions in the Management Business Review meeting of the Integrated Business Management process and the software should provide them capacity views of any work center on the system in seconds. Both rough-cut processes easily correlate families with key resources, thereby enabling quick assessment of the impact of changes in the plan. For example, in Figure 7.4, we can see that a 10% increase in the Supply Plan for the small tractors is not a serious problem, since it would not impact on the shavers. The other work centers are well within their capacity capabilities. On the other hand, as we have seen, a 10% increase in medium-tractor production causes trouble.

At Hayes, the Product Sales manager would frequently come into the Integrated Business Management meeting and inform the group of a new opportunity. One day he said, "We've just broken into a new segment of the market that we didn't anticipate. After talking to these customers, our assessment is that we could get between a 12 to 20% gain in business with our medium-tractor family. Should we pursue that?" The figures were immediately put into the Resource Requirements Planning model to determine if it was at least feasible to get the resources for the job.

Shortly after implementing Resource Requirements Planning at Hayes, Lenny's first words at these monthly meetings were usually "What if?" Since it was relatively simple to run a Resource Requirements Planning analysis on any new possibility, the management team could address the situation virtually in real time.

RESOURCE REQUIREMENTS PLANNING AND
ROUGH-CUT CAPACITY PLANNING LIMITATIONS

These processes have plenty of things working in their favor, but there are also some limitations to be aware of. First, the Resource Requirements Planning approach assumes that the Resource Profile chosen to represent the family is typical of all of the products in that family. This, of course, does not address those environments where product variability within a family is significant. In such an environment, Rough-Cut Capacity Planning takes on a greater significance since it deals with individual products.

Resource Requirements Planning also assumes that the production lot size is equal to the Supply Plan, and that the company will produce exactly what will be required for that particular month. Rough-Cut Capacity Planning takes into account lot sizing at the Master Schedule level but not at the component level. Since different lot-sizing rules are often used at the component levels, the actual capacity requirements may differ from the Resource Requirements Planning and Rough-Cut Capacity Planning calculations. The consequence would be that no capacity is used because there is inventory from a previous month or that the capacity requirements are three months' worth because the lot size established covered that period of time. Resource Requirements Planning and Rough-Cut Capacity Planning also amortizes the setup time over a typical run. In reality, as the Supply Plan and/or Master Schedule is either increased or decreased, the actual setup times for component jobs can vary.

The Resource Profile and the Load Profile can provide an approximation of lead-time offset. In companies that have long manufacturing lead times (greater than one month/four weeks) the lead-time offset should be used. We know there's going to be some lead-time offset in the work centers that appears at the beginning of the manufacturing process. This, however, can usually be accommodated in the mechanics of the process by offsetting the required capacity to the appropriate week/month. At first, Brian didn't recognize the impact of the lead-time offset issue. But, once he did, it was relatively easy to resolve it. Typically, all four of Brian's work centers worked on the product four weeks earlier than the product was due to ship. By offsetting the required capacity four weeks earlier, Brian was able to give himself a better representation of the timing of the capacity requirements. Mickey's work tended to fall in the month the product would be shipped, but some of Dan's had to be offset as much as two months from the Supply Plan.

The Resource Requirements Planning and Rough-Cut Capacity Planning processes ignore component inventory. It assumes we have to make all the parts necessary to build the product. This usually does not cause a problem, but it can be a problem if the company is planning to reduce the inventory levels of the family or if a product or family is being phased out or has become obsolete. By design, it also only considers specific, designated key work centers, not the total process. Conceivably, a potential bottleneck work center could be left off the list. Generally, this is only a temporary problem, since once an additional work center is recognized as a key work center as evidenced by information from Detail Capacity Planning, it is merely added to the list of key resources. These limitations result in the inaccuracy of the Resource Requirements Planning and Rough-Cut Capacity Planning in the short term. To compensate for these limitations, Resource Requirements Planning is used over the longer term (typically 4–24 months). Rough-Cut Capacity Planning should be used over weeks 2–52. Detail Capacity Planning over weeks 1–13 will be required, by day in the immediate horizon.

COMPARING RESOURCE REQUIREMENTS PLANNING, ROUGH-CUT CAPACITY PLANNING, AND DETAIL CAPACITY PLANNING

A question often asked is, "Do we need to do all three: Resource Requirements Planning, Rough-Cut Capacity Planning, and Detail Capacity Planning?" In most cases, the answer is yes. Each technique has its own purpose, time-frame, strengths, and weaknesses. Let's compare the three techniques.

The primary difference between Resource Requirements Planning, Rough-Cut Capacity Planning, and Detail Capacity Planning is that their focuses are different. Resource Requirements Planning receives its demand from the Supply Plan, Rough-Cut Capacity Planning receives its demand from the Master Schedule, and Detail Capacity Planning receives its demand from Material Requirements Planning.

The horizons of the three processes also differ. Because of its limitations mentioned previously, Resource Requirements Planning is a medium- and long-term monthly planning process. Since Rough-Cut Capacity Planning can use more detailed routing information and lead-time offset, and is based on specific master scheduled items and quantities, it provides a more precise view of the capacity requirements than does Resource Requirements Planning. Consequently, the Rough-Cut Capacity Planning is more useful in the near to mid-term time frame. Typically, Resource Requirements Planning operates over months 4 through 18; Rough-cut Capacity Planning operates over weeks 2 through 13, and over a longer horizon when needed to support a proposed change to the Master Schedule. Detail Capacity Planning operates over the shop-floor execution horizon, by day or by shift, out to a horizon to support shop-floor Planned Hours commitment as discussed in Chapter 5.

Because it deals with monthly periods, Resource Requirements Planning typically is run only monthly. Rough-Cut Capacity Planning can be run either weekly or monthly, and displays information in either weekly or monthly buckets. Detail Capacity Planning is normally run weekly and displays information in weekly or daily periods.

Different people use the three processes. Resource Requirements Planning is a tool the Supply Manager uses to identify long-term problems and display them to top management; Rough-Cut Capacity Planning is used primarily by the master schedulers. Detail Capacity Planning is a tool by the Capacity Planner, middle managers, and first-line supervisors.

Resource Requirements Planning and Rough-Cut Capacity Planning look at only the designated key resources, whereas Detail Capacity Planning considers all work centers established on Routings. Resource Requirements Planning and Rough-Cut Capacity Planning are run before Material Requirements Planning is run. Detail Capacity Planning is done after Material Requirements Planning, because that is where key data reside. With Resource Requirements Planning and Rough-Cut Capacity Planning, inventory on hand or on order is not netted out from the capacity requirements calculations. This inventory, however, is netted out in the Material Requirements Planning process before Detail Capacity Planning is run. Resource Requirements Planning typically has no lead-time offset applied to the timing of capacity requirements, whereas lead-time offset is a standard feature of Rough-Cut Capacity Planning and Detail Capacity Planning. Also, Resource Requirements Planning can be done on a personal computer. Rough-Cut Capacity Planning should be included as a module of the full Enterprise Resource Planning system because the number of items in the Master Schedule are normally so many that it makes manual manipulation difficult. Detail Capacity Planning requires complete Material Requirements functioning as well as routing and work-center files.

Resource Requirements Planning and Rough-Cut Capacity Planning should be periodically compared with Detail Capacity Planning to be sure they are reasonably consistent with each other.

In summary, Resource Requirements Planning and Rough-Cut Capacity Planning have the advantages of speed, flexibility, and simplicity. Detail Capacity Planning has the advantages of thoroughness, detail, and accuracy.

Once Resource Requirements Planning and Rough-Cut Capacity Planning were properly implemented at Hayes, surprises in the capacity report rarely reached Brian's desk. Through Integrated Business Management, Pete and his staff assumed responsibility for deciding what aggregate levels of product would be supplied each month. Through Master Scheduling, Material Requirements Planning, Detail Capacity Planning, and the Dispatch List, Brian and the other production managers would receive their production schedules. It was then up to him to execute the schedules and deliver on time.

The Shaver problem that started the whole focus on Resource Requirements Planning and Rough-Cut Capacity Planning at the beginning of the chapter should have been resolved at the Rough-Cut Capacity Planning level. As soon as Lenny requested a mid-term mix change in tractors, Roy, the Materials Manager, should have run Rough-Cut Capacity Planning and taken the output to Ralph for his commitment. Of course, we wouldn't suggest that Ralph make the decision without consulting the owners of the resource— Mickey, Dan or Brian. In the case where Lenny wanted to increase the overall schedule, that should have been handled at the Resource Requirements Planning level. As soon as Lenny had an inkling that he wanted to increase the schedule, he should have introduced it into the Integrated Business Management process. That way the Resource Requirements Planning process could identify possible constraints and investigation on how to solve capacity problems could be completed well in advance of changing the schedule.

Chapter Eight

Joining Forces

Life seemed to be getting better by the day for Brian. His shortages were going down, as were Dan's since he started using the Dispatch List, Summary Capacity Plan, and the Input/Output/Queue Plan. Many problems were being exposed using the Resource Requirements Plan and Rough-Cut Capacity Plan, but they were now exposed with time to resolve them. Ralph was a lot easier to live with, but he kept saying "enjoy it now because tomorrow the bomb will hit and the shortages will be back." Brian was more optimistic.

Hayes had made good progress on reaching Class A behaviors with the Integrated Business Management process. They weren't quite there because they needed to refine some processes, improve the forecast accuracy, and do some Resource Requirements Planning with suppliers. There was some resistance from Harold Bloom, the Purchasing Manager. Brian wasn't concerned because he felt that finally he had complete control of his capacity, and Dennis Jones, their coach from Effective Management, was giving him accolades that rough cut for production was the fastest and best one he had ever seen.

Pete had decided that the Class A process was working so well for Integrated Business Management that he was going to expand it to the rest of their processes. Roxanne from Effective Management, who was coaching Pete, suggested that they identify some business milestones that would result in a Class A milestone Planning and Control. Pete jumped at the suggestion. The first business milestone was Integrated Business Management and the second was on-time delivery. Roxanne was working with Pete and his staff regarding the follow-on milestones.

Accurate routings and bills of material were a part of the second business milestone. Once he figured out how easy it was to get the routings correct by the operators in the shop working together with Manufacturing Engineering, Brian applied the same concept to the bill of material. Mickey resisted at first but once Lloyd Adam, the Design Engineering manager, started supporting Brian and Dan with quick changes, Mickey jumped on the bandwagon. Dan joined the effort and it wasn't long before they all were above the 95% minimum level for routing and 98% for bills of material. Dennis Jones threw a damper on their enthusiasm when he said that those levels of accuracy would meet the requirements for the first Class A milestone Planning and Control, but Class A business excellence certification required a minimum of 99.5% for both. This scared Brian until he started to see an occasional 100% accuracy for both the routing and bill of material. When Brian dug into the details, he saw that both engineering groups and the production people were really acting as a team. Whenever a problem arose the engineers were going online and fixing it right then. By the time the auditor arrived it was fixed. In addition, the teams had started to employ their six sigma black belts to solve the more difficult problems.

Another measurement the Effective Management required for Class A was inventory accuracy. Roy O'Brien, the Materials Manager, had been working on the stock rooms to make them more accurate for several months. The Effective Management coaches had helped Roy overcome a few "sacred cows," like keeping the production people out of the stockrooms, and their accuracy rose quickly. The shocker was that Class A required that "work in process" also be accurate. Dan and Mickey dug their heels in on that one, saying that their people's job was to make product, not do paper work. Brian started to side with them but decided to trust the Effective Management coaches because they hadn't led him astray before. Brian wondered how Dennis Jones was going to convert Dan and Mickey and get them to understand why. The answer was simple: education. Through education, Dennis showed them how inaccurate inventory hurt them because they would have to respond quickly when a count was short, and how they could be making something early when a count was high and that could keep them from making the right part. Dennis then went on to show them how to get the inventory accurate without overburdening the operators.

The Materials Department was making huge strides getting their plans valid. With the bills, inventory, and forecasts more accurate it made the master schedules and material plans a lot more stable. That meant they could work any messages that the systems sent them everyday. It meant fewer shortages to chase; more time to plan. The vicious circle was actually starting to go in the right direction, toward the virtuous circle.

Brian was getting lots of praise recently and was really feeling good. The praise wasn't just for delivering on time, but it was also because his productivity and quality were both going up. He knew that the improvements were because his supervisors were spending less and less time expediting and more time working with their people to solve problems. Life was really starting to feel good, but unknown to him, Ralph was right about another disaster being right around the corner.

Lenny was correct about the tractor market going up. Each month he increased the forecast and of course he wanted it right now. The Class A process recognized that the supply organizations couldn't always respond immediately. They therefore recommended establishing time zones to operate within when considering a change. They called the first zone the *firm* or *red* zone. Firm meant they were in the final stage of completing the product and that it would be very costly to change. The next zone was called the *trading* or *yellow* zone and meant the material was on order and that capacity had been established but there was some flexibility. The last zone was the *adding* or *green* zone and meant capacity was available except where capital equipment was required with a long lead time. That meant that if they were to change anything in one of the zones they would have to examine the situation to see if could be accomplished and at what cost. *Red* zone changes required detail analysis by part number. The *yellow* zone and *green* zones could use Rough-Cut Capacity Planning and Resource Requirements Planning to research the issues. It was really working well for the production areas. Whenever Lenny came up with a new forecast it was put into the system and the constraints were quickly identified. Sometimes they just decided not to go after a particular demand because it would require significant capital and the chances of actually getting the orders just wasn't that high. Pete kept saying that the Resource Requirements

Planning analysis was the easiest way that he had ever seen to do risk analysis.

Resource Requirements Planning unfortunately hadn't been completed for suppliers. Harold Bloom always had a stream of reasons why he couldn't get them up. Pete, with constant reinforcement from Dan, kept asking Harold if the suppliers were able to support the increased demand. It was a constant conversation in the Supply Review and Management Business Review meeting of the Integrated Business Management process but Harold stuck to his guns that the suppliers had better, or else. Even Roxanne, the Effective Management coach, couldn't get Harold really to address the situation or get Pete to take action.

Brian got some unusual insight from Dan on the situation. During Ralph's last staff meeting Dan started pushing Ralph real hard.

"Ralph, you know as well as I do that Harold is taking us down the path to disaster," Dan began. "He doesn't know what the suppliers can or can't do and they aren't about to tell him. They aren't going to be honest when he threatens them all the time about losing our business. So they are taking the same approach they have always taken. In the past we have always been the one to fail to meet the schedules because of lack of internal capacity. We were never able to meet the increased production so we were the scapegoat. Yeah, some of them look bad once in a while but they never really shut the line down for long. They would always react quickly to get it going again and they would be heroes. That doesn't take into account the additional amount of work that the parts handlers and Mickey's assemblers have to do when parts show up late. Nor does it account for the scrambling that Brian and I have to do when the raw material shows up late. That is a real loss of productivity."

Both Mickey and Brian sat in stunned silence as Dan continued. "But the kid over there introduced capacity planning to us and we have our arms around it now. I'm confident that Brian and I are going to have the capacity to support this ramp up if we get the material. That is what is going to kill us—lack of material. I'm already starting to see it. How about you guys?"

Both Mickey and Brian agreed that they had started to see more and more of their purchase material show up late. They then both got behind Dan and started complaining, even if they were stretching the truth a little. That did it for Ralph. He went to see Pete behind closed doors. They worked on a strategy to get Harold moving, yet at the same time provide him with a path to get there. The getting-Harold-moving part was relatively easy. Pete called Harold into his office and gave him an ultimatum. Pete hated doing it, but it seemed that that is what it took to convince him to take action. What Harold confessed was that he just didn't know how to do it and therefore resisted it. Pete was quick to understand where Harold was coming from and assigned Joan and Brian to a small project team to develop the plan and to support Harold.

The first step was to invite the suppliers to a conference where Joan and Brian explained both rough-cut and detail capacity planning processes. They then went on to demonstrate the Resource Requirements Planning tool that they bought from Effective Management. Next was detail showing how the resource profile was developed.

Harold then took over. "We can not afford to miss this next upturn in business. It is our opportunity to increase market share and Hayes is determined not to miss it. As you saw from Joan's and Brian's presentation, Hayes has made huge progress with our planning and control processes. Many of you have commented to me that our schedules are finally believable and the number of inside lead-time requests is at an all time low. We need you to have good planning and control capability because without you we can't meet our customer demand. Therefore, I expect each of you to be able to demonstrate your ability to plan your capacities in the future. We also want the resource profile like Brian just showed for your critical machines that we can put into our Resource Requirements Planning system. If there is a request to increase production, I want the ability to check your available capacity quickly and see if and when we might cause you a problem. If there is a problem I will contact you immediately. This makes life a lot easier on us and easier on you. In addition, we will be making visits to assess your capacity planning capability, much like our quality audits. I will be bringing an in-house expert like Joan or Brian to do the evaluation on your capacity planning capability."

Harold's last remarks set off quite a stir. Brian couldn't determine if it was positive or not.

The supplier visits Brian made varied all over the map regarding their capacity planning ability. Most of the companies had very inadequate planning and control systems and no Resource Requirements Planning process. He always referenced Dennis and Roxanne but sensed he was receiving "lip service" when told they would give them a call. When Brian touched base with Dennis, he confirmed Brian's suspicion. Brian sensed that most would just apply a lot of pressure on manufacturing to make sure that Hayes got what they wanted. It was the environment that Brain was just transitioning from: Focus on the customers that had a lot of clout and let their other customers suffer. To get the supplier to change was going to be a long haul, but it needed to be done if they were going to get their Class A certification because it was one of the topics addressed in 'Managing the Supply Chain.'

When Brian made the comment to Dan regarding priority at the suppliers he just laughed. "They have been ignoring us for years because we have been so screwed up. It's about time we got the top priority."

"But Dan," Brian countered, "that just isn't right. They need to fix their problems."

"Some will because they have some smart kid like you. Most won't. They will just throw money at it and will never get it. A few will end up going out of business. That's life," Dan said, shaking his head as he walked away.

The key suppliers came through with resource-profile data so that Joan could load it into the Integrated Business Management software. The number of resources grew significantly, but Harold assigned one of his best buyers to the review for the Integrated Business Management cycle. It only took her a few minutes to review all the key supplier's critical resources and identify capacity constraints. That is when the real work started.

Harold's Purchasing department wasn't the only area that the improved planning and control processes applied to. Carol Barrow, Manager of Quality Control, had been watching and listening with great interest to the changes happening at Hayes. She had seen how the production departments had gotten their schedules and capacities under control. Her operation, however, was still out of control and she couldn't figure out why. Finally, she decided to talk to Brian about it. "I'm getting buried out there. I never know what a priority is until Mickey needs it, which means I constantly have to move people around at the last minute. I'm always working overtime, which isn't the most economical way to run the organization. When I go to Pete to try to hire more inspectors, he always puts me off by telling me that things will get better and I probably won't need more inspectors. Then he goes off on the Juran tangent saying we should fix the process and get rid of the inspectors. I couldn't agree more, but you have to fix the process first. You are starting to make progress here in the machine shop but we are a long way from getting there. In the meantime I need enough inspectors to keep you, Dan, and Mickey off my back. Now, to my way of thinking, the capacity planning process that you installed in the Machine Shop could improve my operations, too. Couldn't I get a capacity plan for QC, like you guys in manufacturing do?"

Brian thought about Carol's request. "What you're asking for is a priority list for inspection and a way to determine how many inspectors you need. . . . You know, I bet we could do that if we put the inspection operations on the routing."

"You mean make inspection a regular operation?" Carol asked. "We've never done that before. I mean we're inspectors, not production," she stammered.

"So what?" Brian shrugged. "The inspectors are a resource, aren't they? We can schedule them just like any other operation."

"You'll have to convince me," replied Carol.

They went to the inspection layout table and picked up a work order. "Look," said Brian, "this part has to come here to be inspected prior to going on to the next operation. We could insert an operation, assign a work-center number, and put in a setup and run time (see Figure 8.1).

Figure 8.1   Routing Showing Inspection as an Operation

594706	Sub. Assy. - Frame				
Part Number	Part Description				
Opn. No.	Dept.	Work Ctr.	Operation Description	Setup	Run
			Release		
			Pick		
10	Fab	53	Weld, Tack	.5	1.00
20	Fab	57	Weld, Finish	.1	1.00
30	QA	60	Inspection, Layout	2.0	.00
40	Mach	36	Mill, Knee	1.0	.50
50	Mach	35	Bore	.5	.25
			Store		

"Do that on all the routings that require the inspection operation, feed it into the computer, and it will give you a Dispatch List just like we have for the production operators. Not only that, but you'll also get a Summary Capacity Plan and Input/Output/Queue Plan for the 12-month horizon. That will be the information Pete is looking for to support your request for more inspectors. Ever since I started using the capacity plan, I've always gotten the people I need. Pete knows the predicted hours are accurate. When I've gotten the people I asked for, there has never been a loss of productivity. Just the opposite has happened. Productivity has improved 11 percentage points since I have started doing capacity planning. I have been able to hold overtime at the planned level. I'm also sure that if I asked for a reduction in people, he'd believe it, because we've shown we can accurately predict our needs through this system. We really understand where the numbers come from and we can support them. I used to have the same exact problems you're having, but not anymore."

"Slow down, slow down," Carol said. "I can't use run times. I don't inspect all the parts. We only do a statistical sample. If you put the time in to inspect one part and multiply it by the order quantity, it will overstate the lead time and capacity requirements."

"You're right," conceded Brian. He thought a second. "Tell me, Carol, is the sample size typically the same?"

"Well, we use statistical sampling to determine the sample size, but in general the sample size is the same even if the order quantity varies a little."

"Then why don't we just figure out how long it takes to inspect the whole sample and put that into the routing instead of using a run time per piece?"

The process that Brian suggested using here is often called a "block" standard—a block of time to do the complete job. Another term that is used to describe this is the "total elapsed time" for the operation.

When Carol told Brian that their software did not provide the "block standard" or "elapsed time" feature, Brian said, "Why can't we just put that information into the setup field on the routing. It amounts to the same thing, a block of time to do the entire job instead of a time per piece."

"You know," Carol said, visualizing how this would come together, "I think that will work, except for one thing. The inspectors aren't going to like having a standard time set on their inspection."

"You're probably right, Carol. I had the same problem with the production people when we asked them to help establish realistic standards. They were constantly asking for them to be loosened."

"How'd you resolve that?"

"We still occasionally have a problem," Brian admitted, "but we worked really hard to educate the operators about how the standards are used for capacity planning, scheduling, and calculating the cost of the product. That helped, but it wasn't until we stopped using the standards as a way to pressure them for better performance that we really started to get their cooperation."

"Wait a minute, Brian. You still use your efficiency performance measures. I hear your supervisors talking to the operators about them all the time."

"You're right," Brian said, "but we are trying to use the correct approach with the operators. Instead of demanding that they improve their efficiency, we ask them what can be done to improve it. For example, when an operator says a standard is too tight, the supervisor asks the operator to call him over while the job is running so they can review it. They try to improve the process to meet the standard time. If they can't, they'll call the manufacturing engineer to help with the process improvement. If they still can't meet the standard, the manufacturing engineer will change the standard. As soon as we started doing this, productivity went up but, believe it or not, the standard times on average have been reduced by over 5% so far, and are steadily going down as we improve the processes. But don't let me mislead you, Carol, it didn't work for everyone. We still have a few diehards out there. But, what's really interesting is that they aren't getting any support from their peers or the union. What you'll find is that if you approach the problem properly, your inspectors are going to see this as a real help to them and not a hindrance."

"What about the roving inspectors?" Carol asked.

"I don't know what to do there," replied Brian. "How do you plan their capacity now?"

"Well, I know a roving inspector can cover about 20 production people. I just don't know how many people you'll have on any one shift. You see, I've got to provide coverage on all the shifts regardless of the number of people."

"Well, that's no problem," Brian said. "I'll give you my capacity plans and you can calculate your requirements from that."

"Hey, Brian, that'll be great. I really appreciate this."

After an intense education session that Brian helped Carol develop, she assigned one of her most experienced instructors to adding the operation to the routings. Elliot volunteered one of his new manufacturing engineers to help. What she originally thought would be a really large task turned out to be a lot easier than she expected. Many of the inspections were similar so adding them was a lot of cut and paste. In addition, the inspectors bought into the process and meticulously reviewed the routings while inspecting the job and adjusted them as needed. Brian told Carol if she felt any of the resources were critical she should inform Joan so she could add them to the rough-cut capacity planning process.

Walking back to his office after helping Carol work through the Summary Capacity Plans and Input/Output/Queue Plan, Brian felt good. He felt that he and Carol had actually accomplished a great deal. They were working together constructively to solve a real problem, and they had done so without any bitterness. Most of Brian and Carol's previous conversations involved arguments over acceptability of parts. Brian had to admit this one was much more satisfying. He realized that Hayes was finally starting to operate like a team. That didn't mean there wasn't more to do, but people had begun working things out together. It also amazed him that he had time now to work on improving processes instead of chasing shortages. "An occasional shortage is a lot of fun to chase and feel the glory of getting it done quickly, but it's just an ego thing—not what I should really be doing," he thought to himself.

Similar problems as Carol's were also cropping up in the area of tooling. It always seemed there were never the right tools available to start a new job. Brian had been running his operations off his Dispatch List, and things were getting better. But they still ran into problems, like the time they introduced a new hub onto the medium-sized tractor. The date for introduction had been changed and changed again, and Brian had been able to reschedule the hub's work centers around management's indecision. Finally, the introduction date arrived and production was ready to begin. There was only one problem: The new tooling hadn't arrived.

Brian knew whom to call. "Elliot, we're ready to start the new hub. . . ."

Elliot didn't need to hear more. "The new hub? Is the tooling ready?"

"That's why we're talking, Elliot."

"Hang on a second," Elliot said and yelled at his coordinator for tooling.

After some mumbling that Brian couldn't understand, Elliot asked, "Is there any way you can make the old fixture work?"

"It's just not possible. You know they beefed up the new hub and it just won't fit on the old fixture." Brian felt some of his old exasperation returning. "Tell me, Elliot, when are we ever going to have the tools done on time, so we can proof run the first production like we're supposed to?"

"What do they expect from me? I mean, how many times have the design engineers changed their minds, and now once again it's just too late to get the fixture altered. I'm sorry, Brian. All I can do is react around this place. I'll have to check on exactly where the hub tooling is, but you can bet it's late because Design Engineering didn't get their design done until well inside of lead time."

"I wish I could help you, Elliot, but I can't get these parts out unless I get my tools from you."

"Look, Brian, I didn't have the slightest idea when these tools were supposed to be ready, especially the way everyone's priorities change around here. I mean, it seems everything is behind. And it's primarily because the design engineers never seem to get the designs finished on time."

The pattern was beginning to seem obvious. The first step to solving this problem was to head up to Design Engineering and figure out what was going on there. They were the ones who caused the delays with the late design releases. This problem stemmed from the fact that the new hub required a fixture for the CNC Drill, and the drawings for the new design were two weeks late, which caused the fixture to be late.

Elliot and Brian tracked down the manager of Design Engineering, Lloyd Adams. When they told him their problem, Lloyd was not very sympathetic. "What do you want from me? We're under the gun to get this new product line out pronto. I'm just trying to get the whole project out. How am I supposed to know which drawing should be done first?"

As Brian and Elliot went through some of Lloyd's method of scheduling, they realized that his schedule was not in sync with production's, and consequently he had been sending out some designs earlier than they were needed and others later. Lloyd reiterated that he had no clear idea what was needed or when, he just saw his workload according to each project. Individual parts requirements didn't come into play.

"Hey, Elliot, you know what's happening up here. We're dealing with customer changes on a daily basis. And we're not even talking about Manufacturing's input for improvements in manufacturability. If you mix that together with your production needs or Purchasing wanting specific designs finished early, it makes it impossible to schedule."

There was no way Brian could argue with Lloyd. He knew there had been numerous times when they might not have had the capacity they needed on one of their lathes, so they decided to proof run a new part early. This meant they needed tooling earlier, along with the purchased material and other components. This became a scheduling nightmare. The priorities were constantly changing, as were the capacity requirements on the lathes.

"Believe me, fellows," Lloyd said as calmly as he could, "I know everything that's supposed to get done and we're getting to it as fast as we can. I keep asking for more engineers but Pete hands out extra head count like his life depended on it."

The only problem for Brian and Elliot was that because of the lead time for manufacturing, some of the designs that were getting done later needed to be done earlier and some of the design that weren't needed till later were getting done early. All Lloyd could do was shrug. "I understand your problem, but the priorities are only being communicated by customer ship date. On the individual parts, I can only do what I think is right."

Later in the day Elliot stopped by to see Joan. He explained the problems he and Brian were having. Joan reached for her notebook from the recent Effective Management course she had attended. The scope for that course was the whole enterprise. She flipped open to the section that dealt with engineering. "You were at the course with me, don't you remember?" she said, showing the section to Elliot. "It's all about how you structure engineering and tooling requirements into the bill of material."

"Yeah, I do remember that, but to be real frank, I just didn't think we would ever get there, so I put it out of my mind. Anyway, I didn't think Lloyd would have any part of it."

"I don't know about you Elliot, but I'm really seeing a change in Pete. He always came across strong on actions required to resolve an immediate problem, but he was never strong regarding strategies and tactics. However, since he has started working with Roxanne he has changed. This Class A stuff has really hooked him and I think he really means business. If Lloyd decides he is going to resist, he is going to get the same treatment that Harold got. To quote what

Harold told me Pete said, 'The train is leaving the station; are you getting on or not?' Harold said he decided to get on before it started moving too fast. He knows that Pete can get the train going fast very quickly once he gets it in his head that that is what he wants to do. To quote Harold, 'It is a lot easier to get on at 5 miles per hour than at 60.'"

The light had really been coming on for Joan. Manufacturing had been using the capacity plan and Dispatch List, so why couldn't Tooling and Engineering? The course had gone into detail about how to use the Enterprise Resource Planning software to aid the various support departments. It detailed how Material Requirements Planning could release past-due messages for activities, as well as parts, and how capacity plans and Dispatch Lists could be provided for these activities, too, reflecting all projects. The simulation capabilities available in the Enterprise Resource Planning system could be used for all activities, not just manufactured and purchased parts. The instructor also explained how changing the Master Schedule causes all activities for a project to be rescheduled in sync via the bill-of-material explosion. A lot of the new software has special software for scheduling engineering or "bolt on" software could be used instead of the more detailed material requirements planning software. The key is to link engineering to each of the component parts and not just at the master schedule level.

As they discussed the methodology, Joan explained how they could use the engineering option that their software had to put the tooling number right on the bill of material. Elliott could then establish operation numbers on the routing for the various steps in tooling, put that in the system, and he could have accurate dates via the Dispatch List and capacity plans for the tool room. Elliot and Joan sat down and structured how it would work on a special design loader they had to produce (see Figure 8.2).

Looking at the proposed bill of material, they could see that the loader required a special bucket. They had changed the shape of the bucket, which required a new back and two new sides. The teeth remained the same. In order for Dan's department to weld it properly, some new slots had to be milled on the locator brackets. Elliot and Joan entered the five steps required to accomplish the modification to the fixture into the routing database (see Figure 8.3).

When Joan brought these ideas to Lloyd, as a way for him to get a handle on engineering resources, he was a little reluctant. "That's

Figure 8.2 Special Product Bill of Material

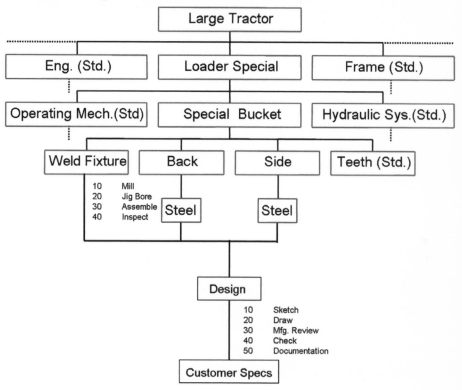

all well and good for machines and mechanical operations, but I'm dealing with people up here. How do you schedule creativity? How can I expect an accurate time from an engineer about how long a project will take?"

Joan explained to Lloyd how it would work. "We have the bill of material for our product (see Figure 8.2). The bucket assembly back and sides are our new engineered parts. Directly under those parts, we list that the assembly needs a drawing to make those parts, and we give that drawing a part number. Then, we create a routing for the process of making a drawing. It may take a sketch, which requires a specific kind of engineer. So instead of saying we need drills or mills, we say we need an electrical engineer or a mechanical engineer, and so on. Then, it should go through a manufacturing review to assess manufacturability. Someone will have to lay out the

Figure 8.3   Tooling Routing

999243	Fixture - Weld				
Part Number	Part Description				

Opn. No.	Dept.	Work Ctr.	Operation Description	Setup	Run
10	Tool	76	Disassemble	.10	3.00
20	Mach	36	Mill	1.00	.50
30	Tool	71	Jig Bore	2.00	3.00
40	Tool	76	Assemble	.10	6.00
50	QA	63	Inspection, Tool	4.00	0.00

drawing, and then someone else will have to check that. Having completed those steps, we document the drawing."

"Hang on a minute," Lloyd interjected. "I need the customer specifications in order to start the design. Why can't that be put on there also?"

Joan painfully recalled the frequency with which the Sales Department asked for product inside of lead time but never seemed to get the customer specifications in on time. "I don't see why not," she replied. "Getting a customer specification is an activity just like anything else. So why not let the computer schedule it as an integrated part of the whole process?"

"Count me in, then," Lloyd said, "this stuff is beginning to make sense, especially if it can help get my customer specifications on time and meet my schedules." Joan and Lloyd sat down and developed a routing that reflected the design steps required to produce a drawing (see Figure 8.4).

Figure 8.4   Engineering Routing

188642	Bucket				
Part Number	Part Description				

Opn. No.	Dept.	Work Ctr.	Operation Description	Setup	Run
10	Eng	80	Sketch, Mech.	12.00	0.00
20	Eng	84	Draw, Mech.	21.00	0.00
30	Eng	86	Mfg. Review	3.00	0.00
40	Eng	88	Check	4.00	0.00
50	Eng	89	Documentation	3.00	0.00

Once the engineering requirements are structured on the bills of material, and routings have been created, the system can be used to plan the engineering resource requirements and schedule the engineering activities.

The planning system was helping to bridge the gaps between areas like Manufacturing, Engineering, Tooling, and Inspection, by linking everyone to the same schedule. It also brought these areas in sync with one another, so they were working together, not as separate departments, not as adversaries, but as a cohesive team.

Manufacturing, Tooling, Engineering, Inspection, and Sales began a pilot project. They made the changes to the bills of material and routings they had developed and used the computer to calculate their schedules. The system worked so well for engineering that within a short time Lloyd was looking for ways to link in his Computer-Aided Design (CAD) systems. Hayes was starting to look, and work, like a competitive manufacturing company.

Ralph was acutely aware of the good advice coming from Effective Management Inc. He had first-hand knowledge of Roxanne Barnes's and Dennis Jones's assistance that had helped them make what he thought of as startling improvements in the Sales and Operations Planning process that had now become Integrated Business Management. But it really seemed to makes sense to expand Class A to some of the other processes, so after the next staff meeting he asked Roy O'Brien, the Materials Manager, for his opinion about expanding the scope of Class A.

To say the least Roy was stunned when Ralph asked him about it. "Well . . . yeah, I think it is a great idea. What do you have in mind?" he stammered.

"I don't know," Ralph responded, "but I thought we should include the things that we have accomplished so far and perhaps some of the missing elements we haven't covered."

"Okay, why don't I have Joan contact Roxanne and see if she might do an assessment of where we are in what they refer to as their Planning and Control milestone using the Effective Management's *Class A Checklist*?"

"Well Joan, you must've read my thoughts," said Roxanne when Joan called her. "You've made such good progress in Integrated Business Management, as well as some of the other areas that you have worked on, that it does seem like a real opportunity to see how good you really are."

"Okay, what do we need to do?" Joan asked.

"First we need to scope out the assessment. You're not ready for a full Class A assessment, but I suspect you're pretty close to what we call 'Capable Planning and Control.' It may not sound like much, but believe me it's the foundation for a whole lot of improvement initiatives."

After working out the details for the visit, Roxanne met the Hayes team to prepare for the assessment. As usual Dan was reluctant to get involved, but Joan and Brian worked hard to persuade him that, as the assessment was looking for integration and performance, he had to be a part of it.

"Hey, even Lenny and his entire sales and marketing team have agreed to participate. You don't want to be the only one that is being bullheaded about it, do you?" Joan had said with the final piece of the argument that Dan couldn't say "no" to.

Later that month Roxanne and Dennis led the entire Hayes team through a three-day assessment using the template for achieving the Capable Planning and Control Class A Milestone Award. It was obvious that a lot was already in place and performing well. It was also clear that some of the processes were not up to the standard. More importantly, few of the metrics had sustained good performance for at least 12 weeks, which was a Class A requirement.

After the assessment they got the Assessment Report and gap-closure recommendations. Pete, the General Manager, and the senior team reviewed the work that needed to be done, and agreed to get the foundation right before trying to drive further improvement.

Four months and a lot of hard work later Hayes was assessed again, and this time the company met the requirements for the Class A Milestone. Amid ceremony and excitement, and with the local press in attendance, Hayes was presented with their Effective Management Class A Milestone Award. Hayes proudly placed this impressive award in a prominent place in the reception area and proudly flew the Class A Milestone flag next to the country and company flags.

What Brian and his colleagues would soon find out, however, was that even though they were now planning and executing well, they still needed to maintain their dedication to becoming better. It was easy to become complacent, but the competition would not stand idly by while Hayes gloated about their accomplishments.

Chapter Nine

Scheduling to Capacity Constraints

Brian was feeling good, not only about the job they were doing with capacity planning and Input/Output/Queue control, but also that Effective Management had certified them on their first milestone. Everyone was excited about the progress they were making. It wasn't just what was going on in the shop but all of the departments. The silos were coming down and people were really starting to work together.

As Brian was sitting and thinking a little bit about the progress Hayes was making, he got a call from Dan.

"Brian, I know I gave you a hard time on this new scheduling and capacity planning stuff. I may have been a little slow in coming around, but I have to admit, it's making a difference. I also know that we wouldn't have done it without your persistence."

Brian was amazed. Another compliment from Dan? He couldn't think of anything to say, so he waited for Dan to continue.

"However, . . ." Dan said.

"Oh, oh," thought Brian. "Here it comes. He was just softening me up."

Dan went on. ". . . I've got a problem in Heat Treat. I'm starting to have difficulty meeting the schedule. I've never had any problem before, but the workload has gradually increased to the point where it's chewed up all of my reserved capacity. I've been watching this coming on the capacity planning report. Some weeks are a little overloaded, some weeks a little under. I figured the overloads and underloads would about balance themselves out. Trouble is, I can't get all the work done during the overloaded weeks, and little by little, I've been falling behind. We're running three shifts, seven days a week. I'm just about at my maximum capacity. In fact, I have been for a few weeks now. I don't have any capacity left."

Brian recalled that this issue had come up during this morning's daily scheduling meeting in the shop. He was starting to have difficulty meeting his own schedules because of jobs coming out of Heat Treat late.

Dan continued, "I'm trying to run to the dispatching rules that we agreed on. You know, when behind schedule, run to the due dates on the Dispatch List. The problem is that running in that sequence forces me to change the furnace temperature and sometimes the atmosphere between almost every job. It takes a lot of time to change the temperature and get it stabilized, and I lose a lot of productive time. If I could run the jobs that require the same temperature back-to-back, I'd get a lot more throughput. You seem pretty up to date on all this scheduling stuff, so I thought I'd call you to see if you had any ideas."

"Can't you send some of the work to an outside heat-treating facility?" Brian asked.

"Sure," Dan responded. "That's what I've been doing. But the cost is half again what it costs us to do it internally. It also adds four to five days to our processing time. The worst thing, however, is that their quality isn't up to our standards. I have to reject a lot of their work."

Hayes had only one heat-treat furnace, and Brian knew it was unreasonable to suggest a second furnace to solve the problem. That equipment was very expensive, and it wasn't in the budget. Brian also knew that it would take months to get a new furnace in place even if they could get it approved.

"I don't want to seem too negative, Brian, but I'm not sure this scheduling method we're using works in situations like this, where the capacity is fixed and sequencing the work properly is necessary to get the work out. I just don't have any flexibility."

"Let me give this some thought," replied Brian. "I'll get back to you."

Brian headed for Joan's office. Maybe she had some ideas on how to handle the Heat Treat problem.

"I've been reading about all kinds of new scheduling techniques, including some that schedule operations within some finite capacity constraints such as Dan has in Heat Treat," Joan responded when Brian explained the situation. "Technology is changing too fast for me to keep up. In fact, Roy and I are heading to an Effective Management course on scheduling next week to try and get up to date on what's going on. Why don't you go with us?"

After Joan explained further about some of the things she had been reading about new developments in scheduling software, Brian agreed that it would be good for him to tag along with Joan and her boss, Roy O'Brien, the Material Manager.

Brian caught up with Ralph as he was headed to the cafeteria for a cup of coffee. He told Ralph about the call from Dan and the conversation with Joan.

"You know, Ralph, Heat Treat has become a bottleneck for us. If we don't do something to nip this scheduling problem in the bud, we could lose everything we've gained. I'd really like to go to this course with Joan to see if there is anything that would help. The course is next Thursday and Friday, and I would need to travel on Wednesday."

"Are you crazy?" Ralph sneered. "I can't have you out of the shop for three days, especially at the end of the month. We're just starting to make some real headway around here. Who's going to keep it all together out in your area if you're gone?"

Brian assured Ralph that the end of the month was well under control barring some emergency. He also told Ralph that his supervisors were well equipped to handle any emergency that came up and that his absence would not cause any problems. Brian was mildly surprised when Ralph, after giving it a little more thought, grunted,

"Well, all right. Go ahead. I keep forgetting about this Class A stuff. Now that I think of it, maybe we don't need you at all!" Ralph replied with a little smirk on his face.

Brian hurried back to his office to make his travel arrangements. He called Dan to see if he wanted to go, but Dan had a vacation planned. "I'll give you an update when I get back," Brian replied.

On the flight to the course, Brian was leafing through some of the materials that Joan had given him on new scheduling techniques. He turned to Joan in the seat next to him. "What do think about all this finite scheduling stuff? The last Effective Management course on capacity planning that we went to cautioned us about using finite scheduling, because it would automatically reschedule the jobs if the work center was overloaded, using some complex algorithms. It'll be interesting to hear what this instructor has to say about it."

"From what I've been able to learn, the advancements in technology have mostly overcome that problem," Joan replied. "Earlier finite scheduling software leveled the load across the entire planning horizon. That meant that you wouldn't ever be aware of any need to increase your capacity because the software would just reschedule the load to fit within the capacity constraint. That would put the Master Production Schedule at risk. Modern software gives you the ability to limit the automatic rescheduling of overloads. Although it seems that each software package has its own ideas about how to do that, it appears that most of them provide an opportunity to put in your own scheduling rules, generate a recommended schedule based on those rules, and give the planner the option of overriding the recommended schedule. You now know everything that I know about the subject. That's one of the reasons that I wanted to attend this course. I want to find out more about it."

As he was settling into his seat at the start of the course, Brian scanned the list of attendees that was among the materials placed in front of him. Just as he had at the earlier course, he noticed the variety of products and manufacturing environments represented by the attendees. Remembering the value of the contacts that he had made from the other course, Brian carefully tucked the list away in his briefcase for safe keeping. He made a mental note to talk to as many of the people as he could while he was there to see if any of them had any experiences they were willing to share.

Amy Shinn, the course leader from Effective Management, began to get into the meat of the subject right after introductions. "The primary goal of plant scheduling is to support the Master Schedule—and consequently customer demands—while making optimal utilization of constrained resources. It is important that the scheduling system provide predictable, stable work schedules."

"So far, so good," thought Brian. The scheduling system at Hayes was doing a pretty good job on this latter point, but maybe there was more they could do regarding their resource utilization, particularly in cases like Heat Treat.

Amy continued. "Production schedules are generated using one of two techniques: so-called infinite capacity scheduling, and finite capacity scheduling. Within each of these approaches are the variations of forward scheduling and backward scheduling."

Brian made a note as a reminder that the scheduling method they were using at Hayes was an infinite-capacity scheduling technique, utilizing backward scheduling (see Chapter 3).

"Infinite capacity scheduling, as you may know, is not truly infinite because the input plan has already been constrained in the master scheduling process. But it works well when the capacities are flexible and can be expanded or contracted, or when resources can be reallocated as needed," continued Amy. "This is particularly the case with labor-intensive work centers or when overtime or alternate processing is a readily available option. Infinite capacity scheduling is based upon the notion that it is possible to adjust the available resources to match the workload.

"Finite capacity scheduling is generally appropriate for use in capital-intensive environments, where it takes longer, and is generally more costly to change the capacity of the resources available to do the work, or where alternative processing is not an option. In this situation, it is necessary to adjust the workload to match the available resources. One of the most important uses of finite scheduling is to assist the factory in getting maximum output from a bottleneck or capacity-constrained work center.

"Most manufacturing companies want to work with a plan that is based on the due date, so that is where they start. They then use a combination of backward and forward scheduling techniques to come up with the optimum solution.

"The use of Finite Capacity Scheduling software—we use the acronym FCS—has increased dramatically in recent years to the point that it is now quite the norm in some industries."

"Oh, boy," thought Brian. "Just what we need: more acronyms."

"It's only fair to warn you," Amy went on, "that this rise in popularity has led to the development of many different software packages. Even though they may all be labeled as finite capacity scheduling systems, not all FCS software is created equal. They do not all have the same capabilities nor all of the features that we will talk about over the next two days. And some may even have features that we don't include in our materials here. While there may be significant differences in how each package performs its scheduling calculations, however, the basic underlying concepts, principles, and practices are similar. Those basics will be the focus of this course. We do not intend to get into the pros and cons of a particular software package.

"It is highly unlikely that any particular finite scheduling software package will meet all the scheduling needs of all of your companies. Each company needs to understand and define its own needs and make sure that the software meets them.

"The scheduling approach used by most finite scheduling software is to start with the order with the earliest operation start date and schedule it with no queue time. This start date is derived by running a backward-scheduling calculation from the scheduled order completion date, using the production routing to determine the operations to be scheduled, and the setup and run times for each operation."

"Hmmm . . . ," thought Brian, "just like we do with our system."

Amy went on to explain the rest of the scheduling process. The setup of the next job in line would be scheduled to start on that machine immediately after the first job finishes. The third job would then be scheduled after the completion of the first and second jobs. This would continue for each succeeding job on the work list until the total workload equaled the predetermined capacity constraint of the work center. "The question is how to determine which job is next in line," she said. "That's the key to finite scheduling, and that's what we'll talk about next."

RULES-BASED APPROACH

Finite scheduling systems use a rules-based approach that defines how the next job is selected for a specific resource. Most finite scheduling packages have a standard set of rules that are typically available and can be specified by machine by the user. Some of the software has relatively simple single-criteria rules such as earliest due date, shortest processing time, shortest setup time, or highest dollar value.

Published articles have claimed that the manufacturing cycle time can be significantly improved by deploying more sophisticated rules (than single-criteria rules) that take into account the Theory of Constraints. The Theory of Constraints is built around the notion that, just as a chain is only as strong as its weakest link, the shop-floor throughput is constrained by a few bottleneck work centers, and the production schedule should be driven by these constraining work centers. The resolution of the constrained situation involves both scheduling within the limits of the constraint and consideration of the removal of the constraint.

Leading Finite Capacity Scheduling software provides planners the option of developing custom, multicriteria rules that are tailored to a factory's unique constraint situations. Conceptually, multicriteria rules are a series of tasks, decision points, and choices that the software logic uses to branch among different scheduling algorithms using "if/then" logic (if this is the case, then do this). For example, the planners might choose "earliest due date" as the first rule. Then they could look for jobs that minimize changeover time. Depending upon the precise situation at the time and the particular company environment, planners might use rules that give priority to urgent jobs, tooling availability, setup time, material type or availability, or preventive maintenance requirements. Rules that consider overlapping operations, parallel operations, variations in queue, and move times are used. Although employee work schedules in manufacturing tend to be relatively static, as flextime becomes more widespread, the scheduling process must deal with planned time off, unscheduled time off, and skills availability.

SCHEDULING BEYOND CONSTRAINED CAPACITY

Once the total scheduled workload has reached the capacity constraint and there is more work to be scheduled, additional scheduling rules come into play. The simplest, of course, is merely to schedule that job to a time period where the capacity is available, either earlier or later. If the operation is scheduled later, then the remaining operations on that job must also be rescheduled using forward-scheduling methods. If the operation is scheduled to an earlier date, then its preceding operations must be rescheduled using the backward-scheduling technique. If the remainder of the schedule cannot be compressed sufficiently to meet the original start or completion dates, then a newly scheduled order start date or completion date must be generated.

A more complex approach is to employ scheduling rules that look upstream and downstream and resequence jobs to optimize the total schedule. This may require several iterations of the schedule by the software, including rescheduling those jobs that have already been scheduled. Modern computers can process millions of calculations per second, so it is not unreasonable to expect it to be done easily.

The use of the computer to aid the scheduling process allows us to take into account a variety of important factors that impact scheduling. Although some software is limited to the extent to which it addresses the interaction of these other factors, other packages provide almost unlimited flexibility in rules development. Carried to the extreme, rules could be developed so that virtually any scheduling decision can be represented using these rules.

"One thing you should know," Amy said. "Finite scheduling is far more complex than infinite capacity scheduling, because it tries to simulate all the possibilities that could happen on the shop floor and incorporate them into the scheduling process. Each additional factor that is considered increases the complexity of and understandability of the rules, and makes the human interface more complex. Computer power has generally increased to the point where processing speed is rarely an issue. Unfortunately this can encourage overcomplicating the rules, which then become unmaintainable.

"A word of caution: Avoid using those functions or features of the software that you don't need just because they are there. It makes it more difficult for the user to understand the nature of the schedule. We call this the 'black box effect': You put numbers in one end, and almost like magic a different set of numbers comes out the other, and you've no idea how it did that. So who's accountable for the schedule? When in doubt, err on the side of simplicity."

During the first break, Brian grabbed a doughnut and a cup of coffee and made his way through the crowd to a young man named Tom Kirk who had been sitting just in front of him. Brian introduced himself and learned that Tom was the Master Scheduler for Supreme Enterprises, a company that made several different household products, including detergents, cleansers, aerosols, and other chemical products. Tom told Brian that he had only recently started working for Supreme Enterprises, having moved from a company that made automotive parts.

Brian was curious about the differences in scheduling between the fabrication and assembly environment and the high-volume process industry.

"I'm pretty familiar with how we did things at my old company," Tom told Brian. "We had a Material Requirements Planning package that used infinite-capacity-based scheduling techniques." But at "Super Soap"—as Tom said they referred to themselves—they were using finite capacity scheduling. Tom said that his presence at this course was part of his company's education program to bring new employees up to speed on finite scheduling techniques as quickly as possible. When he got back to the plant, he was scheduled to begin a hands-on training program to learn their system.

"So," Tom said to Brian, "I'm afraid I can't tell you much about how we do it. But my boss is very charged up about our scheduling system, and I'm sure he would be more than happy to talk to you about it. Why don't you give him a call and see if you can set up a visit to our plant?"

Bingo! Touchdown on the first possession! The course was not even two hours old and Brian had his first lead on a user visit.

Tom gave Brian the name and phone number of his boss, Joe Crowe, the Production Manager at Supreme.

Back from break, Amy started the session again right on time. Brian followed the presentation in his notebook, highlighting the pertinent points and scribbling notes.

In a material-driven environment, the scheduling focus is on meeting demands, and due dates are the controlling variable. In a capacity-driven environment, the scheduling focus is the utilization of resources, and resource capacities are the controlling variables.

"In any company," Amy said, "situations are likely to be encountered where a constrained resource will force an adjustment to the component schedule that mandates a change to the Master Schedule. Typically, in a material-driven environment, every effort is made to avoid this situation and to preserve the Master Schedule due dates. While it may be undesirable to change the Master Schedule, we must admit that it does happen. The starting point for creating or updating any Master Schedule is the demand from the demand management processes. The reality that we may face is that the when the first iteration of the Master Schedule is reviewed, using Rough-Cut Capacity Planning, it is not achievable because of one or more capacity constraints. Then a new schedule must be worked out. It doesn't matter if you use finite or rough-cut capacity planning, you'll face this situation on occasions. In the next iteration the master scheduler must try to find supply capability. This could be overtime, running an additional shift, offloading to another company, or whatever options need to be examined. But when this fails and the overloaded resource cannot be adjusted to fit the work in, the demand must be adjusted by the demand manager. With finite capacity, scheduling the difference lies in how much computer support is used in making the change.

"Before we got to this situation at the Master Schedule we would first have tried to see it coming, by getting the capacity in the 'ball park' and by doing Resource Requirements Planning on the aggregate Supply Plan as a part of the Sales and Operation Planning process. That's before you enter the cumulative lead-time horizon. Once you enter the cumulative lead-time horizon, control passes to the Master Schedule, and you use Rough-Cut Capacity Planning, or some companies try to do this with finite scheduling.

"But where there is an issue inside cumulative lead-time horizon, the master scheduler will have seen this in the Rough-Cut Capacity Planning process. So the master scheduler will be able to review all the calls on the resources causing constraint, to ensure they're all valid. If a constraint still exists the demand manager will need to adjust the mix so that a doable schedule can be created. The load profiles that Rough-Cut Capacity Planning uses are based on input from the production people accountable for the resources, so they should be realistic. Having finally created a master schedule where supply can meet the adjusted demand, the Master Schedule essentially is an achievable finite capacity schedule. But notice that master scheduling is a people-based process. People made decisions. In using finite scheduling software, the software may make the changes based on the scheduling rules, but without involving people, especially the demand manager. We call this effect, 'rescheduling the customer.' This is rarely a good idea!

"The question becomes not one of '*Can* the computer do it?' but '*Should* it?' Even though a computer can perform any process that can be programmed, planners, schedulers, and shop supervisors are not likely to respect the results if they don't understand the process. This is what the late Oliver Wight referred to as the 'principle of transparency.' It is critical that your people understand the concepts and principles of your scheduling system," Amy stressed.

Tom turned around to look at Brian. He gave him a knowing look that said "That's why I'm here."

SIMULATION

Good finite capacity scheduling systems have simulation capability. The software provides a simulation module that is capable of running through different scenarios of your scheduling rules without changing the active plant schedules. This module should use the constraints and decision rules from the active factory scheduling system.

The doable Master Schedule is input to the Material Requirements Planning system that creates material plans. These are already doable against all known constraints. It is when orders start to get released into the real shop-floor world that the work-order schedule may need validation against the latest status and priorities. This can be done through detail capacity planning and scheduling, but some companies choose to go via the finite route. The Finite Capacity System (FCS) can simulate the effect of the plan with all the constraints and decision rules to verify its feasibility. The sequence of the orders at each work station is then determined by FCS based on the scheduling rules.

The FCS software will run through the various forward/backward-scheduling iterations within the constraints of the capacity of the work center until it has a best-fit schedule. This best-fit plan is displayed for the planner's review and approval before being loaded to the active schedule for the factory. This is often on an electronic planning board—like an electronic Gantt chart. This is an attempt to make the output more understandable. If the software cannot schedule the jobs to meet the planned need dates and fit within the capacity constraint, it must send the planner a message to that effect, along with its current best-fit plan. The planner then must make adjustments, using his or her experience to help find solutions, if the demand is not being adequately met. In this sense, finite scheduling is a "predictor" of pending problems, and it is up to the planner to address the situation. The key to success in scheduling manufacturing is having people make the final decisions, not the computer.

The simulation horizon should be variable so the user can ask for assistance in solving a specific future problem. The FCS simulation should be used to address shop operation scheduling problems. Simulations where multiple components, subassemblies, and assemblies are involved, especially in job shop environments, are better done by the Material Requirements Planning process. Material Requirements Planning uses simple logic that starts with the item due date and back schedules using fixed move and queue times between work centers, a single setup time for each operation, and a run time (time required for one piece multiplied by the number of pieces) for each operation. While not considering all the variables, this simple approach is easy to understand. In an environment like a job shop, where there are many different steps an item must move through, it is often the preferred method of scheduling because the capacity planner can better estimate what will happen.

REAL-TIME RESCHEDULING

When executing the schedule, some performance variance to schedule is expected to happen. In the infinite capacity scheduling approach, this variance can typically be absorbed in the queue and move times or by flexing the capacity. Since capacity cannot be flexed in a capacity-constrained environment, finite capacity scheduling must schedule operations much more tightly.

Brian asked Amy, "What happens when a job does not arrive in the work center on schedule, or the setup takes a little longer than planned, or the scheduled run time is exceeded due to problems?"

"Finite capacity scheduling systems typically will rerun the scheduling algorithms to create a new schedule," Amy replied. "Some software perform these reschedules in real-time as input is received from the shop floor. Depending upon the scheduling rules, this rescheduling could alter the sequencing of the jobs that are in the work center in real-time. There is a concern on the part of some people that this makes the schedule very unstable. It is constantly changing. As I said at the beginning, it is important that the scheduling system provide stable work schedules. Frequent rescheduling may be a symptom that all is not well with either demand control, or the planning system, or the execution of the plans. The issues mentioned previously infer a lack of execution control, but they could also be caused by inaccurate data. If frequent rescheduling persists, it is best to determine the cause and correct it, not just tolerate the symptom.

"The biggest concern, however, when operating in the real-time mode is that we have delegated the responsibility to change the schedule to the computer, with no human intervention. Success in this environment is dependent upon the accuracy of the scheduling rules, the frequency of rescheduling, the degree to which schedules are changed, and the ability of the people to understand and cope with the changes."

ACCURACY OF INFORMATION

The "garbage in results in garbage out" adage has never been more applicable than with FCS systems. The precision of the FCS approach uses a tremendous amount of detailed information. The quality and timing of the input information will be reflected in the quality of the schedules. Therefore, production models must be extremely accurate. The 95% routing-accuracy threshold commonplace with Enterprise Resource Planning systems should be raised in order to support Finite Capacity Scheduling.

In the infinite capacity environment, variances to standards are compensated for by the use of demonstrated capacity and load factors, as discussed in Chapter 4. Both of these factors have much less significance in the FCS environment. More emphasis is placed on the precision and accuracy of standards. Demonstrated capacity is often tracked by part number rather than by resource.

Many FCS systems require the precision of the operation time standards to be in one-minute increments or less. If the actual operation run times for each job are not repeatable within that sort of range, or if they vary from the standards by more than that, then it is difficult to produce a reliable, stable schedule.

OUTPUT

Most FCS software produces Gantt charts, business graphics, and statistical reports to assist planners in analyzing and presenting the results. The graphical output is particularly useful for people who are able to work better with a graphical representation of the schedule.

A typical output from FCS is displayed in Figure 9.1.

This particular report is for a two-week period in daily increments. If appropriate (for example, each resource processes several jobs each day), the output can be displayed in hourly increments for each day. Each job is typically represented by a different graphic pattern, a different shade of gray, or a different color for easy identification. Note in this example that preventive maintenance periods are scheduled on each machine. In environments where work orders are not used, the product or part number is displayed on the schedule instead of the work-order number.

"What about assembly operations," Brian questioned. "Do they need the capability of a finite scheduler?"

"You'll love this answer," Amy laughed. "It all depends. That's a standard answer from a consultant in the sales mode. Seriously, it depends on the complexity of the assembly environment. In a simple environment, there just isn't a need. However, we're seeing more and

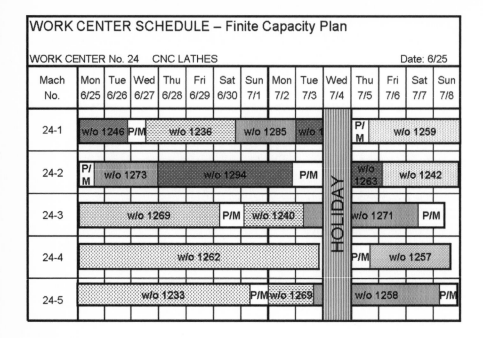

more companies that have long assembly lines, with lots of variable products going down the line, starting to use FCS. They are trying to balance the line so they have a consistent flow of product down the lines. That does mean that they have to develop routings and all the work-center data required for the FCS system to work. How'd I do, Brian?"

"Great," Brian responded, "It just makes sense, like most of the stuff."

When they returned from the course, Roy, Joan, and Brian met with Ralph in his office to decide where they should go from here. They told Ralph that two things were clear to them. First, the power of finite scheduling is unquestionable. Today's computer technology makes it possible for software to simulate numerous situations on the shop floor and aid in making decisions to improve productivity and throughput. Secondly, there are many approaches to scheduling in a constrained capacity environment, and each software supplier seemed to have some unique ideas.

After listening to their report, Ralph said, "Let's not rush into anything. It's clear to me that we need to know a lot more than we do before we make a decision on this. Brian, when we were starting out to fix our scheduling and capacity planning processes, you and Joan got a lot of benefit from talking with and visiting other companies. See if you can find a company or two that has implemented finite scheduling successfully and then pay them a visit. You know, it may be technically feasible to do all this with the computer, but let's look at the practical side of it. I think it would be best if we talked to someone who has actually done it, and. . . ."

"Actually," Brian broke in, "I'm way ahead of you. I picked up a couple of leads at the course, and I've already contacted one company who is willing to have us visit their plant."

"Good." Ralph responded. "Why don't you and Joan go talk to them? In the mean time, Roy, would you work with Information Systems to pull together all the information you can get on the various finite scheduling software packages? This doesn't sound like something that we can modify our current software to do, but maybe there is a 'plug-and-play' package that is compatible with what we have."

The next week, Brian and Joan went to Supreme Enterprises. Joe Crowe met them in the lobby. "Welcome to Super Soap," he chortled. "I believe you know Tom already," he said, as the Master Scheduler joined them and they all shook hands.

As they made their way out to the factory, Joe told them, "We are a high-volume, make-to-stock company. Most of our processes involve very expensive capital equipment. We work three shifts, seven days a week. Our business is so competitive that we can't afford to let any of our high-capital equipment not to be utilized. In addition we can't send any work outside because no one has the capability."

Brian smiled. "Sounds just like our Heat Treat situation—except for the make-to-stock part."

Joe added, "We are very excited about what we have accomplished with finite scheduling. Before we put this system in, it would take us days, depending on the amount of change, to develop the Master Schedule, what with all the trial fits and gyrations we had to go through. Now it can be done in less than an hour. Our software takes the requested Master Schedule and schedules it around our constraining resources, which are the aerosol packaging line and one of our chemical processing tanks.

"On the aerosol line, the changeover time between different products is quite long because of the cleanup required. The changeover of can sizes can also be quite lengthy as well. We need to schedule all the runs of a particular product and can size back-to-back, regardless of the label or final package size, which we call campaigning. The FCS system knows all the sequencing and changeover rules, so it schedules the best way to do it based on the parameters set in the software. Of course, this means that we have to schedule the bulk product production to coincide with the aerosol line schedule, and we have to coordinate the labeling station and the boxer and palletizer with the line schedule. Then, of course, wouldn't you know, we run smack into the capacity limits of that one chemical processing tank.

"We're no different than any other manufacturing company. We could put together the best schedule in the world, and it probably wouldn't last five minutes. Things are constantly changing around here. Line breakdowns, process problems, and things like that. So one of the big benefits we get from our software is the speed with which it reschedules the factory. We are able to feed a whole host of variables into the scheduling system and then select the schedule we like best. And we also . . .

"Oh, man," Joe sighed, "there I go again. I just get so charged up I can't shut up. Tell me a little about your operation."

"Well," Brian said, "as you know, we make tractors for both the agricultural industry and homeowners. I'm not sure how that relates to soap and cleansers, but I've learned not to be too narrow-minded about things like that.

"First of all, we're able to flex the capacity of just about all of our work centers," Brian continued. "Until recently, a constrained-capacity resource has not been our problem. Our capacity planning system loads the work into daily buckets just like your FCS system does. And we use the backward-scheduling logic that is common to most of the software packages, finite or infinite. However, we don't try to have the software do anything more than back-schedule from the order due date from Material Requirements Planning. Our scheduling software doesn't consider all the variations and permutations possible on the shop floor—just simple, straightforward, backward scheduling. We believe that the shop supervisors can—and should—sort out which job should be run next. This has worked well for us in most cases. What we use is pretty simple logic, but it makes some assumptions that are not always true, like fixed queue sizes and setup times and, of course, infinite capacity. My take on it is that our infinite capacity scheduling approach is fundamentally about the same as your finite scheduling approach. The difference is in how we handle an overload condition."

"I'm not so sure that it is all that simple, Brian," Joe piped in. "Let's take for example the assumption you mentioned about queue time. The logic of your system assumes that the queue level for a specific work center would always be relatively the same. But in reality, the queue varies day by day, based on the amount and type of work moving to and through the work center on that day. Finite capacity scheduling systems consider the actual jobs scheduled through the work center and calculate the amount of queue that will be in front of the work center when a specific job arrives. Therefore, a job scheduled via finite capacity scheduling may be scheduled to start sooner or later than it would if scheduled with a fixed queue, depending on whether the actual queue was less than or greater than the fixed queue data. In either case, finite scheduling would more accurately simulate what would be expected to happen on the factory floor.

"The second assumption that you mentioned—that the setup time will always be the same for a particular part number—is similarly flawed. There are numerous reasons why the setup time will vary, the most predominant of which is that the prior job running has a similar setup. If that is the case, then the amount of time allocated for setup could be significantly different. Finite capacity scheduling systems can recognize this situation and adjust the schedules accordingly. To predict the setup time more accurately, FCS systems can use multiple setup times for an individual item, depending on the sequence of the items in the schedule. We created an options table showing the different setup times for every item that could precede this specific item—that means if we run 10 different products through the work center there would be 10 setup times, 1 for each item. But the system then looks at the sequence and can adjust the times, and so more accurately predict the expected setup times. If we're on schedule or slightly ahead, the FCS can suggest the most effective sequence to run. The FCS system takes data from the database—typically group or sequence codes—to identify those parts that have similar setups and also to note the degree of similarity. They can then schedule them to run in a sequence that minimizes changeovers. This is the feature that we use to schedule the aerosol line."

Joan was concerned about the apparent complexity of FCS and the detail required to generate realistic schedules. "Finite capacity scheduling requires a tremendous amount of information. For instance, we have some machines that can run over 100 different products across them. That would mean 100 different setup times. It's not just in the routings, but in the scheduling rules as well. Isn't it difficult to create and maintain this much detail and precision and keep it accurate?" she asked.

Joe had a ready response. "When you have capacity flexibility, and can absorb schedule variations in your move and queue times, you don't have to be as concerned about very precise queues, moves, and setup and run times. However, when you don't have the luxury of flexible capacity, you are forced to be more precise in your data. Sure, it's more difficult, but it's the price you have to pay to get better schedules. Besides, you should be trying to control those queue and move times and reduce them anyway if you are going to be competitive in a global market. The pressure for more accurate scheduling is becoming greater all the time."

Joan followed up on her point. "Finite scheduling is more precise in its scheduling logic than is infinite-capacity scheduling, and therefore the schedules and capacity requirements are more precise also. However, because the finite scheduling process is much more complex, and the computer has to crunch a lot more data, aren't the computer run times much longer, and doesn't it require a significant increase in computer power?"

"I am aware that some companies had reported long run times with older FCS systems, but that has not been a problem for us, and we're running on the same computer we had nine years ago," Joe answered. "Now, I understand that we don't have a large number of end items, and even fewer components and subassemblies to schedule, so we probably have it a little easier than you might. Of course, you have to have the processing capability. If you can't complete the scheduling runs in time for the factory to use the information, you would just be wasting time and money. We are able to process our rescheduling in much less than an hour, even with a major upheaval in the schedule. In many cases, it takes just a few minutes."

Joan walked over to watch a molding machine that was spewing out plastic caps. She turned back to Joe. "I understand that there are occasions when the computer isn't able to come up with a schedule that is practical, or at least preferable. Once the finite scheduling system has produced a plan or schedule predicting undesirable results, such as rescheduling an order out, isn't it difficult for planners to determine what changes must be made to improve the plan, because they don't understand how the computer came up with its plan?"

"Let me add to that thought," said Brian. "We've got some folks who aren't all that comfortable with computers. They'd rather do without them. I'm concerned with the rescheduling aspect of FCS. I don't want to have the computer rescheduling operations and orders without some involvement of our people. It takes the decision making totally out of the hands of the supervisors. How do you hold people accountable for the schedules? Don't they just blame things on the computer?"

Joe looked first at Brian and then at Joan, trying to figure out which question to answer first. After a moment's thought, he said, "Both of your questions deal with related issues: understanding and accountability. The interesting thing is that you can't have one without the other. People will accept accountability if they have the understanding. And they will go out of the way to build an understanding if they know they will be held accountable. We put a great deal of stock in giving our people the best opportunity we can to get them to understand the scheduling system. That's why Tom here was at the course with you. We want him to have a solid understanding of the basics before we immerse him in the details of our system.

"On a similar note," Joe went on, "it becomes obvious when someone doesn't have a good handle on the process. Perhaps they need additional training, or maybe they aren't cut out for that particular job. It is management's responsibility to step up to these issues and correct them."

Joan had another question. "How do you cope with the fact that the schedule changes by the software may alter the completion date of the order, which in turn may impact on the Master Schedule due dates?"

"We have not found those changes to be very big—maybe a few days at most," responded Joe. "Since we are a make-to-stock company, we can absorb those fluctuations in inventory. We may dip below the safety stock level from time to time, but isn't that what safety stock is for—to protect against problems with schedule execution?"

Brian introduced a new thought. "We need to have visibility of the real future capacity requirements so that we can do something about future increases in business. I wouldn't object to finite scheduling the short term as long as we are able to see the actual future capacity required in order for a work center to support the needs of the Master Schedule."

"That can be done," replied Joe. "Our FCS software provides the option of infinite loading to display that information so that you can see the actual capacity required to support the schedule as it is presented. You can then specify the horizon over which you want to finite schedule within the constrained capacity. But this is mostly unnecessary, and this can cause very long computer run times. We think it more effective to use Resource Requirements Planning and Rough-Cut Capacity Planning (see Chapter 7) to predict our mid- and long-range capacity requirements. These processes do not consider the day-by-day capacity constraints."

Joe shifted topics. "You know, there are a few special situations that we have to deal with that you should be aware of. I don't know if they are issues for you, but let's talk about them. Some of our operations experience significant losses during processing. To schedule the operation times properly, our FCS system uses yield data on each operation instead of only at the part-number level. As each operation is scheduled, the quantity of parts is reduced by the yield shown for that operation and the run time calculated based on that lower quantity."

"We have that situation in our shop, too," Brian said. "Our software doesn't handle it too well now, but our Information Systems Department told me that the latest upgrade modules have this feature if we need it."

Joe continued, "Another consideration is that in order to do finite scheduling effectively, each resource needs to have its own scheduling calendar. In addition to including allowances for holidays and weekends, scheduling calendars for finite capacity scheduling need to provide for shift differences, planned down-time, or other factors that affect the availability of the resource."

Joan jumped in with another question. "What about raw materials and component parts needed for the manufacturing process?

They are potential constraints to the process. Do you consider material availability in your scheduling algorithms?"

"We tried to do that, but we decided that it was too complex for the benefit obtained. Besides, our Material Requirements Planning system provides a capability for checking material availability before an order is released, and the planner has the option of releasing the order or not. We think it is better to have that decision made by the planners rather than add that level of complexity to the scheduling system. This should be an issue only with jobs that get released inside the normal material or component lead time. If the material planners have valid material plans in Material Requirements Planning, and procurement is holding the supplier accountable for on-time delivery for that valid plan, then it is reasonable to assume that the material will be available for jobs that are planned outside the lead time. You remember the 'silence is approval' principle the Effective Management people are so insistent on?"

Both Joan and Brian nodded as Joe continued. "Well to make sure the suppliers don't forget, we use the internet for the supplier to communicate when they ship. If the 'ship date' in Material Requirements Planning isn't met, the Material Requirements Planning system sends the planner a message that it was missed. The planner then follows up to see why they weren't told before the ship date was missed. Talk about a behavior change! Little things like this are allowing us to get closer and closer to the 99.5% on-time delivery the Effective Management people are always talking about.

"One final caution," said Joe, as they headed for the cafeteria to get coffee. "Unplanned activities wreak havoc in a finite scheduling environment. We don't usually have any problems in that regard as far as product schedules go. All of our production is planned through the Master Schedule and then fitted into the factory schedule via FCS. What we have learned, though, is that you have to be very careful to manage any Marketing or Sales promotions formally. They sure can cause havoc when they come out of the blue!"

"We don't have promotions, we just have a few knee-jerk managers who want to make the decision fast, and skip the 'consideration of fall-out' bit! But I can see what you mean," Brian said.

Joe continued, "Nobody can get a job into the factory without going through the Master Scheduler. However, we learned the hard way that preventative maintenance and equipment overhaul should be scheduled rather than be treated as an unplanned activity. It needs to be a part of the planning and scheduling system."

Brian was elated to report that this was one situation that Hayes had under control. "We've got that covered. We create routings for maintenance work and put work orders into Material Requirements Planning. Our scheduling system then schedules it appropriately and puts it on the Dispatch List like any other job."

"That's just what we had to do," replied Joe. "Beyond that, you still have to be prepared to deal with unplanned events. Any scheduling system is built on the premise that all of the scheduled events will happen as planned. Unfortunately, unforeseen events do occur. Although you try to keep them to a minimum, they will occur. That's where the dynamic update feature of finite scheduling is a plus. Our software lets us update the FCS model in a dynamic and timely fashion."

During the rest of the tour, Brian and Joan had the opportunity to talk to some of the production supervisors and planners. They spent some time at Tom's desk going over his master scheduling process. He pulled up the schedule for the aerosol line. It was very similar to the sample from the course. It was in color so that it was easy to differentiate the different jobs. It had the projected inventory displayed on the bottom of the screen so that he could see the effect of the schedule changes. Tom showed them how he could "drag-and-drop" jobs around on the screen to adjust the inventory if it was necessary to do so.

The work-center schedules were also available on-line. Joe pointed out that they could get hard-copy printouts, but if the schedules changed during the shift, they would need to print out new ones, so they only printed them by exception for meetings or other times they felt they would be beneficial. The supervisors all had terminals at their desks, and there were several others throughout the shop.

Brian was impressed with how well everyone understood and liked the scheduling system. Several people said that even though they didn't totally understand the details of all of the manipulations the computer went through to produce the schedule, they all knew what the scheduling rules were that were used by the software. They had either participated in establishing the rules or were given subsequent training on the rules. They were very confident that the schedules generated by the computer were valid schedules, and they readily accepted the accountability for their execution.

As they were headed for the lobby to leave, Joe added one final thought. "The biggest hurdle with FCS is preventing people from thinking that it is a magic cure-all. Management shouldn't perceive finite scheduling as a solution to bad data or bad disciplines. You still have to have valid plans driving the FCS system and long-range capacity planning to know when you should expand facilities or buy more equipment."

Joan and Roy thanked Joe for his help and headed for their car.

The day after the visit to Supreme Enterprises, Ralph scheduled a meeting with Brian, Joan, Roy, Dan, and Mickey. "Well," he drawled, "tell us about the trip."

Joan summarized what they had learned from their visit. "Those folks at Supreme really have their act together. They seem to have made finite scheduling work quite well for them in their environment. But, before we jump to any conclusions about changing our scheduling system, we've got a lot more work to do."

"Well, let's review what we are doing now in comparison to the finite capacity scheduling approach," Ralph began. He had clearly done his homework before the meeting and summarized the situation for the group.

"We've learned that the purpose of capacity management is to identify and solve capacity issues before they become problems. We use the infinite loading technique as part of our Detail Capacity Planning process to identify potential capacity constraints and resolve them before they hurt us. And I must say we've been doing a pretty good job at it." Brian smiled to himself as Ralph continued. "If we need more capacity than is expected to be available, we've only got two choices: Either we get more capacity or we reduce the requirements. And you all know how reluctant we are to say no to a customer. Where we have the flexibility to increase capacity, it seems to me that our infinite-loading-based approach is perfectly fine. On the other hand, in situations where we cannot increase the capacity or we want to use the capacity better, it seems that the finite capacity scheduling approach would be helpful. According to what I've been reading, other companies are utilizing their equipment better, reducing lead time, and improving their costs."

Picking up on Ralph's lead, Roy, the Material Manager, jumped right in. "Detailed Capacity Planning has been very effective in most of our work centers. We've scheduled overtime, changed the shift schedule, and added people based on what we saw in our detail capacity reports. We've been watching the situation in Heat Treat closely and sending the overload to an outside shop. But their quality and delivery has been unreliable, and it has put us in a bind. We're likely to face more of these situations as our business grows and we don't have the luxury of extra capacity. Things are going to get more competitive in the marketplace, and we have to continue to drive our costs down. This finite scheduling technique sounds like just the ticket."

Ralph sat up a little straighter in his chair. "Now let's not get ahead of ourselves. This could be a pretty big undertaking, what with all the education and training we would have to do. And I'm not sure we have to do finite scheduling across the whole shop. Can we do it on just a few work centers like Heat Treat?"

Roy looked at Brian and Joan before speaking. "I think we will need a little coaching. I'll give Roxanne Barnes from Effective Management a call and see if we can't get Amy, our course instructor, to help us. Roxanne has always steered us in the right direction before and, if Amy is the right person, I'm sure she will make sure we are able to use her. From the information that I've gathered so far, there is a wide range of software features and functionality available on the market. We'll have to be very careful how we approach this and the Effective Management people are really unbiased."

"It sounds like this could take a while," declared Dan. "What about my problem in Heat Treat? I need to do something right away. I can't get blood from a stone."

"Yeah, and how about me in assembly?" Mickey asked. "I don't want someone jamming some crazy system down my throat."

"Let's take one a time," Ralph cut in. "I'm not really worried about you right now, Mickey. It's Dan that I'm most worried about."

"Anybody got any ideas about Heat Treat?"

"I got a couple," Brian said after a moment of silence. "First off, we could increase the queue time in front of Heat Treat. That would get the jobs moved to Heat Treat earlier to assure Heat Treat never runs out of work and also give Dan's people time to sequence them properly. Of course, that would extend the lead time through the factory. We'd rather not do that, but we have to do something short-term to alleviate the capacity problem in Heat Treat.

"The second thing I thought about is based on something we learned at the course and we saw in action at Supreme Enterprises that just might help us out here. Finite capacity scheduling systems use a code to identify those parts that have similar setups. The software then uses a 'same setup rule' to schedule those jobs sequentially. I think we can use that notion in our scheduling of Heat Treat by using a code to identify heat-treat requirements. We can put a code on the routing for each part that has to be heat treated so that we can identify those that require the same combination of temperature and atmosphere. We can then modify our Dispatch List to print that code. We could then extend the visibility of the Dispatch List to the amount of queue days. Then Dan, your supervisor can look ahead at what's scheduled for Heat Treat and schedule all of those with the same code back-to-back. Again, in the short-term, you could also have the capacity planners look into the future to try and pull work up to run similar jobs. By just increasing the queue there is no manual effort other than sequencing them in the proper order. If the capacity planners start pulling work forward, it will be quite a bit of work. Remember, if you start rescheduling work, you will have to maintain close communications with Joan's planners and the shop schedulers so that the jobs you pick to run early can be rescheduled as necessary."

"Interestingly enough," quipped Dan, "we were trying to run jobs with the same heat-treat requirements before we got behind schedule. We didn't increase the queue and didn't have the code on the Dispatch List, so we had to spend time figuring out which jobs to run together. It sure would be a lot easier with that code on the Dispatch List. Let's start with increasing the queue first and then, if needed, we can work on manually scheduling further in the future."

Joan nodded in agreement. "Of course, this may be only a temporary thing until we figure out what we're going to do about new FCS software. We have a couple of fields on the routings we don't use. I'll talk to Laura Sanderford in Information Systems about switching one of the unallocated fields back on to use for sequencing codes, and make sure the code is printed for each job on the Dispatch List to help the supervisor. I can get on it first thing Monday morning."

"Okay, let's see how that works. Let's schedule a meeting in two weeks to see how your idea in heat treat works out. In the meantime let's all think a little more about Mickey's assembly area," Ralph said summing up the meeting.

Two weeks later they all got together again.

"So far I've heard some pretty good things about Heat Treat," Ralph kicked the meeting off.

"Yeah," Dan picked up on the lead in. "We're getting caught up slowly but surely, and it looks like we will have a little excess capacity in the future. We just have to hope that nothing too drastic happens."

"How much extra work has it been?" inquired Roy.

"We haven't had to try and pull up work with the capacity planners yet. We will probably have to do it at some point in time if we have equipment problems or get a bad mix along the way," Dan answered.

"That only leaves finance complaining about the extra five days of queue you put in front of the furnace," Ralph added.

"With the finite scheduling system we could reduce that at least a couple of days," Joan put in. "Seems worth while to investigate."

"Let's discuss Mickey's application," Ralph moved on.

"Joan and I have been talking about that," Brian said.

"I'm in trouble now," Mickey moaned.

"Mickey's right, if he doesn't need a detailed planning and scheduling system, we shouldn't force it on him," Brian continued.

"A lesson we have been learning is that if the user doesn't want something, don't jam it down his or her throat because it just won't work," Joan followed. "However we have a couple of ideas that might interest Mickey."

"Okay, I'm all ears," Mickey said.

Joan continued, "Mickey, for the large tractor you could use a Line Rate Schedule right from the Master Schedule. We would download it onto a simple PC-based spreadsheet, pulling the routing data from the pseudo bill of material/routing steps. We need to keep the Master Schedule valid, and since the Effective Management folks got us focused on Class A, we have rigorously done that. Should be easy."

"Okay, what about the small tractor line?' Mickey tentatively asked.

"For right now we would use the same technique, but we would want to investigate using a finite schedule, especially if the line rates continue to go up and the variations continue to expand," Joan answered. "It is our understanding that some companies are really doing some really great stuff with them. However we would want you to visit a facility that is using it successfully before we try to implement it here."

"Sounds good to me," Mickey said enthusiastically. I really like the simplicity of a line spread sheet, and going and visiting other companies sounds exciting. It's high time I started learning a little more about what's going on in the outside world instead of you guys getting all the glory."

There was just a stunned silence after that little outburst, but Ralph got them back on track.

"Okay! Here's what I want you to do," said Ralph as he stepped to the white board on the wall and picked up a marker. He wrote:

1. Queues and dispatch codes

"First, as a stop gap measure until we figure out if and how to take advantage of finite scheduling, we continue with what we are now doing in Heat Treat."

Then he wrote:

2. Assembly Capacity Planning

"We help Mickey with the spread sheets to help with line scheduling Assembly."

3. FCS Software

"Joan, finish up your investigation of the software. Find out if finite scheduling can be used on some of our operations while continuing to do what we do now with the rest. Then, based on what you find out about that, come up with a short list of software packages that seem to be best suited for our environment and we'll look further into each of them. Get some preliminary cost estimates. Joan, then you can work with Brian, Mickey, and Dan to put together a proposal for education and training." He wrote the fourth item on the board:

4. Education and training

He then followed it with a fifth:

5. Proposal

"Then the three of you put together a cost proposal for putting it all in place. Give Roy and me a proposal for each of two approaches: (1) a plant-wide implementation of finite scheduling and (2) finite scheduling limited to a few selected work centers, if that turns out to be feasible. If this is something we decide we want to do, we'll put it in the budget for next year. Let's simply call this initiative Finite Capacity Scheduling. Build your plan on these four items. I will get Finite Capacity Scheduling listed as a project for the Managing Products and Services process and send it through the 'stage and gate' process until we reach a decision."

It was late as they left the meeting. Brian and Joan chatted about how it had gone. They were impressed with the way Ralph had handled it. He was beginning to show a noticeable change in his behavior. In the past, he would have probably made a snap judgment and either told them to go ahead immediately with finite scheduling, or even more likely rejected the whole idea—since he had never been much of a computer fan—and told Dan to just "do the best you can." They knew that they needed to learn a lot more than they knew at that moment, and Ralph had shown a willingness to take the time necessary to do so.

It appeared for once that they were going to make an intelligent decision based on facts and information, rather than on emotion. "Maybe all this effort is beginning to pay off in more ways than just our planning and control systems. I'm beginning to see some real changes around here," Brian said to Joan as he headed out the door for the weekend.

Chapter Ten

Eliminating Waste and Variability

Pete Smith, the General Manager of Hayes Tractor, had been re-ceiving pressure from the corporate Business Improvement Group to work on business improvement initiatives. The chairman of the board had heard a lot from other companies about continuous im-provement and was using the Business Improvement Group to push the various divisions for implementation plans. As you might expect, the stuff always rolls down hill and Brian, Dan, Mickey, and Joan got the brunt of it. The Quality Control manager, Carol Barrow, was also added to the team, ostensibly to ensure quality was not compromised in any changes. But the hidden agenda was to make sure Carol would be part of the "build quality in" approach that would, later, significantly impact the role of QC. They assembled as a team and tried brainstorming to get ideas. The usual candidates appeared: Kanban, Lean, Agile, Six Sigma, Demand Pull, and so on. But what next? It could not be like choosing any cookie; there must be some sort of logic, surely.

"There must be some sort of logic to where we go next," Brian offered.

"From my point of view I like the idea of Lean," said Dan.

"Yeah, with your body I can see why!" chimed in Mickey.

"Okay guys, let's get serious here. What's next for us?" Brian said. "Is it Kanban, like some of the Business Improvement gurus are pushing?"

Uncharacteristically, Dan suggested they talk to Roxanne Barnes, their Effective Management coach, about their dilemma. Roxanne was delighted with the call and said she would ask her colleague Les Johnson to visit them. What they did not know was that Les was really hot about companies taking Class A improvement much further than Capable Planning and Control.

The day Les arrived they were all in the management conference room, coffee and doughnuts on the side.

"How's that for Lean!" joked Joan.

"Hey! Leave the chocolate one for me," said Brian. "I need it."

As Brian was speaking, Les walked in the door—looking tall and stern-faced. "Okay," Brian thought, "now to business."

"That chocolate doughnut's for me," said Les, grabbing a coffee and Brian's doughnut before Brian could get his hands on it.

"Oh! Oh!" thought Joan, "Now the fun's going to start." Brian looked at where his doughnut had been, and smiled. "A man after my own heart," he said. With that they all settled down to business.

"Let's get straight into this." said Les. "We've got a lot to cover." With that they all looked expectantly at him, and Les started to speak.

"The supply chain is where manufacturing companies make their money. It should be the cash generator. And so Supply Chain Management needs to be considered the highest strategic priority. And the Supply Chain needs to be kept under control!

"The supply chain might be likened to a pipe where money comes out the other end. Yet most supply chains are so leaky they need serious plumbing work. Just see how much inventory business writes off each year. It runs into billions of dollars, and that's after the creative footwork (and costs) to avoid writing it off.

"Today we have Enterprise Resource Planning (ERP) systems, Manufacturing Execution Systems (MES), and Advanced Planning Systems (APS), as well as Configurators, Optimizers, Simulators, and so on. They appear not to have helped. Yet these systems can provide all the tools we need to support us being smarter and to control inventory and customer service within bounds. So that's not the issue. Okay, guys, what do you think the problem is?"

"Hold on a second," Joan said. "We have gotten some great results with our Enterprise Resource Planning system."

"I'm sure you have," Les shot back. "But are you getting all you can get?"

Joan paused. "No, I don't think we really are."

"Okay, then, what's the problem?" asked Les.

"Maybe we need more Kanbans?" Mickey suggested.

"How about an optimizer?" Joan added.

The room fell silent after Les shook his heard after each suggestion and had a very sad look on his face. "Those are possible solutions, but if you don't know what the problem is, then you will start using the solution like a hammer looking for a nail. No other ideas?" Les challenged.

"Well, I've heard of a company that implemented Kanban and reduced their work in progress," offered Dan.

"We're getting closer," said Les.

"I don't think we've focused enough on the supply chain," said Joan. "Sure we've got our Capable Planning and Control Milestone Award, and we were told then that it's like a ticket for a journey. My guess is we've got to focus on making the supply chain less leaky. That's our journey."

"What's another word for 'leaky' when we talk about supply chain?" asked Les.

After a pause Brian said, "I'd say it's waste. That's what leaks from our supply chain."

"You're getting there, but what's behind all this waste? What's stopping you from being the best?" asked Les.

"We need better machines." said Mickey.

"Better suppliers." said Joan.

"Better specs." said Dan, who'd recently had a run in with Carol Barrow, the QC manager.

Les looked them straight in the eye. "Don't you see what the problem is?" He said. Everyone looked puzzled. Les continued, "It's right in front of you, with you everyday, but you haven't recognized it yet. The universal enemy to cost and effectiveness is time—the 'time in your system,' to paraphrase Deming. So let's pause to see where we are at, and where we need to go."

Brian looked puzzled. "Where is he going? Our planning and scheduling is helping us to go as fast as we can, but we live in the real world," Brian thought. "What about waste, then?" Brian asked out loud.

"Okay, but waste is an effect, not a cause," Les replied. "Have you thought about what happens when you have waste? And I'm talking about Deming's view of waste: Anything that is not absolutely necessary that is applied to the product, and that a customer would be willing to pay for."

"I guess he'll want inspection, then." said Mickey. "That way he's sure to get good product."

"Hold on," said Les. "Just think about what you said. Why do you need to inspect?"

"Well," said Dan, "sometimes things don't go quite the way we'd expect, and we need to check to be sure that we don't let bad product get out."

"But you do let bad product out!" challenged Les. This got everyone a bit angry.

"The hell we do!" said Dan.

"Okay, let's see what you make of this," said Les, and he drew a diagram on the interactive panel (see Figure 10.1).

Figure 10.1   Expected Output Quality vs. Specification

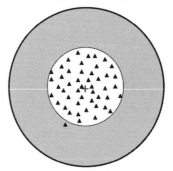

Last 50 Releases: 49 of 50 within Control Tolerances = 98%

"The '+' in the center represents ideal product according to the spec. The outer circle represents the specification tolerance. The dots are incidences of where the product fell within the specification. The inner circle represents the product with the upper and lower control limits. The outer circle represents product within specification. There shouldn't be very many of these because if we are using the control limits properly we should be readjusting to come back to the inner circle. And pieces outside the circles are out of tolerance, which should be reworked or scrapped. Well, that's the theory. Is this the way your charts look?"

"You got to be kidding me," Carol interjected as she jumped up, grabbed the pen from Les, and drew another chart (see Figure 10.2).

Figure 10.2   Actual Output Quality vs. Specification

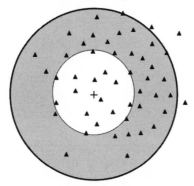

Last 50 Releases: 47 of 50 in tolerance = 94%

"This is what most of our parts looks like when we plot them! The concept of upper and lower control limits is foreign to this place. In practice we use everything in tolerance and the parts that are out of tolerance Dan and Brian bring to me to get Engineering to do a Temporary Deviation on. If Engineering doesn't accept it, Brian throws them away but Dan sits on them until Mickey is out and raising hell. Then the engineers are pressured to use them."

"I'll be damned," Brian thought, "another trick from Dan that I have missed."

"Now what do you think about the quality?" asked Les.

"As I told you, our quality's good," said Dan confidently, looking at the others—but he was not so sure after that run in with Carol. "Hey, we're here to make money, not to get all excited when it's just a little out."

"I rest my case." said Les. "You release product that doesn't meet Engineering specification and then put pressure on them to accept it. Worse still, because you don't understand waste, everyone thinks 'a little bit out' is okay. But it's not okay!" Les glared at them. "Ever do any rework?"

"Sure, doesn't everyone?" Dan said. Brian looked thoughtful, and Joan smiled at Dan's obvious discomfort.

"You only do rework if you choose to," replied Les.

"I don't choose to do it!" exploded Dan. "It just happens."

"As long as you guys think like that, you've missed it." Les said. "Come on, what's the ideal waste level?"

They all looked at Joan—she was bound to know the numbers. "Sure, some of our processes are 5 to 8%, and our best is on the machining center—it's only 1.2%." said Joan.

"It's that thinking that's holding you back," said Les.

"How come?" they mumbled together.

"You've got to think zeroes," said Les. "The ideal waste is zero."

"Get real," said Mickey. "Any process has got waste."

Les responded gently, "Okay, let's look at that. 'Any process has waste.' You've just admitted that waste is okay. And it's not! It wastes time inspecting, reworking, scrapping, dealing with customer complaints, and it uses your valuable materials and resources.

"Roxanne mentioned to me that you have a constraint in Heat Treat," Les continued, looking at Dan.

"Yes," said Dan. "It's operating at near maximum capacity. However, we just implemented some improvements in the way we schedule the product through the heat-treat process, so we're not falling behind any more."

"Bet you increased the queue to accomplish that," Les shot back.

"Yeah, but we got results."

"Maybe we should look at the waste in the process to gain improvements also," Les suggested.

Joan suddenly spoke out, "I get it. That process has 3.4% waste, and it uses about 5% of its time on rework. If waste were zero and rework were zero, we'd probably have about 8% more capacity. That means we'd get about 8% more output. Hell, we could start losing sales if Lenny and his sales guys got an opportunity to make some short-term sales when we really have the capacity, only it's being lost on waste!"

"And capacity is also an aspect of time," said Les.

"As you should know, at Effective Management we recognize there are clear paths to business excellence. The paths are a series of steps to logical levels of performance we refer to as stages." (See Figure 10.3.)

"Your Capable Planning and Control Award is the third stage and has allowed Hayes to gain control of your planning processes.

Figure 10.3 Class A Planning & Control Journey

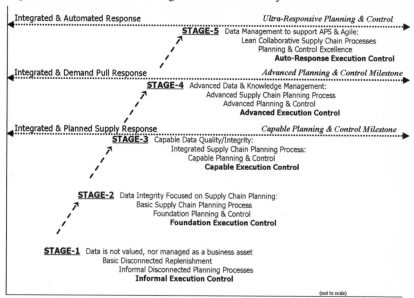

Integrated & Automated Response   *Ultra-Responsive Planning & Control*

STAGE-5 Data Management to support APS & Agile:
Lean Collaborative Supply Chain Processes
Planning & Control Excellence
Auto-Response Execution Control

Integrated & Demand Pull Response   *Advanced Planning & Control Milestone*

STAGE-4 Advanced Data & Knowledge Management:
Advanced Supply Chain Planning Process
Advanced Planning & Control
Advanced Execution Control

Integrated & Planned Supply Response   *Capable Planning & Control Milestone*

STAGE-3 Capable Data Quality/Integrity:
Integrated Supply Chain Planning Process:
Capable Planning & Control
Capable Execution Control

STAGE-2 Data Integrity Focused on Supply Chain Planning:
Basic Supply Chain Planning Process
Foundation Planning & Control
Foundation Execution Control

STAGE-1 Data is not valued, nor managed as a business asset
Basic Disconnected Replenishment
Informal Disconnected Planning Processes
Informal Execution Control

(not to scale)

It would seem that your next logical step would be Stage 4—Advanced Supply Planning and Control. Are you all familiar with Stage 4?"

"Sure, I remember Roxanne going through that," Joan replied.

"Maybe we should remind ourselves of what's in Stage 4. Is everyone in agreement?" Les asked.

All nodded their heads.

Les opened his computer, hooked it up to a projector, and put up the definition of Stage 4. (See Figure 10.4.)

After a good discussion on Stage 4 Les said, "Now we need to decide what today's priorities are, and then we can spend some time creating a path that will help you deliver against those priorities.

"Let's back up a little and start with the basics. The ability of a company to take these paths is governed by the synergies or conflicts between People, Process, and Tools. We've said that the Tools are there. So the problems lie in the Processes and in People issues.

"So how does time fit in? Time is invisible, and so we may be unaware of the insidious nature of time, because inventory hides its threats. As Robert Hall said, 'Inventory is Time's shadow.' Let's consider the Supply Chain—our moneymaker.

Figure 10.4   Definition of Stage 4

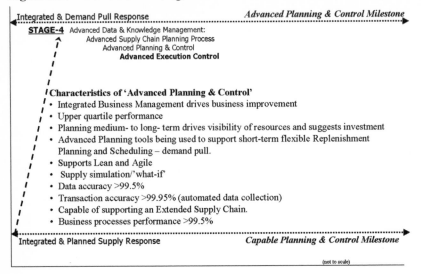

"First a few definitions:

Planning is about the future. It lays out what we expect to happen, and commits the Supply Chain to provide the resources (people, equipment, and facilities) to support the plan. Most Planning in this sense is done automatically by the Enterprise Resource Planning system, using your rules based on inventory records and master data, such as item, routing, work center, and bill of materials masters.

Scheduling occurs when a Material Planner decides to commit the supply chain to a specific product and so takes control of a replenishment or manufacturing order. This will provide detailed consideration of availability and uses all resources to create a workable solution that meets the specific demand. This is a manual process triggered by reminders (action messages) from the Enterprise Resource Planning system.

Execution follows. This is where the shopfloor (internal or supplier's) sequentially works to the prescribed workflow by transforming input parts and components to the relevant manufactured item. This direction is typically provided by the Dispatch List.

On the journey so far you have established the capability to plan and control your internal Supply Chain, with 95% confidence that the planned event will happen, on time and in full. Where necessary you redesigned your processes to integrate them so that they worked together to minimize hand-offs along the supply chain. Remember all the changes you made to gain control of capacity planning, as just one example. You found that you needed the Enterprise Resource Planning system as the supporting tool. But you also learned that performance was based on the behavioral aspects of the people, from top to bottom of the organization."

Brian thought back to Dan and Mickey's journey from hostility and resistance to commitment.

Les continued. "The overriding need then was to gain integrated control so that what you planned to happen would happen—and that meant redesigning your processes and measures to align with supply chain and business performance. So now you've achieved 95%+ performance; you're ready to move on.

"We need to talk about the changes that will need to happen to Planning and Supply Chain Control as you continue your journey. Now that you've gained control you've got to stay in control.

"Because time is the enemy, you need to attack the things that take time in the supply chain. You don't want unscheduled stoppages, so you implement Total Productive Maintenance; then later Total Predictive Maintenance, so you just about eliminate unplanned stoppages.

"And you take out the inventory that buffered those stoppages. It's there somewhere, or you'd never achieve 95%+ service.

"You know that rework is time wasting, so you need to make your processes so capable that they produce near invariant, on spec product. That usually involves the methodology of Six Sigma." Carol glared at Dan, whose products had recently been noticeably more out of specification.

"Then you take out the inventory that buffered the rework time.

"Oh, and you've stopped referring to performance as percentage, and start to see performance in parts per million (ppm). Now I'm not talking about the more precise Six-Sigma definitions, but to simply make a few key points. That 95% we referred to you can mean 50,000 potential failures per million—hardly excellent, is it?"

Carol really paid attention here. It made her think. She was well aware that many companies were starting to use parts per million, but she could not get anyone at Hayes even to start thinking along those lines. Everyone, including the people in the Quality Control Department, still thought 95% was pretty good. She could see they'd all need to change their views on this and Les might just be the one to help.

Les continued, "Your most exciting journey is going to be tracking down waste in all its forms, because waste also equates to 'time in system,' and is also buffered by inventory. So you start to do Value-Stream-Mapping to track down those nonvalue-adding steps in the Supply Chain. You'll talk about doing 'Lean' as the banner for the many waste elimination initiatives. You'll begin to understand that inventory, far from being an 'asset,' is waste, that inventory levels (i.e. waste) are directly connected to lot-sizing and replenishment frequency. You see the need to make 'smaller more often' the challenge.

"And you'll take out the inventory that buffers today's wasteful steps.

"People will start talking about 'demand pull'—that's where customer demand is met by Production making product, rather than pulling it from stock, and ideally this principle extends upstream through the internal supply chain, giving everyone an experience of being customer centric. You'll recognize that you may have trained your customers (internal and external) to order large quantities, such as in full pallets, or full truckloads, or four-week's worth at a time, or whatever the item ordering policy is. What you'd really like to know is the rate at which your customer consumes product, and thus not be confounded by your imposed rules. You declare that you're going to be customer centric! This completes the challenge on the size/frequency decisions.

"And more inventory will be taken out.

"Now you'll be so close to the customers' real needs you'll recognize that you may have to be more flexible (ability to respond to short-term volume changes); and maybe more agile too (ability to respond to short-term customer choices).

"And you can make little further progress if you do not take into consideration the velocity (measure of time), flexibility, and agility of the extended Supply Chain. You'll need your suppliers to be part of (or partners in) this high effectiveness Supply Chain. And you'll need these steps between your company and the end consumer also to share your desire to serve the customer/consumer. All this will make big changes to Planning and Control.

"As companies progress through Stage 4 in the journey they must increase velocity (drive out 'time'), and that always shows in inventory reductions. As a consequence, as they go faster there is less inventory buffering the errors in Planning and Execution, potentially weakening the control processes, so these processes must become more effective, and faster.

"This has little impact on Enterprise Resource Planning (in our definition) other than to simplify it, but it does affect execution control (Scheduling, Kanban, Takt, and Flow). At some point companies find that the ultimate constraint to velocity is the speed at which Execution Control occurs. After all, if you are selling online, is it reasonable to expect the customer to wait until an Order Entry Scheduler comes in Monday morning to accept the order and a material planner to schedule it? Of course not! And so you'll start to see the need to automate the supply chain execution-control systems, even directly linked to customer order entry.

"The main enablers for automation are going to be building a model of the supply chain, the precision of the data that the system uses, and the speed at which the system can schedule across the internal and extended supply chain. If the data lack adequate precision, then automating the scheduling will produce exciting but disastrous results.

"At this point it probably makes sense to consider investing in a capable tool, such as an Advanced Planning and Scheduling system (APS)," Les observed.

"We're actually looking into that as we speak," Joan said. "In fact we're having Amy Shinn from your organization help us."

"Great choice and I'm really glad you're moving forward," Les responded. "However, let's just continue the thought process while we're at it. You would want to include memory-resident processing (for super high-speed calculations), multi-constraint-based scheduling capability (to calculate viable solutions), and simultaneous calculation of material and capacity/constraint needs. So a scheduled event (could be an order) is doable within the supply-chain model and its rules. You'd need to use Capability-to-Promise (CTP) to support the many supply points along the extended supply chain in order to ensure the supply chain can deliver what you promise. And the Manufacturing Execution System (MES) tool completes the feedback loop by tracking actual performance in synch with predicted performance, and to provide alerts where planner intervention is needed.

"To work together, the companies that constitute the extended supply chain would operate in negotiated and agreed collaborative supply planning arrangements."

Les looked around the room at the faces of this group of intelligent people. They were all deep in thought, taking all this in.

"Now comes the sting in the tail. If you cannot develop the required model and precision, beware! Automation of imprecise data will produce incapable schedules—and it all happens very fast, and invisibly. No one is going to check the Schedule—there's no time. It must be correct straight out of the system.

"One caveat, where the system faces a 'logical bind,' that is it cannot find a solution within the rules, experience suggests that, rather than trying to make the rules more comprehensive, you use a knowledgeable capacity planner. Capacity planners can find creative solutions much faster than you can create model changes.

"Using our simple view of performance, data accuracy at 95% (potentially 50,000 ppm inaccuracy!), and even at 98% (20,000 ppm inaccuracy), is not going to be good enough for automated execution control. At each step in the Supply Chain defined in your model, the Advanced Planning and Scheduling (APS) system will calculate time-phased events (orders, operations, shipments, etc.). The more extended the supply chain, the more times the Advanced Planning System is going to calculate, and it can be a massive amplifier of errors.

"So if the four steps in your internal supply chain operate at 95%, the effect could be 95% $\times$ 95% $\times$ 95% $\times$ 95% = 81%. Today you make up for this shortfall with inventory.

"But you've 'leaned' the supply chain. So let's try for 99.5% performance: $(99.5\%)^4$ gives 98%. That's barely acceptable if your customer is on Vendor Managed Inventory (VMI), or worse, has gone lean too.

"But for the extended Supply Chain to operate in an automated manner, with maybe 10 or more steps, this means 99.95% performance at each step (remember there are very few inventories buffering errors now), so that's $(99.95\%)^{10}$ = 99.4% for the extended supply chain."

Carol thought, "I understand now. I'll need to bring the Quality Control department up to speed on all this. We've never seen it this way," but she agreed with the thinking.

"Your current Class A milestone Planning and Control needs an operating minimum of 95%. You'll need to move up to the next step of 99.5% as the operating minimum."

There was total silence from all the participants as Les roared ahead.

"While we suggest that an Advanced Planning and Scheduling type system investment will be necessary to move to Stage 4, full exploitation of its capability in the extended supply chain needs to wait until you have developed the precision of master data and transactional data to at least 99.95%. And all of this potential can remain unrealized if your process capability isn't excellent also. Did you notice in your release performance chart (Figure 10.2) that your process average performance was not centered on the specification? That's also lack of process capability. That's why a Six-Sigma program is so important if process variability is an issue, which actually means it's the constraint to going faster.

"You'll have to learn to 'build quality in,' so the operator is aware of quality at every step of the production process. After all, it's too late when Quality Control puts a Quarantine Order on the latest batch!"

Carol spoke out, "Then what do we in Quality Control do?"

"How about Quality Assurance? You should consider taking on the role of assuring quality throughout processes, not forgetting your own test methods and test plans. We haven't got time to explain it all, but some general areas are how you intend to build quality into design, make quality visible, ensure mistake-proofing so common problems cannot occur, and ultimately challenge design and manufacturing against the dangers of complexity. Of course, Quality Assurance also means being the customer advocate to ensure only truly fit-for-use product is shipped to customers."

Carol nodded to Les. She'd need to follow up on this after the course. She had been telling Pete they shouldn't call her department Quality Control because they didn't control anything—the operators did. Maybe she could get Pete to change the name to Quality Assurance—that would at least be a start.

Les continued.

"The reward for the journey will be Inventory turns maybe exceeding 40X—let's call them 'spins' so we don't confuse them with slower companies; closer collaboration with customers, maybe leading to the elusive 'loyalty'; the ability to introduce new products much faster; outperforming your competition; massively reducing your operating capital and increasing cash-flow. Ultimately, it may be a question of survival."

"Wow!" said Joan. "That's a lot to take on board." The others looked dazed.

"Know how to eat an elephant?" asked Les.

"Yeah! One mouthful at a time!" said Brian.

"Here is what I suggest you do. I tried to focus this session on awareness. You really need to get a deeper understanding of the subject. I suggest that we do a course to get not just the five of you, but the whole organization up to speed. Once the education is done we can proceed more rapidly because everyone has heard the same message. As we go through the various techniques we can do workshops to talk about the applicability and decide what we want to work on. How do feel about that?"

"Makes perfect sense to me," spoke up Mickey immediately. "I think I'm really going to enjoy this. What about the rest of you?"

It was hard to figure out whether all the affirmative nods were because they were in agreement or just shocked.

Even though they all agreed, they knew that they had to get Ralph and Roy to buy in. Roy wouldn't be a problem, but then there was always Ralph. They scheduled a meeting with Continuous Improvement as the subject.

Ralph showed up to the meeting a little late. The team had planned on letting Mickey open the subject, but before Mickey could say a word Ralph started. "Listen up to what I've got to say. Even though things are better than they used to be, we need to get a lot better if we're going to remain competitive in this market. We've lost a lot of small-tractor business to overseas manufacturers. There is still plenty of room for improvement around here. I also want to be one step in front of the corporate group."

"Yeah, they have been complaining about what we're doing about waste, or rather not doing," Roy said.

"I'm glad you brought up the subject of waste," Ralph said. "I think there's a lot of waste around here. For one thing, we still have too much inventory around to suit me. We just seem to cover up our problems with inventory instead of solving them. We're going to have to change that. Now that we've gotten our shortages down and our on-time delivery performance up, we need to refocus our priorities. We're going to, that is, *you* are going to eliminate waste. How's that for a challenge?"

There was a gasp round the table. It was obvious that no one had told Ralph about Les Johnson's visit. Trying to cover their tracks, Mickey said, "Well, how do you expect us to do that?"

"That's not what I wanted to hear. You know me better than that. I've just read an article about Lean Manufacturing that talks about eliminating waste in a manufacturing company, end to end. It sounds like something we should look into. We need to learn more about it, see how it applies to us, and then see how we can do it. Looking back on the benefits we got from the Effective Management education, I think we ought to get them to educate us on the whole subject of Continuous Improvement. You just had someone from Effective Management in here to talk about Continuous Improvement, so why don't we see what they can do for a complete education program."

Mickey, who seemed to know how to handle Ralph the best, jumped at the opportunity. "Hey boss, I'll jump right on it. Do you have any idea how much you are willing to spend?" Mickey knew that Ralph was so tight that he sometimes squeaked when he walked.

"You know me, Mickey," Ralph responded. "I don't want to waste money and I know Effective Management isn't cheap, but I do know the value that they have always given and they don't try to sell what's not needed. All of you use good common sense on what you agree to but let's get this under way as quickly as possible."

"That was a short meeting," Joan said to Brian as they left the conference room.

"Anytime a meeting is less than 10 minutes and it gives clear direction, it's a huge success as far as I'm concerned," Brian replied. "I'm not sure what's going on with Ralph and Mickey, but it sure is nice."

Les Johnson arrived a week later.

Les's opening statement got a thoughtful nod of approval, although they hadn't seen it this way before. "First, I need to say that the most effective Lean implementations cover Lean Supply Chain. That involves all the steps between the end-customer, and your first- or second-tier suppliers, but most companies will start with Lean Manufacturing. You're probably expecting me to say that our focus will be on eliminating waste, but actually Lean is about avoiding waste in all its forms. Obviously, when you avoid waste you reduce existing waste, but, more importantly, you open your eyes to hidden waste and potential causes of waste. In this course we will include discussions on eliminating waste in manufacturing and some of the techniques to assist in waste elimination."

Les continued, "As we try to increase the velocity of the flow of work, problems are revealed that impact on quality, delivery, or cost. These problems are typically caused by the presence of constraints that appear in the form of waste. In this context, waste is defined as any activity that does not add value to the products. It's the use of resources in excess of the theoretical minimum required, whether of people, equipment, time, space, or energy. Waste can be in the form of excess inventory, setup times, inspection, material movement, transactions, or rejects. Anything that can stop production—such as faulty material or missing material, tooling, or specifications— causes wasteful activities. Any activity that is not actively involved in a process that adds value is waste.

"Lean Manufacturing is a methodology that drives change in the company. It is built on the philosophy of continuous avoidance and elimination of waste, leading to continuous improvement. While our focus today will be on the production departments, the principles, concepts, and practices of Lean apply equally well to the order entry, engineering, accounting, and all other functions in the company. And, as you probably realize by now, Lean assumes you've got a handle on quality throughout, from design to disposal. Lean expects quality to be there, rather than inspection being used to filter out the bad stuff.

"To work effectively, Lean requires valid plans. I know that Hayes has an Enterprise Resource Planning system and Material Requirements Planning as a planning and scheduling methodology. Having reached your Planning and Control Milestone for Class A, you already know that Material Requirements Planning is a time-proven superior methodology for providing valid plans. But let me point out to you that improper or ineffective use of these planning tools can also contribute to waste."

Les pointed out that as you move to Lean Manufacturing, things are definitely going to change on the shop floor. Lean is characterized by small lot sizes, short setup times, and small, often zero, queues, all of which lead to short lead times.

"There have been statements made by others that Material Requirements Planning does not work well in this environment, but that is not true," he said. "It works perfectly fine with small lot sizes, short setup times, and small, often zero, queues, although it does increase planner workload unless different processes are implemented. The Lean process starts where you are today and works its way toward these characteristics a little at a time. So don't throw your Material Requirements Planning system away."

Brian suddenly felt a lot better. He glanced at Joan, sitting to his left, and saw her nodding in agreement. At least all the work they had done at Hayes wasn't going to go for naught.

Les continued with the course by explaining that Kanban is part of the waste-eliminating process, reducing "time in system." The basis for Kanban is the technique used to authorize the movement or the making of product. Kanban (rhymes with bon-bon) is used in place of a Dispatch List. Loosely translated from its Japanese origin, Kanban means visual signal. When the operator sees a Kanban, it signals to a work center to replenish the work in progress or inventory—raw material, parts, semifinished product, or assemblies—that have been withdrawn by a downstream work center or a customer. Kanban is a physical signal that replaces the need for work orders and Dispatch Lists between operations, and often the need for scheduling levels in the bill of material where parent and child are linked by a Kanban.

"Kanban is not just used in manufacturing!" Les continued. "In Nairobi, Kenya, there's a restaurant not far from the airport that runs the service to tables on Kanban. When you arrive you'll be shown to your table and the host will inquire about which language to use. Next, plates are placed on the table. The plates signal the next step, and soon arrives a tiered tray of chutneys, sauces, and other accompaniments. Atop of this is a little country flag that signals to the servers the language to use. The tiered tray also signals for a tray of vegetables, potatoes, and rice to be placed in the middle of the table. This in turn signals the meat servers, who were going from table to table, to call at your table. Each meat is on a Sword with an animal badge on the handle: pig, antelope, crocodile, and so on. You select the meat you want and the server carves meat off the sword, and moves on. Then the next server with a different meat arrives, and so on. When your table has eaten all you want you simply pull out the flag. This signals to clear the table and get the check. The Kanban was also working earlier in the process. At any time there was only one Kanban (sword) per meat in process at the tables, and one full sword awaiting its turn. The sword in use left an empty hook at the meat station. This signaled that the meat was in service. When the sword being used for service had no more meat on it, this sword went back to the central kitchen where its arrival indicated 'cook some more of this.' The refilled sword now goes back to its hook in the meat area. If the restaurant is very busy then extra swords (Kanbans) can be included for the more popular meats, thereby increasing the meat flow. Although I was distracted by studying the Kanban flow, the food was good too!"

"I'd like to practice some quality assurance there, then," said Carol. They all laughed.

Les continued explaining that Kanban signals what needs to be done. "The Kanban is the signal to replace what has been used, or what needs to be moved to line. If the Kanban authorization is present, you do the job. If it is not, you don't. The Kanbans themselves can come in many different forms including empty shelf spaces, squares taped on the floor, cards, electronic signals, and even swords. And like the sword, the Kanban also signals how much to move or make.

"Kanban differs from operation scheduling and finite scheduling in that it authorizes a work center to perform its operation only when the next downstream work center has used a predetermined amount of material. In the operation/finite-scheduling approaches, work is moved into a work center's queue, knowing that the downstream work centers will need it, because the product flow is all driven by the Master Schedule requirements. The Master Schedule anticipates customer demand and in make-to-order or assemble-to-order companies includes customer orders. While often referred to as 'push,' this is a misnomer. The issues are the speed of response and the synchronization of parts production to the final build stages. Scheduling and Input/Output/Queue Planning is a largely manual route to synchronization between upstream and downstream work centers, but this is only approximate, resulting in work-in-process stocks.

We've learned that this means time. Note that the typical Kanban is also work-in-process stock, but it is highly controlled and limited by an absolute ceiling. It controls input and output from work center to work center without the need for detailed Input/Output/ Queue Planning, other than at the process-line gateway. When applied properly, the Kanban approach can result in much lower WIP inventories and smoother production flow. It does mean, however, that when a downstream process stops and the queue is used up, the upstream processes must stop also.

"One fact about Kanban is often overlooked. Although it is a very powerful execution-control technique, it is not a planning technique. The Kanban technique can communicate to the shop floor what to make, when to make it, and how much to make—but only for the present time frame. Kanban cannot predict what materials or how much will be needed in future time periods, nor can it predict what future capacities will be required. A planning process is still necessary to predict material and capacity requirements. Short-term capacity planning needs to be more precise because the WIP buffers are much lower. Variation needs to be taken out of the processes; repeatability is one of the key enablers of Kanban. Planning of material and capacity happens in the Enterprise Resource Planning system. Consequently, many companies are learning how to use the Enterprise Resource Planning system to support mid- to long-term planning, and to let Kanban control execution in the very short term.

"Kanban, when used properly, has certain advantages over the operational-scheduling/dispatch-list approach. It is simple, provides visual indications of requirements, and controls material movements, and it readily exposes problems in production operations and quality. It creates a sense of urgency to resolve problems and encourages reduction in inventory and lead time, thereby increasing the velocity through the process steps. This last step is what is normally executed poorly in companies.

"Kanban execution control by itself can improve results, but the real benefits come from employment of a concept of continually striving to 'economically manufacture one less at a time.'[1] By reducing lot sizes, queues, safety stocks, and setup times one less at

1. "Purchasing in the 21st Century," by John E. Schar, John Wiley & Sons.

a time, problems are revealed that impede the acceleration of the work flow. This is a process of continuously identifying and removing constraints one by one—whether they be inventory, quality, production, or administrative procedures—and continually improving the manufacturing process. One of the essential ingredients of the process is the participation of the direct-labor work force. They have excellent ideas for improving their operations, the processes, and the product itself.

"One overriding aspect that companies should be aware of with Kanban is that it requires significant changes in the traditional shop-management philosophy. The success of Kanban is based on the principle of fixing problems as they occur, rather than working around them. This can result in line stoppages that are contrary to traditional management thinking. The long-term effects of such practice are problem elimination and productivity improvements. However, if management hasn't made the commitment to alter their thinking and habits, and to take an aggressive approach to fixing the problems, Kanbans aren't going to help. On one level, fixing the problems is one of its greatest advantages. However, some companies that have yet to get their planning systems and data under control may not be ready to make such changes."

Les went on to talk about the "zeroes culture." He explained the "zeroes culture" as a list of goals that include:

- zero defects (eliminate causes of defects)
- zero excess (make only what is necessary—one at a time)
- zero changeover time (eliminate causes of changeover time—"Single Minute Exchange of Die")
- zero breakdowns (don't let processes fail—Total Preventive/Predictive Maintenance)
- zero accidents (there's no acceptable goal other than zero)
- zero handling (flow)
- zero lead time (eliminate causes of nonvalue-adding time)
- zero waste (eliminate causes of waste)
- zero flexing (level production schedules and stable product mix)

At first these seemed crazy, but Les explained that you need to believe in these goals to keep continually improving. If your ambitions run out at 99%, then it's doubtful if you'll even reach 99%. If you open that door, the unwanted will rush back in.

Les then shifted gears to Agile. "Agile," he explained, "is a different approach than Lean. Agile's focus is on quick response to change; customer choices; market changes; and any new areas the company needs to leverage quickly. Notice 'needs to,' not so much 'wants to.'"

Les went on to explain the vital role that Six Sigma plays in process variability avoidance—looking for opportunities for variability, and closing them down.

"We will not attempt to teach Six Sigma at this time, but it is an important enabler to achieving the Stage 4 of Class A.

"We have brought you through a lot in the last two days. How do you feel?" Les asked as he finished the course.

"Like I've been fed with a fire hose," replied Mickey, to which everyone agreed with a laugh.

"It's okay for you guys, but it sounds like I've got to reshape and refocus my Department," Carol said. She got no sympathy from the others—she didn't expect it either. She knew what everyone thought of Quality Control.

Brian took over, "The education was good and required, but to me the most powerful parts of the last two days were the workshops where we clearly identified what we need to go off and do."

"Thanks, Brian." Les replied. "Remember, you've got to practice this stuff. Learn by doing, we call it."

At the end of the two days the team felt exhausted but elated. All action items that were defined during the session had teams assigned to them. One of the assignments was to implement Kanbans in the hub cell in the Machine Shop.

Hayes had implemented Kanbans in a few areas, but the corporate Business Improvement Group wanted to see a more widespread application. Some of them were even making predictions that the Enterprise Resource Planning system could be replaced by the Kanbans. After the session with Les, Brian, Dan, and Mickey knew that just implementing Kanbans wasn't the answer. Implementing them in the right place with the correct processes was the key. They all felt that the Business Improvement Group in general was too philosophical in its approach and didn't have the real hands-on experience to understand the real impact of implementing these concepts. They wouldn't be held accountable if the product didn't ship on time—Brian, Dan, and Mickey would.

Brian, Dan, and Mickey all decided that they wanted to take a first-hand look to see the things Les described actually in action, so that they could avoid some of the pitfalls others had made. They decided to ask the Business Improvement Group if they could recommend a company using a wider application of Kanbans that they could visit. The Business Improvement Group was more than happy to provide Brian with the names of several companies and people to contact. One of the companies they strongly recommended was Mercury Electronics. Mercury built computer printers, and their Lean process had been online for nearly a year.

"I have to tell you," Brian confessed as he spoke to George from the Business Improvement Group, "I'm not too sure how making computer printers resembles making tractors . . ."

"Trust me on this one, Brian," George assured him. "You're about to enter a new world."

The day of the Mercury tour arrived, and Rob Erickson, the Production Manager of Mercury Electronics, greeted Brian, who was accompanied by Elliot, Dan, Mickey, and Joan, in the lobby. Rob took them to a conference room where he gave them a brief overview of their Kanban implementation. Then they moved out into the plant. Mercury had arranged their shop layout so that production moved as a continuous flow, a single part at a time, throughout the shop. Everywhere they went, there were manufacturing cells—groups of operations linked together to produce a high-velocity flow of production. The whole place was a mini version of Mickey's assembly area, with work moving through cells and down production lines, just a lot smaller. Rob pointed out that this layout had helped them to practically eliminate queues and the product throughput time had been shortened from weeks into hours.

In one cell, Brian watched them change over a circuit-board assembly line to accommodate a different-size board. The complete setup was accomplished in less than 10 minutes. Brian was amazed by the efficiency of the process, and he wondered about the planning that had obviously gone into it. Rob also showed them a dedicated line that Mercury had established on their most popular circuit board. It was never changed over, even if it was idle at times.

They saw the Kanban technique in live action. The printer assembly people pulled completed circuit boards from small boxes resembling the old mailbox slots (pigeon holes) they'd had at Hayes before email took over. Whenever a board was removed from one of its boxes, it authorized another board exactly like it to be replaced by the circuit-board assembly area.

In all areas, the components and subassemblies were pulled directly from the production floor as they were needed. The assembly line had been linked with the packaging cell and the shipping dock. Finished printers were built and shipped in one day. There were no component or finished-goods stockrooms.

Since there were no stockrooms, Brian asked Rob where they stored their purchased materials.

"We keep them right on the production line. Our suppliers replenish the stock using the Kanban approach. The suppliers deliver our high-usage items daily. Lower volume items are replenished less frequently. We have reduced our purchased material inventories significantly, and we have cut our material handling costs to practically nothing," answered Rob.

Controlling production at Mercury Electronics was done completely with Kanbans. The schedule was given daily to the Assembly department. It told them what models to build that day. When the subassemblies and component parts were pulled by Assembly to build the printer, the empty Kanbans signaled the production areas to build replacements.

Brian commented to Rob, "This process seems to be okay when you build a few standard models all the time, but we build a lot of special tractors and spare parts."

Rob told Brian that, in addition to their standard models, they often built products from a choice of options, and that they also got occasional orders for customized printers. Rob said that they did not schedule the option or special subassemblies with Kanban, but instead they inserted a special *order* Kanban Card, colored blue, into the production flow. He showed him the schedule for that day, and it had two specials on it. The bills of material for the special configurations were attached to the card, so that when the assembly line got to those items they knew what parts to use. Then, when the Assembly Department pulled the components and built the subassemblies as needed, that would initiate the Kanban process throughout the rest of production to replace the parts used on the special printer. If nonstandard or customized parts were required, or if they got an order for some spares, a production authorization card (Kanban) was sent out to the production area that built them. They took advantage of the forward-looking capability of their Enterprise Resource Planning system to do their planning of future material requirements and used Kanban as the release mechanism to actually produce the parts or receive them from the supplier.

"But how do you plan your capacities?" Brian asked. Rob showed him his capacity plan (see Figure 10.5).

Figure 10.5   Mercury Electronics Capacity Plan

Work Center: P1			Date: 2/04
Description: Printer Assembly			
	Demo.		Max.
	No. Operators: 10		12
	Shifts: 1		2
	Hrs./Shift: 8		10
	Rate/Day 80		192
Week	Required Capacity Printers per Day	Planned Capacity Printers per Day	Deviation
2/04	80	80	0
2/11	80	80	0
2/18	80	80	0
2/25	80	80	0
3/03	80	80	0
3/10	80	80	0
3/17	80	80	0
3/24	80	80	0
3/31	100	80	-20
4/07	100	100	0

Rob said that his current plant staffing level in each cell was geared to produce 80 printers per day. The required capacity on the capacity plan was for 80 printers per day for the next eight weeks. This number came directly from the Master Schedule. Rob said that his required capacity was directly proportional to the total volume of printers scheduled, since each printer consumed about the same amount of labor resources. He pointed out that several weeks ago the report signaled him that the Master Schedule had been increased and he would have to start building 100 printers per day in April, so he had sent requisitions to personnel for additional manpower, starting April first. The current capacity plan (see Figure 10.5) now showed him that the increase in the master schedule had been pulled up one week, so he was going to have to call personnel and have those hiring dates moved in.

"We send the same Master Schedule to our supplier so they know how many printers we will be building in the future. It does not authorize them to make anything; the Kanban does that."

After they completed the tour, Rob said to the group from Hayes, "Let me make it clear that there is a great deal more to making this process than just the Kanban. We've done a lot of things, such as standardizing our product designs, rearranging our shop layouts, eliminating inspection by focusing on the concept of quality at the source, reducing setups, and crosstraining workers. We've changed our whole outlook and attitudes about how to run this place. The Kanban technique is a very important part, but it is only the most visible aspect of the process."

Brian was more than impressed with Rob's operations. Still, it seemed to Brian that building printers was easy to adapt to this kind of flow manufacturing. Hayes made tractors. (We can't repeat what Mickey had to say about the comparison!) To Rob's credit, he emphasized that though the applications might differ, the concepts that drove the process were the same.

Back at Hayes, the group discussed what they had learned from the course and had seen on the tour of Mercury Electronics. They talked about the concepts of Lean Manufacturing, especially the problem-solving attitude and the one-less-at-a-time process.

Mickey did finally admit that he had some subassembly areas that could operate similar to Mercury. Brian also admitted that he, too, could begin to look for ways to simplify and streamline to continually improve his operations. Dan was not so sure.

Elliot said that, in order for them to be able to reduce lot sizes, they needed to reduce the setup times. He offered to look into the technique of SMED (Single Minute Exchange of Die) that they had heard so much about.

Brian and Dan could also see that Kanban would help them to decrease the shop-floor transactions.

"Now you're talking," Mickey said. "That's one of my big objections to Enterprise Resource Planning systems—too many transactions."

Brian reminded them that they had already reduced queues significantly with the queue-reduction program, but they could undoubtedly make them even smaller. "There's plenty of fat left in the process, even though we've cut our queues by 40%. Remember that Les Johnson from Effective Management showed examples of companies that had been able to reduce their work-in-process inventory by up to 95% after improvements had been realized."

"Don't forget," Elliot reminded them, "we need to encourage and facilitate progressive thinking by all of the people in the company if we're going to pull this off. I'm sure they've got plenty of ideas that will help. We've just never given them the chance before."

Back in his office, Brian thought over all he had learned. As he recalled the operations at Mercury, he thought about what Les had said about the application of the concepts. He began thinking about where he might begin using Kanban at Hayes.

The hubs, which fed directly into Mickey's assembly line, were a perfect candidate. Mickey was constantly complaining that the lead times were too long. "I can't understand the problem," he'd say to Brian. "Every tractor that goes down the line takes two front hubs and two rear hubs. We make three different tractors. That's a total of six different hubs. Is this too difficult to get right?"

Brian got together with Elliot and his first- and second-shift supervisors. They explained how Kanbans worked and began discussing the possibility of starting a pilot project for wheel hubs. They reviewed the existing routings to determine which operations were required (see Figure 10.6).

Figure 10.6   Typical Hub Routing

163726	Hub, front Wheel					
Part Number	Part Description					
Opn. No.	Dept.	Work Ctr.	Operation Description	Setup	Run
			Release		
			Pick		
10	Mach	24	Turn	1.5	.10
20	Mach	24	Turn	3.0	.20
30	Mach	22	Drill & Tap	2.0	.10
			Store		

Their first step was to set up a manufacturing cell to make hubs. They calculated that producing the quantity of hubs they would need per month would require two CNC lathes and one CNC drilling and tapping, all running about two-and-a-half shifts. The first step would be to relocate the machines close together to create a flow from one machine to the next. They figured that the two lathes would have to run at 80% capacity, but the drill would be idle about

40% of the time. Elliot expressed concern about machine utilization. Brian pointed out that, if they could meet the production requirements for hubs with only 80% utilization of the lathes and 60%
utilization of the drill, why should they run them at 100%? That
would be wasteful since it just created inventory. That was enough
justification for Elliot, who finally saw the problem of using 'utilization' to drive production performance. Les had told them about this,
but now they could see it for themselves.

They agreed to combine the three machines into one work center
and use the Kanban technique to pull the parts through the cell and
into Assembly (see Figure 10.7).

Figure 10.7   Hub Cell Layout

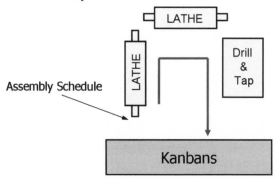

They would also eliminate the need to put the hubs into stock by
linking the hub cell directly into Mickey's assembly operations via
Kanbans.

"If we're going to do this," Brian said to Elliot and José, as they
walked around the shop floor, "we'll have to change the Bills of
Materials and the routings to reflect the changes in the manufacturing process, the work-center assignments, and the setup and run
times." Currently hubs were stocked, and so were a bill-of-materials
level that required planning and reporting. They'd heard about "de-
leveling the bill," but were not sure how this was done.

They phoned Les to talk about their proposed Kanban pilot. Les
was pleased they were following up on the challenge, but explained
that they had to earn the right, as he put it, to implement Kanban.

"When Kanban is implemented, it must be safe for it to work automatically to its Kanban rules. In other words, the process steps covered by Kanban need to be consistently repeatable or reliable. If product quality or yield varies much in the process being pulled, you must fix that variability first. The process doesn't need to be perfect, just repeatable. The Kanban sizing can take care of the repeatable nonperformance, such as near constant 5% waste. And it is tolerant of variable run times. Until you've made the process repeatable you need a person, a scheduler, to manage those links between the process and it's nearest upstream and downstream processes. That means the operation must still be in the routing.

"When you're happy that you have these characteristics you can consider de-leveling the bill of material, and also de-leveling the associated routing. But a preferred approach is to convert a Kanban-controlled level to a pseudo-item in the bill structure. This means that the level is still visible on the computer—very useful for engineering control—and the routings are still available for costing rollup. But the Enterprise Resource Planning system does not create any material orders or schedule operations; it sees a pseudo-item as a mathematical conversion from one level to another."

Brian was happy to report that the processes they were going to use for the pilot were in fact very suitable. They had very low failure rates and only one rework in the last six months. Brian wanted to check with Les, their Effective Management instructor, about the operational Kanban rules to confirm that they were going to be in the training for everyone, especially the operators. He got the rest of the team together to see if they wanted a coaching session with Les before they continued much further. They all agreed it was a great idea.

During the coaching session, Les talked about the rules he'd referred to, and reminded them there are some "no choice" Kanban Rules. "Break these, and you'll lose control. The two most important of these rules are: never start work or move material without an 'open' Kanban; and never pass on a known defect.

"There are other rules and some guidelines to bear in mind. Work to keep the Kanban level within your rules, and never let the Kanban run out. There is no perfect math to size Kanbans—at the start ensure you err on the side of having a generous Kanban size. You do not yet know all the problems that your current stock is hiding. Then let the operators start a program of reducing the number in a Kanban. Gradually reducing Kanbans will expose problems,

prioritize opportunities, stimulate problem-solving, encourage cus-
tomer/supplier communications, get people thinking about the right
things, provide visible feedback on progress, and increase velocity.
And it's very motivating for the production people as they see their
own success.

"Be prepared for 'line-stop.' Kanbans assume all the product is fit
for use. The operator, seeing a problem, would need to stop production. If this is an issue, consider what you think is the worst
problem?

- Continuing to make bad product?
- Hiding problems with inventory?
- Temporarily stopping production to fix the root cause?

"The guidelines are simple. You will need to set the starting Kanban sizes. Setting the number of Kanban squares or cards sets a ceiling or limit on the amount of inventory, which is time, in the system.
The best Kanban is a natural Kanban, such as one at a time; a fixed
number of pieces; standard containers or totes; a size that reflects
an inherent attribute of the process, such as a 10-liter mixing vessel;
or a standard sheet of material. Whatever the number of Kanbans,
it should permit a gradual reduction.

"Have only active material at the work place. That's why you still
plan to enable supplies to be called as required into the Kanban or
line-side. Make a place for everything and ensure that everything
is in its place. Again, this generates a visible signal if something is
missing, or out of place. Process Kanbans on a first-in/first-out basis
or according to a Line Rate Schedule if mixed products go through
the line. When a Line Rate Schedule is used, the sequence must be
followed. It is best for the customer to pull material from the direct
supplier, and continue this process internally—that's called 'demand
pull,' you'll remember.

"Kanbans are simple and efficient to use, and easy and inexpensive to implement. They set a known upper limit on inventory and,
as I said, reducing the Kanban size exposes problems and prioritizes
opportunities for improvement.

"Just remember the key rules: Never move material or begin work
without an open Kanban; never pass on a known defect."

This gave Brian and the team the input they needed to plan the
Kanban implementation properly, to avoid losing control.

"But if we're not going to use a Dispatch List," José said, "why can't we just eliminate the routings for the hubs altogether?"

Brian reminded José that they needed them for engineering control, to do costing, and calculate future capacity requirements for the hub cell. "We'll still need the routings, although they will be simpler. You see, unlike Mercury Electronics, where every model uses similar amounts of capacity, the capacity required to make our large hubs is significantly more than that required to make small and medium hubs. And since the mix in the master schedule is never constant, I think we still need to use detail capacity planning to tell us what our future capacity requirements will be."

It didn't take them long to realize that the constraint on their capacity was the slowest operation in the cell, namely, the second turning operation. If the slowest machine had sufficient capacity, the other machines would also. They set the run time for the cell by timing how fast the parts came out of the last machine. This, of course, was the run time of the slowest machine, because it was the one that paced the cell. The setup time was drastically reduced because only hubs were now being run in the cell and the variation from one setup to another was very small. In addition, instead of having one operator set up all three machines, a second operator was added during the setup. The net result was an average change-over time of only 15 minutes. The reduction in the setup time also allowed them to drastically reduce the lot size, which was no more than one-day's worth of any hub, even the lower quantity large tractor hubs. The routing could now be used to tell Brian how many hours of operation were required by the hub cell as a unit in order to meet the Master Schedule (see Figure 10.8).

Figure 10.8   Revised Routing as Hub Cell

163726	Hub, front Wheel				
Part Number	Part Description				

Opn. No.	Dept.	Work Ctr.	Operation Description	Setup	Run

10	Mach	C1	Release
			Pick
			Hub Cell
			    Turn
			    Turn
			    Drill & Tap
			Store
				.25	.20

They realized that they only had to schedule the input to the first machine (the first lathe) because whatever hub started there would flow through the cell. The Assembly Schedule that was sent by the master scheduler to Mickey every day was now also sent to the hub cell (see Figure 10.9) to tell them what to start.

When Mickey took hubs from the Kanbans, they would authorize more hubs to be produced in the cell. Within the Hub Cell, the Assembly Schedule and Kanban had replaced the Dispatch List as the priority tool.

Brian, Joan, and Tony put together an educational program and began teaching the supervisors and operators the concepts and tech-

Figure 10.9   Assembly Line Schedule

| Work Center: A1 Assembly Line | | Date: 3/10 |
| Description: Small Tractors | | |
Date	Part Number	Plan Qty.
3/10	21349	1
3/10	26874	4
3/10	36492	2
3/10	32846	2
3/10	25173	5
3/10	31962	1
Total		15
3/11	21349	1
3/11	26874	5
3/11	36492	3
3/11	32846	1
3/11	25173	4
3/11	31962	1
Total		15
3/12	21349	1
3/12	26874	4
3/12	36492	2
3/12	32846	2
3/12	25173	5
3/12	31962	1
Total		15

niques of Kanbans. At first, there was some resistance. But when the operators started seeing their ideas immediately incorporated into the process, they all began to offer more suggestions. This was the manifestation of the employee involvement concept that the corporate Business Improvement Group had been pushing. The results were incredible. After only a few weeks of operation, setup times and lot sizes were being reduced significantly. Unfortunately, most companies focus on techniques like Kanban and forget the most powerful piece—people engagement.

Brian now got a single detail capacity plan for the hub cell instead of individual reports for turning and drilling. The master schedule was set for approximately 25 tractors per day, depending on the mix of tractors. This meant that the hub cell needed to produce approximately100 hubs per day. But, since the mix of hubs would vary according to the mix in the master schedule, and since the large hubs required more time that the small ones, the hours of required operation of the hub cell would vary week to week. It wouldn't vary a lot: The variation around the 25 tractors per day was because Mickey had the same mix problem as Brian; large tractors took longer to assemble than medium tractors; medium tractors took longer to assemble than small tractors. Brian could see from the report how his requirements would vary over time. Since the report covered a full 12-month horizon, he could also see whether he would have to increase or decrease the capacity of the cell and by how much and when (see Figure 10.10). He continued to manage the capacity in the cell in the same manner that he managed prior to establishing the cell.

After they started the pilot, one of the critical moments that tested their resolve came when the Assembly Department had to shut down the assembly lines because of a quality problem. Since they were not starting any more tractors, they were not pulling any more hubs from Brian's hub cell, nor sending back Kanban cards, so the hub cell also shut down. And, wouldn't you know it? Just at that time, Ralph came walking through the shop and saw the hub cell at a standstill.

He immediately found Brian and screamed at him. "What in the blazes is going on down there? I thought Lean Manufacturing was supposed to reduce waste. What I see is valuable capacity going down the drain. Why isn't that cell running?"

Figure 10.10   Hub Cell Summary Capacity Plan

			Summary Capacity Plan			

Date	3/10	No. Machines	1	Hours / Shift	8
Work Center	C1	No. Operators	3	Shifts / Day	3
Description	Hub Cell	Mach / Oper	1	Days / Week	5
Demo. Cap'y.	110	Max. Cap'y.	130	Load Factor	90%

	MACHINE CAPACITY			LABOR CAPACITY		
Week	Reqd. Cap'y (Hrs)	Plan Cap'y (Hrs)	Load vs. Capacity(%) 50 100 150	Reqd. Cap'y (Hrs)	Plan Cap'y (Hrs)	Load vs. Capacity(%) 50 100 150
8/06	116	108	xxxxxxxxxxx	116	108	xxxxxxxxxxxx
8/13	103	108	xxxxxxxxxx|	103	108	xxxxxxxxx|
8/20	106	108	xxxxxxxxxx|	106	108	xxxxxxxxx	
8/27	123	108	xxxxxxxxxxxxx	123	108	xxxxxxxxxxxx
9/03	111	108	xxxxxxxxxx|	111	108	xxxxxxxxxxx
9/10	101	108	xxxxxxxxx		101	108	xxxxxxxxx|
9/17	128	108	xxxxxxxxxxxxx	128	108	xxxxxxxxxxxx
9/24	110	108	xxxxxxxxxx|	110	108	xxxxxxxxx|
10/01	109	108	xxxxxxxxxx|	109	108	xxxxxxxxx|
10/08	122	108	xxxxxxxxxxxxx	122	108	xxxxxxxxxxxx
↓						
7/28						

Brian explained that as long as the assembly line was down, there was no need to make more hubs, since they weren't needed right away. As soon as the line started up again, the cell would be back in full production.

"But, in the meantime," shouted Ralph, "you've got people standing around drawing pictures on a flip chart! We're paying them to work, you know, not to goof off."

Brian said, "They're not goofing off. They are discussing an idea one of the operators had to reduce the run time on the second turning operation. If they can do it, it will increase the output of the cell because that's the slowest operation. I think that will prove more valuable to the company than pumping out hubs that are only going to sit in inventory. Remember, we started this whole process in the first place to make the company more productive over the long haul. We can't just look at the short term. You've got to give it a chance."

"Well, all right, Miller. I see your point. I just don't like seeing idle equipment. I understand we have to change our way of thinking around here. I just have to get used to it, I guess."

But that wasn't the end of it. Mickey's quality problem turned very serious on the large tractor line. The latest delivery from the supplier for the material in the roll-over protection device was out of specification and was causing cracking problems. Mickey had to stop producing large tractors for five days while new material was being brought in, the existing frames were cut apart, and the defective material was replaced with material to specification. Finally, when Mickey could start up the large tractor line again, he was doing everything possible to get back on schedule. He started running 10-hour shifts along with Saturday and Sunday. He knew he could run at this rate for a short period of time. It wasn't long before Mickey had used up all the large hubs that were in the Kanban and, as Brian tried to catch up, they started running out of hubs for the small tractor line also.

At the regularly scheduled meeting in the morning to review the production status, the same old behaviors surfaced when Mickey jumped at Brian. "What's going on over there in the Machine Shop? Are you guys on vacation? I'm out of hubs!"

"Yeah, I know," replied Brian. "When you shut down for five days, my queue filled up in less than a day and I shut down per the Kanban rules."

"I knew we shouldn't have people standing around drawing on flip charts," Ralph interjected with a growl and frown Brian hadn't seen for quite a while.

"When you started up assembly with all of the overtime, I was just not able to keep up," Brian continued. "We're running all three shifts along with Saturday and Sunday, but that is not enough to keep up with Mickey, who can assemble tractors a lot faster than I can make hubs. In the meantime Mickey will have to synchronize his overtime with me so he doesn't work himself out of hubs."

"What are you going to do to keep this from happening again, Miller?" Ralph shot back.

"Elliot, Joan, and I are working on it," Brian said, as he thought about going back to the drawing board.

"You know," Joan said at the meeting with Brian and Elliot to sort out the problem, "whenever you have an area that has to work multiple shifts to support an area that works one shift, you will run into this problem. "I don't know why we don't let the Kanbans control the work through the cell, but let the Line Rate Schedule that Les talked about control not only what the cell starts, but also what they are supposed to produce every day. When we calculated the amount of queue for the Kanbans it was about two days. What we should do is set the due date out of the hub cell to be two days ahead of assembly and then measure the cell to see if it is producing on time via the schedule. Then, if Mickey falls behind, we can either leave the schedule the same if he is going to catch up right away, or change the hub-cell schedule to reflect what we want it to produce, to keep this problem from reoccurring."

"Let's give Les a call," said Brian. "I'd like to make sure we're getting this right."

Les called back that afternoon near quitting time. Brian linked Joan into the call to hear what Les had to say. Brian explained the issues around Assembly, the hub cell they'd set up, and their latest problem. Joan then explained the approach they wanted to take using the Line Rate Schedule.

"That makes a lot of sense to me," Les agreed.

"I have another situation that has come up since we met last, Joan," Brian interjected. "In reviewing the Summary Capacity Plan we noticed a spike in demand in three-months' time. It is actually more than we can handle. By looking at the source of demand using the detail capacity plan we found that we are introducing a new design of hub for the large tractors. That is consuming a great deal of capacity for the 'prove in.' We were just wondering how we would handle that."

Joan said, "We could smooth out the load by pulling some work forward. We'd do this for that period of time by decoupling demand from supply. Then in Material Requirements Planning we would add in the prestock demands. This would then appear naturally in the Line Rate Schedule. Our Material Planners know how to do this; they do it for any machine planned shutdown."

"Great," said Brian. "Everything would be a lot simpler because then the supervisors would just have to manufacture in the sequence and volume of the Line Rate Schedule."

Les agreed, but added one final comment. "We are getting to the point in this partnership I really enjoy. You are really starting to get it. I'm turning more to the role of a coach instead of instructor, and it won't be long before I will be learning from you. Then you'll throw me out because I'll have accomplished my objective—you standing on your own two feet and driving the improvement."

Everyone laughed, but Brian countered, "We appreciate your comments on our ability to think for ourselves but we need your constant prodding Les. So we're not going to throw you out. Who would I have to battle with over the last chocolate-covered doughnut?"

The next day Brian and Joan reviewed their conversation with Les for Dan and Mickey. These two remained skeptical, but that was normal for manufacturing managers of their service!

"What about the 'one less at time' approach we wanted to do with Kanbans?" Elliot asked.

Brian thought for a moment. "Well, we'll continue to use the Kanban between the machines, just like we have. Now that they've had the training, we'll tell the operators it's their job to reduce the number of pieces in the Kanban, one at a time, until they find the optimum level. And I bet they'll find more things we could do to reduce them even further."

"I reckon those guys will see better ways to lay out the processes for better product flow," said Joan. "Let's think back to when we were fed with a fire hose. Didn't Les say that, through educating the operators—which we've done—through learning to listen to them—which we need to do much better—we'll learn to empower them to take ownership of their processes? Our job is to give clear objectives and define what constitutes success, a bit like a team coach. We don't run the plays ourselves."

"This is going to take a lot of getting used to," said Dan.

"You can say that again!" agreed Mickey.

Joan's face lit up. "Why don't we learn by doing? Of course, we'll have to let our people know what we're trying to achieve, or they'll think we're going crazy."

"Oh boy!" exclaimed Mickey. "Ralph is going to love this. But I'm going to try to get him to understand—he's a smart manager, and he empowered us to make improvements."

Later that day Brian moseyed into Ralph's office. "Just wanted to let you know that by the first of next week we will be caught up with Mickey and we've figured out a way to stay out of trouble in the future."

"Glad to hear that, Brian," Ralph responded in a consoling voice. "Mickey has already spoken to me about what you guys are going to do. It's okay. Didn't mean to jump on you like I did, because I know you have made a lot of improvement this year. Screwing up once in a while is worth it, so long as we don't do it too badly, we recover from it, and we learn from it for the future."

Brian was shocked, but decided to take advantage of the situation while Ralph was in a good mood.

"Thanks, Ralph. There's something else I wanted to talk to you about," Brian said. "If we keep making the kind of progress on reducing the run and setup times, we are going to have a lot more extra capacity. How about taking in work from the other plants to utilize that capacity?"

"And take a chance on missing our schedule because of them? No way!"

"Come on, Ralph," Brian said, "We have our capacities under control. If we keep making these improvements, we're going to have to start reducing our work force. That's going to start sending the wrong message to the operators, and they'll quit making the improvements."

Ralph nodded. "Yes, I can see what you mean. Maybe we should take on some outside work."

"I just happen to have a proposal in my office that Elliot and I put together," Brian said, smiling, "for your approval, of course."

Ralph laughed. "I'm going to learn to quit agreeing with you until I've had a chance to figure out how you're setting me up."

By changing the manufacturing environment in the hub cell, the scheduling and capacity management process was greatly simplified, yet still provided the same control as before. Many other areas were picking up on the lessons learned at the hub cell. Where it made sense they linked Kanban directly to the assembly line. In more complex situations like the hub cell, they combined the best of Kanban along with the Enterprise Resource Planning system to get a process that was as simple as possible yet provided the information to operate effectively and efficiently.

The Mercury Electronics tour had really opened everyone's eyes and provided the Hayes team with the initiative to make some real progress. Brian started to wonder if there was more to be learned. The more he thought about it, the more he wanted to visit another user of Kanban. He gave George Turner at the Corporate Business Improvement Group another call, asking to visit another company that was more like them. George gave him the name of McNally Machine Tools, saying that they would be an interesting contrast to Mercury Electronics.

Brian picked up the phone and called Buster Jones, the contact name that George gave him. Buster was very cordial, and two weeks later Buster was able to arrange for Brian to join a tour of their plant that had been set up for one of their customers. Brian was excited because McNally had a machine shop and a sheet-metal fabrication shop, so some of their operations would be similar to Hayes.

The McNally Machine Tools tour started off with an overview of the Lean Manufacturing project. Buster explained that the initiative was driven by the senior vice president of their division. Their charter was to implement product cells, reduce lead times, and cut the cost of production.

Buster went on to say that they had consultants from an outside firm on site helping them make the changes. At first that really sounded like a good idea to Brian because it meant that there would be additional resources to help with the implementation.

After the briefing in the conference room, the group headed out to the factory. As they approached the Fabrication Shop, Buster explained that they had installed an Enterprise Resource Planning system a few years ago, but that they had never really got it working well. Brian could understand that, since that was the situation when he first took over his job at Hayes.

McNally had identified six different product groups and had arranged all of the machines necessary to support the manufacturing of those individual products into product cells. However, the parts still moved from one machine to the next in batches. They had not accomplished the single-part flow like Brian had done in his hub cell. They had accomplished a reduction in travel time and had gained some improvement in quality, but there had been no reduction in the move and queue times between operations, nor were there any provisions for overlapping or parallel setups or runs. This meant that they hadn't gotten the reduction in lead time that Brian did when he created the hub cell. When Brian asked him about it, Buster said that they planned to address that in the future.

Brian could see that they were having problems meeting schedules. Hot tags were visible on several jobs, and there was a constant stream of people moving around looking for parts. Brian asked Buster how they set priorities in the shop. He responded that everything moved on a first-in/first-out basis. Then Brian asked how they planned capacity. The response was that they planned capacity based on a rate basis and that it was not really an issue. Brian could see that things were not moving first-in/first-out; he recognized expeditors when he saw them. It also appeared to him that capacity was indeed an issue at some of the machines since there was quite a lot of work backed up there.

Brian moved back to talk with Randy, one of the other people from McNally who was helping with the tour and who seemed less than enthusiastic. Brian and Randy drifted farther to the back of the group, carrying on a side conversation between themselves. Brian felt Randy was giving him the straight story and had hands-on shop knowledge. While Buster, the tour guide, droned on about how well the process was working, Brian asked Randy if he could talk to the supervisor of the area. Randy looked around and spotted the supervisor talking with his area manager. Buster led Brian over to where they were talking and introduced him to the pair. Brian asked them how the shop was doing from a scheduling standpoint. He then got an earful.

The supervisor explained that they previously had routings with individual work centers prior to creating the cell, and that they used their old Enterprise Resource Planning system to schedule the operations. The supervisor told Brian that when the Lean Manufacturing initiative was launched, they had discarded their shop-floor scheduling system because they had been advised that anything that was on the computer was not lean. The manager and the supervisor both agreed that creating the cells was a good idea, but they hadn't realized how much they had depended on the data that the Enterprise Resource Planning system had provided. They readily admitted that the data had some accuracy problems, but even in spite of that, they felt that they had been better off before than they were now. They had just begun to make some progress with their performance when the turnabout to Lean Manufacturing came. Now they felt out of control with no expectation that they could get back into control.

Brian asked them about creating single-piece flow cells to get the lead-time reduction. They said that they had talked about doing single-piece flow cells, but the higher-ups didn't want to take the time to do the proper design. Management wanted action now. In addition, nobody in the company, or any of the consultants, had come from an environment where shop-floor systems worked well, and therefore they were all convinced that it couldn't work. The supervisor and manager felt they were not in a good position to argue the point even though they recognized the importance of good schedules in attaining on-time delivery.

Brian asked about capacity planning. They explained that the Enterprise Resource Planning system had provided that information in the past, but they had eliminated the detailed capacity planning system and installed a capacity planning process based on rates. In some areas of the factory, the rate-based capacity planning process worked fine. In the case of this particular cell, however, they were having trouble because the work wasn't coming to them at a steady rate and the run times varied considerably, depending on which specific parts they were running. The new capacity planning system did not adequately account for the fluctuations in orders, mix changes, engineering changes, or problem parts. Even with less-than-accurate setup and run times, they felt that the detail capacity planning system had given them much better visibility.

Brian got an idea. "Why don't you come visit us at Hayes? It might give you some ammunition to use to get back some of the information that you would like to have to manage your area. Then you can work on single-part flows instead of chasing parts."

They thought that would be a good idea and thanked Brian for the offer.

Brian and Randy caught up with the tour group. Brian saw some areas that were running very smoothly and had clearly made positive strides with Lean Manufacturing. Other areas he saw were similar to the Fabrication Shop, and were struggling with scheduling and capacity issues.

On the drive home, Brian started thinking about some of the things he had learned on his trips, from Les, from the Business Improvement Group, and from his own experiences. Brian wondered why the Lean process was working so well at Mercury Electronics but was struggling at McNally Machine Tool. Why was McNally so convinced that they had to back away from computerized planning and scheduling tools when they were working so well at Hayes? Was it because the products were different? Or the manufacturing processes? Brian didn't think so. Fundamentally, things were quite similar in all of these plants. The only real difference was the people.

"That's it!" Brian shouted, as he slammed his palm down on the steering wheel and almost drove through a stop sign. "It's the people!"

Using Enterprise Resource Planning based shop scheduling and capacity planning isn't any different from any other system or process. Bad data, bad schedules, misguided decisions, and/or poor discipline will destroy any system. Brian nodded to himself. No system will provide good information to manage with if you don't put the right processes and accurate data in place.

If people don't understand the concepts and principles of the various systems and techniques, they are likely either to go down some wrong paths or resist the changes altogether. By understanding each process thoroughly and its relationship to and impact upon other processes, people will be able to compare new ideas with the current processes in place on the shop floor to see if a new approach would, in fact, provide an improvement. Understanding the processes and techniques is what is important, not the buzzwords and acronyms.

It is important to align the current planning system with the manufacturing process. If you are operating in a batch environment, you need to recognize it and use the planning system effectively to help manage the business. As you leaned out the processes, then you could eliminate those pieces of the planning system that became unnecessary. Brian could see how critical it was to get the manufacturing processes and the planning processes in alignment, or else you could end up wasting a lot of time and effort using the computer to help you when it wasn't needed or, like McNally Machine Tools, not having the tools to run the business with.

Reflecting on it all, Brian realized that Hayes had done the right thing up front to get the education and training so they could continue to build the disciplines and controls and make headway with the continuous-improvement process. To get control, they had to have the planning provided by the Enterprise Resource Planning system and Class A processes. And he knew that in order to properly compete globally, the company needed to adopt the philosophies of continuous improvement and elimination of waste.

The success of the hub pilot and other pilots that Dan and Mickey had started got everyone throughout the plant excited about Lean and, in particular, the cell approach. Brian and his colleagues discovered that the philosophy and process of Lean caught on like wildfire. Even in the offices things were changing, mostly in Joan's area. It motivated people to begin looking at how they could simplify their process and procedures. There were some areas where the cell approach was straightforward. The hub cell was one. In other areas, it was hard for Brian to envision making the flow process applicable. That didn't mean Brian stopped trying to apply it, because sometimes the solution didn't just pop out. It also didn't mean that many of the other Lean concepts weren't applicable as well. Brian had learned that Lean was more than Kanban and creating cells. It was reducing and eliminating non-value-add activities—anything that added time instead of value. Things like avoiding setups, minimizing movement of parts and fixtures, a new look at measuring performance, and new problem-solving techniques. Where did it stop? He realized that it never did.

The basic concept of Lean Manufacturing—the continual and relentless avoidance and elimination of waste—was firmly fixed in everyone's mind. In fact, it was starting to become an obsession. "Why hadn't we done it sooner?" he asked. It all made such perfect sense.

Earlier, he had mistakenly thought that Lean just meant zero inventories and lead times of one day. At the time, those notions were so completely foreign to him that he quickly dismissed Lean as not applicable to Hayes. Therefore, he simply never took the time to learn more about it. Why? He then remembered the good old days of chasing parts, battling verbally with everyone, and constantly defending himself from all quarters. It was a time of never having what was needed and never knowing what was coming next. It was like a perpetual walk in the dark. Things had had to get better before Brian would ever have had the time to consider something like Lean.

The key was having the time to work on improving the process. He had to have a valid—accurate and feasible—schedule to give him the control he needed so that he could attend to process improvement. They would never return to the bad old days of constant expediting.

Chapter Eleven

Advanced Planning, Optimizing, & Scheduling

Seven months had gone by since Les ran the Continuous Improvement workshop and the focus on the elimination of waste was going well. Brian was really overwhelmed by the successes achieved so far at Hayes. Life had been a lot easier in the last year. He could see it in the whole management team. They were more relaxed and weren't pressing so hard any more.

One evening Brian was sitting in front of the television, watching his favorite baseball team the Detroit Tigers play the Seattle Mariners in Detroit. It was the ninth inning and the score was four to nothing Seattle. This was no surprise because Detroit hadn't been playing well this season. Detroit's problem was that they had a lot of young players and they just didn't have the experience to win consistently yet. Brian noticed the confident looks on the faces of Seattle as they ran out on the field. Brian could see the team knew they'd done enough—they could just coast through the rest of the game. A lot of the Detroit fans in the bleachers were getting up and leaving as if the game was over. "Been here, seen this too many times" was their attitude.

"Hey, the game's not over until the last one's out," Brian yelled at the television.

Brian's wife stuck her head in the room to see what he was yelling about. Upon seeing what Brian was watching she said, "Brian, you

283

need to give up on Detroit. And while you're at it you need to quit talking to the television. It isn't what I would think an 'up and coming' executive would do."

Brian gave her the sign language that said to leave him alone, to which she just laughed and went back to fixing dinner.

But Detroit wasn't finished yet. In the dugout you could see the manager energetically encouraging his players, not raving at them, but almost as if reminding them of what the coaches knew their players could do. Everyone in the dugout turned their hats inside out and put them on their heads—now they had their rally hats on!

The first batter in the top of the ninth came up to the plate. The pitcher, somewhat relaxed, delivered a fast ball that was meant for the outside corner, confident he'd hear "Strike," thinking he had intimidated the young hitter. But the ball went soaring out to right field, to the surprise of the outfielder who'd also relaxed and didn't get a good jump on the ball. It got by him, went to the wall and ended up as a double. The next batter surprised everyone when he laid down a perfect bunt down the third base line. The third baseman, the pitcher, nor the catcher, was able to get to the ball in time to throw either runner out. There were runners at third and first. The next batter was down in the count one ball and two strikes, but hung in there and hit a little blooper to center field that allowed the runner from second base to score. The score was now one to four, and runners at first and second.

Brian could see the pitcher really starting to stress. The pitcher was paying too much attention to the base runners and lost his focus on the batter. On the other side of the field the Detroit players were shouting encouragement. The next batter walked. With the bases loaded and the winning run at the plate and no outs, Seattle's manager called in his closer who had been almost un-hittable. The next batter struck out. One out, bases loaded. Brian was really excited—his wife closed the door to the television room.

The next batter ripped one, but unfortunately straight to the left fielder. There were two outs, one batter left. Confidence returned to Seattle and especially to the reliever. The Detroit manager pinch hit with a new player from the minor league. The announcers were talking about a great try by Detroit but too little, too late. However, the young Detroit team was ecstatic and screaming encouragement to their new player. The Detroit fans were starting to return and the whole place was electric. First pitch, home run, Detroit wins!

Brian couldn't believe what he saw. He couldn't wait to give Dan and Mickey a hard time because they're loyal Seattle fans. He was so glad to see that arrogant Seattle team get beat by the lowly Detroit Tigers. You could just see Seattle's over-confidence.

Just then, another thought flew into Brian's head. Could that be what's happening with Hayes top management—confident they'd done enough? And he suddenly remembered that saying: "Achievement is the death of endeavor" (Ambrose Bierce). It really shook him—how had he forgotten that, he wondered? He knew that there is no end to the quest for excellence. That's what those "zeroes" goals and continuous improvement meant that Les Johnson from Effective Management mentioned. It was time to look for the next exciting step on the journey.

The next morning after giving Dan and Mickey a hard time about the game, Brian went to see Joan.

"You know Joan, I'm getting a little worried about how complacent the management at Hayes has been over the last six months," Brian started.

"Well, that is because you haven't been involved in the Constraint-Based-Scheduling implementation."

Brian interrupted, "Remind me about that."

"Well, you know we talked about Finite Capacity Scheduling (FCS)? You remember, defining your process capacity limits and creating a plan that works within them, but using a computer to do the iterative calculations to get the best fit?"

"I guess so" said Brian. "We've been through lots since that discussion!"

"Well," continued Joan, "Once the total scheduled workload has reached the capacity constraint and there is still more work to be scheduled, FCS either forward schedules—reschedules out—to load the work, or alerts the planner for help. With a Constraint-Based Scheduling approach, additional scheduling rules come into play. We would need to define those rules; such as optimized sequences and changeovers, alternative possibilities, etc. This is a more complex approach requiring significant computer support to do the math. It uses our scheduling rules to look upstream and downstream, seeking to resequence jobs to optimize the total schedule.

This may require several iterations of the schedule by the software, including rescheduling jobs already scheduled. As you can see it's quite complex, and so we need to learn how to work with a tool like this before we start towards fuller Advanced Planning and Scheduling system (APS) capabilities."

"Why's that? What's it got to do with APS?" asked Brian.

"Constraint-Based Scheduling is one of the core features of an APS system." As Brian seemed satisfied with the answer, Joan continued.

"As you know, we got approval in the capital budget last week to for a limited Constraint-Based Scheduling project so we can learn how to use this new technology. And you well know from the capital budget spending process, that only means you really have to do all the hard work to define in detail what you want to do and justify it. I have Amy Shinn from Effective Management coming in next week to help us get started. Look at your schedule; I have you as a part of the process."

"Now I remember. Well I guess we deserved a little break, but it's good to know that we are not getting complacent."

Joan invited Brian, Dan and Mickey to the opening session with Amy on her coaching visit.

Joan started the meeting trying to get Amy up to date, "We're getting some improvements from the manual Constraint-Based-Scheduling processes we have put in place, but they take too much time so we need to automate them now. And management has now said they want to achieve closer ties to customer needs. I know we could do even better if only we could engage more of our supply chain in our quest for superior, cost effective service. Where would you start?"

"Well Joan, given the nature of your business—fairly stable demand, and manageable number of product offerings, especially now you've designed and organized for options and manufacture—as we have discussed before, I think you need to consider taking the integration of customers, production, and logistics further; much further. I'm talking about advanced Supply Chain Management, supported by Advanced Planning and Scheduling software; and this includes optimization as well. First you need to have a much more detailed understanding of the pluses and minuses of Advanced Planning and Scheduling, and then we'll see where you should consider applying advanced techniques that might help Hayes Tractors."

"But let's back up a minute," said Amy. "I think we need to review what's involved in advanced supply chain management.

"First, the word 'supply' in advanced supply chain means the end to end supply points that enable delivery from the supply chain to the customer. To do this you need to involve more than just your own supply points. Demand and supply at this level are complementary aspects of the same thing—delivering to customer request as often as possible.

"This means such techniques as Collaborative Supply Planning[1]— where companies work together for mutual benefit, to make each other successful through leveraging the supply chain, focused on the end customer/consumer. And to do this, the integration and communication between companies in the supply chain need to be absolute. Information, transactions, and event data needs to be exchanged and processed at ultra high speed; so fast, in fact, that there's no time for anyone to validate the data. It must be right first time. Further, this means the supporting system must be very flexible as data speeds through company systems software, often on different platforms, with differing supply chain capabilities and flexibility. This is where the Advanced Planning and Scheduling (APS) software comes in."

Amy asked, "Why do you think some companies are looking at and are drawn to APS?"

"From the brochures I've seen, it sounds really attractive," said Brian. "It's got all the stuff in it to solve our problems—if the software providers are to be believed."

"And do you think implementing APS software will solve your problems?" asked Amy.

Joan chipped in. "Well, we've been down this path before. When we bought our Enterprise Resource Planning system we thought that it would solve the problems we had then. We've learned though that, rather like a coffee pot, if we don't put the right stuff in, the pot isn't going to make coffee by itself. It's about how we understand our business and our people, and how we use the tools to achieve our objectives."

"Right on," said Amy. "There'll be many reasons companies are drawn to APS. Maybe they heard it was 'miracle planning.' Maybe

---

1. *Supply Chain Collaboration,* by Ron Ireland and Coco Crum, published by J Ross and APICS.

it sounds good—you know, 'advanced.' But the more realistic reasons are to do with the increasing pressure on companies to respond faster and better to customer demands. And the customers are smarter and more demanding than ever before. They want choice, they want it now, and they want it cheap. This results in shorter product life-cycles, a greater range of product options, the need for faster reliable deliveries, and the pressure to optimize supply chain costs to sustain margins. Enterprise Resource Planning can support preparing the supply chain for action, as we've said before, but it can be cumbersome and slow in its response time to an actual customer order. You consider today how long it actually takes from the customer deciding to call you, and actually having the product. APS can provide the necessary speed of response by simultaneously scheduling all activities and events that need to take place to fulfill an order to request, taking into account supply constraints. And it can do these calculations in a few seconds. The bad news is that there's no agreed definition of what APS means. It can be anything the software house thinks it should be, but almost all of the APS systems include finite scheduling. Now don't go throwing out your Enterprise Resource Planning system! APS has a high focus on scheduling and execution, but little in the way of planning and business process capabilities. Some don't even have a database, assuming it'll get its data from Enterprise Resource Planning system. In most cases APS systems are an add-on to your Enterprise Resource Planning system." Amy checked that they were all getting this.

"APS is a system-based approach with the focus on execution and delivery. It deliberately links supply and demand. Unless you've got really good demand control processes this is dangerous, as raw demand ignores your capabilities and costs. We can contrast this with master scheduling, which is a people-based process, supported by software, that focuses on realistic commitment and delivery, and formally manages the demand to supply link. Formally managed demand, even using Available-to-Promise, is essentially manual. That is why it's slow! The reality is, you'll need both Master Scheduling and APS. Master Scheduling will help to manage the mid- and long-term, and it prepares the supply chain for execution. It ensures that materials and capacities are lined up with anticipated demand. APS more typically is calculating solutions to actual demand, and very fast. So APS operates most effectively in the very short-term. APS systems must calculate solutions extremely quickly. They take advantage of today's cheaper memory and high speed processors to enable memory-resident processing. They use mathematical optimizing equations such as linear programming; they base their logic on the Theory of Constraints; and utilize XML[2] and other protocols to enable APS to 'talk' across systems and platforms. Many companies just use the finite scheduling capabilities for one key process, or even across several linked key processes. But I know of no company that exploits all of the possible scope of APS, not surprisingly, because any use of a tool must be tailored to the business needs of the company."

Amy continued. "But to implement APS effectively, safely, you will need in-depth accurate knowledge of your business processes, all the driving and alternatives parameters, all interactions and constraints that you know about. There are two views about how accurate data needs to be. One view says that your data accuracy needs to be extremely high, at least 99.5% by data master. The other view says that such precision is higher than the capabilities of the processes, and so 95% is OK. This latter view may be so for one or two processes being finite scheduled, but where APS is being used to model the supply chain (see Figure 11.1), potentially including first tier suppliers and customers, the 99.5% precision is necessary. And if APS is expected to be driving robots, as can be the case beyond Business Excellence Stage 4 capability, then even higher precision may be required."

Brian made a note to talk to Lloyd Adams, Design Engineering Manager, about this.

"The next issue that becomes apparent is the need for the processes defined in the model to work repeatably, time after time. This means you've attacked process variability and waste. There's no point in automating waste, or having fast schedules that are fouled up by lack of control of the processes. Of course, if a process is somewhat unreliable, for example if quality yield varies from 95% to 100%, you can always rerun the model with the actual yield. And that may work fine for a single process, even though we would recognize this as 'rework,' a deadly waste. But when the model includes multiple partners and supply points, it just will not do. Reducing

2. XML (Extensible Mark-Up Language) enables the definition, transmission, validation, and interpretation of data between applications and between organizations.

Figure 11.1   Control Needs Are Related to the Scope of APS

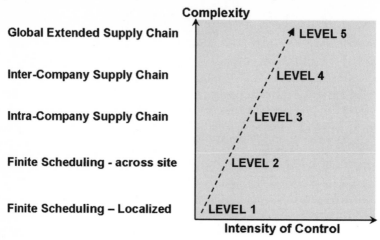

process variability to Six Sigma levels makes both product quality and promising quality most secure."

"Hear that Dan," Mickey teased. Amy just smiled.

"APS systems are equipped to handle not just Available to Promise (ATP), but also Capable-to-Promise (CTP). Available-to-Promise works very well at the single key interface with a customer, for example at end item, the stuff you sell. But without Lean, there tends to be a lot of stock held either at the end item level or the option level to make it happen. In a Lean company, there is very little stock—just enough to cover the defined flexibility. So using Available-to-Promise without considering all the supply points in the chain can be unreliable to customer service. And Available-to-Promise usually only considers stock or projected stock based on the planned orders in the Material Requirements Planning generated by the forecast. What about capacity? In the Lean supply chain, the major buffer to safe promising is often in capacity. Capable-to-Promise simultaneously assesses material and the capacity elements of flexibility at all key supply points in the chain. Further, if your model defines this, APS can examine alternative priorities, such as 'Customer Service first,' 'Cost first,' 'Speed of delivery first,' and other rules that you can define. So if speed is your priority for this customer with this order, then APS will seek the fastest supply

Figure 11.2   The Need for a Virtual Model of the Supply Chain

Supplier   Mfg-1   Mfg-2   Distribution   Customers

ISSUE:
How to plan the complete Network as a 'whole', allowing
for constraints, synchronizing all supply points along the
supply chain, and meeting promises to customers – fast
and cost effectively?

path, taking into account alternative supply possibilities, such as
routings, factories, getting parts or even the product from a com-
petitor, fastest logistics, etc. And it can tell you the cost of doing
this versus the standard or 'primary' path. Capable-to-Promise can
look across your multi-national company for the desired solution,
if that's in the model. How is this helpful? When your customers
engage in e-Business, experience suggests they expect almost instant
promises—reliable promises—they don't expect to *wait* for a reliable promise!"

"I know I expect instant promising when I use Internet shopping,"
said Joan. Amy continued.

"The basic requirement for APS to produce the best answers is
that you must describe in master data and rules a virtual model of
the scope of the supply chain over which APS will control execution automatically (see Figure 11.2). And someone in your company
must completely understand this model in order to maintain its validity over time."

Amy explained. "APS Systems come as standalone, or integrated
for use with existing Enterprise Resource Planning software. The
purpose of APS varies from system to system. The most fully fea-
tured versions support demand forecasting, customer order entry,
order configuration, order promising, supply planning (short-term),
supply and execution, and transportation planning, constraint-based
scheduling and supply chain optimization against business determined criteria such as, for cost, for customer service, for speed, etc.

The APS System is integrated most often to an Enterprise Resource Planning system and uses its database. This means it has no database of its own nor reporting, relying on the Enterprise Resource Planning system for data warehousing, etc. Some APS systems include elements of shopfloor execution control through routings, and they should also support self-managing execution control, such as flow or Kanban. All can interface with capable shopfloor execution systems, such as Manufacturing Execution Systems, to receive just the transactions APS needs to sustain its on-line capabilities, its event tracking, and alerts. Other shopfloor transactions pass through to the Enterprise Resource Planning system for planning control and management reporting, especially costs. The advantage of doing this is to keep APS freed up from transaction processing that could slow it down.

"What becomes apparent is that APS feeds on timely, accurate transactions. Transactions need to get back to APS near real-time. You'll need to look at data-loggers, bar-coding, Radio Frequency Identification, and direct links to Logic Controllers and robots. The Enterprise Resource Planning system can wait a bit for screen updates, maybe up to 15 minutes, but not the APS system, if it's to be an active and interactive controller.

"At the heart of APS is a very accurate model of the supply chain, including its capabilities and constraints. We referred to that earlier (see Figure 11.2). At its simplest, APS may only have a combined BOM + Process steps (Routing), Work Centre parameters, and basic finite scheduling rules based on demonstrated capacity. This is probably the most common implementation and provides functionality to move the supply chain command and control forward, while having inherent capabilities to support the journey through further APS Levels, if the business needs to go that way."

Joan caught Amy's attention and asked, "This means we will still be using Master Scheduling and Rough-Cut Capacity Planning, and Material Requirements Planning to plan our materials and resources. But what about logistics? After all, there's no point making it fast if it sits on our shipping dock for hours or days."

"Glad you asked that," said Amy. "APS can (and often should) include distribution and transportation models, and may provide on-line triggers to external hauliers to help synchronize picking, staging, loading, and shipping. The distribution model can include the company's own logistics, alternative use of 3PL[3], and even use of 4PL, if you can specify the rules in the model. However, it is usually preferable to support your warehouse management and operations using dedicated Warehouse Management & Control Systems."

"Rules, rules," said Brian. "Sounds like a lot of work to me. And I'm not sure we know enough about these rules you talk about to specify them in an APS system."

"Then you're not ready to use APS," said Amy. "Most people starting out think it'll just be a matter of copying master data from the Enterprise Resource Planning system to the APS system. But that's not the way it works. The good news is that, in fact, your people do know the rules. They use them every day to do their job, especially when things don't go perfectly. But they don't know they know them."

Brian responded to that. "I know what goes on at Hayes, and I don't see any rules anywhere. What's that mean?"

Amy shook her head. "Maybe I've not explained that right. The 'rules' are also known as experience, skill, and judgment. I know you've heard of that. It's just that we've never had to articulate and codify them before. But you're making a good point. One master scheduler I know took nine months to translate, if that's the right word, his knowledge gained over the years into a codified set of rules of what to do when this goes wrong, that goes wrong, and so on."

Brian asked, "How did that work?"

Amy was waiting for that question. "Well, he had a really complex chemical manufacturing plant to schedule. They're some of the most difficult places to schedule that I know. And they were 95% loaded. Any waste of capacity was lost sales. Before they put in an APS system it took 200 hours to schedule the plant for the next eight weeks. And that forced them to very long customer lead-times because the product was too expensive to consider high stock levels. This made them look inflexible and slow from the customer perspec-

3. 3PL refers to Third-Party Logistics providers, i.e., outsourced logistics providers. 4PL (Fourth-Party Logistics) is where an alliance of 3PLs forms to increase truck utilization through optimizing shared destinations and loads. For the company contracting a 4PL alliance, this enables increased shipping frequency of less than full truck loads much more cost effectively.

tive, and the customer had other suppliers, and so it hit sales. Using their supply model they'd defined as data and rules, put in APS, they could create an optimized schedule for those eight weeks in 35 minutes! This meant they could actually get down to weekly Master Scheduling, use any flexibility they had to be more responsive, and drive higher performance to the customer. In addition they realized 7% extra capacity through smarter changeover management (in the model rules). That's potentially 7% more sales.

"Its real value came about six months after cut-over when the external safety inspector came on site and discovered a tiny crack in a glass-lined reactor. He certified it as unsafe, and it was put out of use as soon as the product in process had been extracted. Before APS, this would have stopped production, taking at least 48 hours to reschedule, and little time to consider optimization, resulting in more lost capacity. But the APS system tackled this event in twenty minutes, including showing them options on which products they might take the hit on until the reactor had been fixed and recertified. Within two hours the decisions had been made, people, including customers, informed, and the show was back on the road—a new road."

"Do the rules ever change?" asked Dan.

"Yes they do. The model is set-up for a moment in time that can and will change," replied Amy. "Because new equipment, processes and products are constantly changing, ongoing maintenance of constraints, rules, and supply chain design are critical and potentially expensive in time and resources."

"Have they got a multiple million dollar life insurance policy on the guy?" Dan persisted.

"No they haven't," Amy countered. "They have another person up to speed, and a third person in training. In addition the rules are documented in layman terms and are well understood by key individuals in the company."

"Let's look at this chart that summarizes the evolution of planning techniques," said Amy (see Figure 11.3). She went on to discuss the chart. It was mostly self-explanatory, but helpful in understanding where they were and some of the things that were possible in the future.

"As you can see by the chart," Amy continued, "depending on the nature of your business processes and supply channels, APS can help to reduce throughput time, provide better promising information, and support decision making—leading to a more responsive supply chain."

Mickey had been listening for the last few hours, saying little at breaks. He'd been very cynical about APS, making an analogy with "user-friendly" software, which meant it was decidedly unfriendly, in his experience. Joan tried to get him to open up, but he resisted. But finally all this talk about APS got too much for him. "I can't buy all this—sounds too good to be true. I need to see it for myself."

Joan joined in, "I must admit it would be good to see this in use somewhere," and Brian shook his head in agreement.

"What do you think you're going to 'see'?" said Amy. "Remember APS works mostly invisibly and automatically. Sure there's an electronic planning board—like a fancy Gantt chart—but seeing that won't help. Another company's model would look nothing like your model."

"APS sounds dangerous to me," said Brian.

Amy had been waiting for this too. "You bet it's dangerous. If you haven't sorted out a valid supply chain model, with real rules and real alternatives; if your data accuracy isn't up at over 99.5%; if your stated capabilities are not based on demonstrated performance; if you are not capable of near 100% transaction speed and accuracy, and there are more caveats—then don't even start to go APS."

"Well, what do we do?" said Mickey. "Sounds like we've wasted our time today!"

"You know the saying, 'the truth will set you free'?" said Amy. "APS systems can enable fantastic responsiveness, can help you increase the effectiveness of the business, and can help you grow. But it doesn't do that just by buying the software. What I've said is that 'APS enables you,' and I mean 'you,' to make a difference. If ever there was a case of the 'A Item' being People, the 'B' being Process, and the 'C' being Tools, this is it."

"I remember that from the other Effective Management seminars, courses and coaching," said Joan. "And in every successful implementation we found that people are always the key element in getting it right, so we can buy in to that. What are you trying to tell us?"

Amy paused to make sure the others didn't disagree with Joan. "Implementing APS needs to be a strategic decision, from right at

Figure 11.3   Evolution of Planning Techniques

Manual Planning Boards with Cards	Laborious and error-prone No simulation No integration between functions Limited future visibility
Batch-Processed MRP Systems	Slow data processing Very slow simulation for limited functions Lacks detailed synchronization Transaction intensive Integrated, but synchronization an issue Good future visibility Complex, but logic is visible
Spreadsheets	Fast data processing Fast simulation for "this function" Often Personal—no supporting processes or documentation Not integrated with other systems Doesn't connect the supply chain Some future visibility Not complex for user that developed spreadsheet, but very complex for others
MRP On-Line Processed	Some simulation for limited functions Integrates through Bill of Material Supply focused Transaction intensive Good future visibility Complex, but logic visible
ERP On-Line Processed	Fast simulation for limited functions Integrated Enterprise focused Transaction intensive Good future visibility Complex, but logic visible

Advanced Planning
  & Scheduling Systems
    Finite capacity
    Constraint management
    Electronic interactive
      Planning Boards
    Optimization
    Simulation capability

Early use—near real-time
  simulation for selected functions
Close integration of multiple steps
Supply Chain focused
Decision support
Transaction intensive—starting to
  automate transactions
Excellent future visibility
Complex, and logic is invisible (in
  the model)

Extended Advanced Planning
  & Scheduling
    Web-enabled
    Extended Supply Chain
    Event management and
      automated response
    Remote Customer Order Entry,
      including Configuration

Mature use—near real-time
  simulation for supply chain
Tight integration of network of
  steps
Extended Supply Network focused
Extensive Supply Network decision
  support
Transaction intensive-extensive
  transaction automation
Excellent near-future visibility
Complex, and logic is invisible (in
  the model)

---

the top. What is the company trying to achieve? How does that fit with their value proposition? Are they prepared to face supply chain redesign? And what about collaboration—do they understand the trust issues? What you going do with this new capability? Where does APS fit into this journey? And what is the journey for Hayes? You know the old saying, 'If you don't know where you're going, any road will get you there,' but you might not like the destination."

The team absorbed this in silence. Amy broke into their silence, "OK. Let's take five, and then we'll discuss how you might want to start, safely, practically. Once you get some experience things will become clearer. You guys OK with that?"

"Good idea. I need a little breathing space," said Brian.

During the break Brian, Joan, and Mickey talked about this idea of a journey. The capital budget had been approved based on their earlier recommendation to buy an APS system, but now they realized it would take a lot more than their recommendation to get results from the APS system. It was no different from the other Stages of Class A that Effective management had taken them through. They must expose their senior managers to the business possibilities that an APS system could enable and get their commitment. Top management must be committed. Then the whole organization needed the proper education and training. That meant there needed to be strategic intent behind a decision to exploit the capabilities of a fully functioned APS system.

"What I suggest is this," said Amy. "Review all we've talked about. List possible scopes of implementation; where you could start, and potential benefits these options would provide for the company. I know this is a bit like a solution looking for a problem, but your managers only know what they know. You are in a position to 'educate' them on the possibilities for Hayes. You need the Integrated Business Management Team to articulate where they want to lead the company, and if an APS scenario would enable some of the things they'd like Hayes to achieve. If you can get some interest, then I suggest we arrange a workshop on APS for them."

"You never stop trying to sell your services, do you?" said Dan.

Amy smiled. "Think about what you just said. Does Hayes ever stop trying to sell? And why do you sell?"

"To make money," said Brian. "And we've got a good product that helps farmers make more money too."

"Well," Amy said a little testily, "My motivation is helping Hayes to be successful, and I've got a good product too, so that my customers make a whole lot of money when they follow my advice."

"Dan and Brian are just giving you a hard time," intervened Mickey. "I know that I've given you a hard time, Amy, and am not really receptive to the APS implementation. But I know how effective your company's education has been in the past and if you do half the job that Les did, we'll get the answer we need to move forward. The fact is that I can really see how much better life could be for me in Assembly if we really got this stuff to work. I'm always pessimistic about people changing because perhaps I find it difficult to change myself. But my experience with you guys tells me that we really need to take that next step. I say we go for the workshop."

After another surprise from Mickey, what could the rest of them say? All nodded in agreement to schedule the workshop as soon as possible.

"Now that we are on a positive note," said Amy. "From what I've read in my colleagues' reports on your business, you would find improved performance from implementing a finite scheduler in parts of production. Where Kanban is effective for you, leave it alone. But where lack of synchronization hurts and where there are production constraints to be managed more effectively—then a finite scheduler could help. And in implementing it you'd get experience of constructing the 'model' and 'rules' I talked about."

Dan jumped right in. "I have the Heat Treat area that we need to get sequencing automated. The burners have the same problem. While they aren't a capacity constraint right now, with some of the new products we're introducing and the customers we are winning back with better on time delivery and shorter lead times, I know I'm going to have a capacity constraint."

"I've got some applications also," Brian replied, "I have the same type of capacity constraint happening to the 5-axis machining centers that Dan predicts with the burners. In addition, we've got problems scheduling around constraints, particularly when things don't quite run to schedule. You know what I mean: the schedule close-couples parallel operations to bring parts together for machining, one part is late, and we now have our constraint without work. Add to that we are constantly trying to reduce the queues and you have to conclude that more accurate scheduling is a must. I'm sure we have a lot more applications in the machine shop once we really know what we are doing."

"Can it really help in the situation that Brian just described?" asked Joan.

"It depends" said Amy. If you're talking about a few minutes late, probably not. But if, say, a feeding operation went down, and recovery may be some hours, then APS could be told to use its model to suggest alternatives, 'what-ifs,' for your scheduler to review. Quite often there is an alternative schedule that can reduce potential lost time at the bottleneck."

"We never worry about a few minutes." Brian jumped in. "In the old days it was a few weeks. We now have it down to a few hours, which is really hard to handle manually."

"Looks like there are some good applications of APS, so we should probably proceed," Amy said.

"What about me?" Mickey interjected. "I have some applications also. You don't probably remember, but after our last session with Amy I went to see an application on an assembly line. It was at one of our suppliers that makes engines. I was amazed at how well they use the APS system. The volume of small tractors is going up—by the way, they aren't really small, but compared to our large tractors they are, Amy—and we are starting to make some of the ones we used to import. I really see the need. I really think I need it more than the rest of you."

Again Mickey stunned them all, this time into a long silence.

As Amy, who like the rest of them was in shock, started to talk again, Joan leaned over and whispered to Brian, "I think Mickey is up to something. I will tell you later."

"OK guys," Amy said, "I need to remind you that you've got to put together a business case as to why Hayes should invest in more software. You've got to get those senior managers to fund both the acquisition of the software, but more importantly the training and implementation. My advice in your case would be," she continued, "to consider buying APS software rather than just a finite scheduler if you think there's any possibility you may want to take integration with customers and suppliers and scheduling automation further. In engineering, most of the APS systems will fit your needs. I have to advise clients in process, FMCG[4], and chemical industries to ensure they select software that recognizes the unique aspects of those industries, such as nesting in the first case, and tank-to-tank management in the other."

Joan looked at Brian, Dan and Mickey, "We need to get on with this fast while our senior team is listening. Maybe we could schedule some time next week?"

"Hold on," said Amy. "APS is not always the right solution. Often developing a Lean-Agile supply chain can be more effective. And remember, using APS there's a tendency to lose visibility of what's going on. People need to trust the 'black box,' as they might call it. But where high speed scheduling and promising is the business need, APS wins hands down. As I said before, implementing APS must be in support of strategic and tactical needs. Look at it like this." Amy handed out a few notes, including a summary page.

---

4. FMCG = Fast-Moving Consumer Goods.

APS APPLICATION

STRATEGIC: —Long-term Supply Chain simulation and optimization

- Requires a higher level supply chain model

—Can support acquisition and merger questions

- Example, evaluating production and logistics merging options

TACTICAL: —Short-term Supply scheduling

- Not to replace Material Requirements Planning

- To support agility and flexibility

—Short- and mid-term demand forecasting based on daily or weekly sales

- To help set very short term damper stocks and Kanban level changes

—Short and mid-term collaborative supply planning if it uses standard protocols

OPERATIONAL: —Immediate line scheduling

- This is the most common use of APS

—Customer order configuration

—Capability to Promise

—Automated Order Promising

—Event notification (throughout network model) and automated solutions

—Assisted recovery from failures

E-BUSINESS: —Interactions across the internet

- Intra-company
- Inter-company

ERP + APS   = Powerful, flexible, fast scheduling

ERP +APS +   = Web-based interactive Supply
  INTERNET   Chain, including Inter-Enterprise

Where speed of response to customers is the issue, properly implemented APS can help you provide:

- Near 100% Customer Service
- Support for growth
- Minimized Cost: operating expense, inventory, ROI
- Maximize return to stakeholders
- And, often unstated: survival in a speed-led economy

Features you would expect to find in an APS system:

- Sequence complex processes—intra- & inter-company
- Simulation via Modeling—what-if
- Evaluate cost impact of decisions
- Priorities are variable
- Automates processes that require complex analyses
- Uses common PC user interface and browser
- Near real-time processing

APS can:

- Save hours of laborious planner work
- Calculate and simulate solutions to problems
- Provide 7×24 planning

Amy let them read through the summary, then continued. "It's obvious that fully-functioned APS is only constrained by your ability to define the model, the data, and the rules.

"APS seeks optimal solutions to supply chain constraints, including planning problems—because constraints do exist. APS focuses on critical constraints and, through modeling, highlights exceptions and recommends actions, but very fast! APS can provide Constraint-Based-Scheduling, near real-time processing, and integration with ERP planning. APS algorithms are more effective where speed and optimization is of the essence (vs. MRP/ERP). APS sounds great, but here are the caveats," and Amy handed out another summary sheet.

APS Caveats

- Wrong model = wrong results
- Who understands the model?
- Who can change the model?
- Getting right priorities in rules-based environment
- Relating APS to ERP/MPS priorities
- Accountability when orders go wrong
- All eggs in one basket!
- APS can change products faster than marketing can promote them!
- Internet security can be an issue
- Can be used in "autopilot" mode—dangerous—skill regression
- Need for partners to trust each other
- Behavioral aspects are largely ignored, so implementation suffers

"I'm not sure where we go from here then," said Brian.

Joan came back. "Sounds like using APS to help finite scheduling and optimization around our bottlenecks is still an option."

"And we could learn from that, and use our experience to suggest extension opportunities. I'd really like to see how this would work for us," said Mickey.

They agreed that this was their preferred short-term option, but they knew they had a lot of preparation to do before going to the Integrated Business Management Team for approval.

Amy stood up, "I think we need to start with the workshop. All of the APS workshops need extensive tailoring to meet each company's specific application, so we should schedule two days to do that. We also need to setup the follow-on workshops. We need to do at least two different ones. One workshop will be for senior management, to identify the areas they want to proceed with. The second will be for the people who will be responsible for the detailed definition of those areas. In the meantime, Joan, you and I need to schedule some coaching sessions to set up a project plan, to pull together the capital budget plan and justification, and the implementation. That's crucial."

"Thanks," Joan replied. "I'm really going to need some help on this."

Amy ended the session by saying, "APS presents great opportunities to do some fantastic things, but also to get it fantastically wrong. Go carefully. I think it was Boris Beizer who said something like, 'In God we trust; everything else gets tested.'"

As they were leaving, Brian pulled Joan off to the side. "What were you going to tell me about Mickey?"

"I think he has a crush on Amy. I kind of noticed it during her first visits but it was really clear to me during this one."

"Well I'll be! Now that you said it, he has been acting a little peculiar," said Brian. "He's been a bachelor way too long. It's about time a woman got him under control."

"I had a chance to talk to Amy on the personal side as we were setting up the visit, and I know she was married but has been divorced for quite some time. I noticed that she spent a little too much time looking at Mickey also," Joan said with a smile.

"How's that for Gaining Control!" said Brian.

The others wondered what was going on as Brian and Joan walked away, roaring with laughter.

Chapter Twelve

Moving Ahead

How time flies! Almost three years had passed since Brian started his job as Machine Shop manager at Hayes. During that period, the pride of accomplishment had settled in throughout the company. From the shop floor to Purchasing, from Engineering to Sales, and throughout the wood-paneled offices of top management, everyone realized that the hard and dedicated work to improve Hayes's processes had paid off in making their lives less stressful and more productive. The company was enjoying its best year of business ever. Sales volume was up, on-time deliveries were routinely made, and profits of this division were the best in the entire corporation.

Brian was called up to Pete's office. When he arrived, Ralph was there also.

"Brian," Pete said, "the changes we have made at this division have not gone unnoticed by Hayes's corporate offices back East. There are a lot of changes being made throughout the company because of our success. I am being promoted to vice president of the Georgia Plant to replace Dave Jennings, who is retiring."

Brian enthusiastically offered his congratulations to Pete. While this seemed like a lateral move, it really was a big promotion because the Georgia Plant, which made all of the large earthmoving equipment, was almost twice the size of their facility.

Pete went on to explain that Ralph was being promoted to General Manager here, taking his place, and that Roy was going to the Georgia Plant to replace their current Materials Manager. Dan would take over Ralph's job as Production Manager, and Joan would move from manager of Production Control to the Materials Manager position. Joan wanted Toni to replace her as the manager of Production Control.

Brian waited for the other shoe to drop. Who else was he going to lose?

Pete continued. "Corporate management has decided to launch a process-improvement initiative across the entire corporation. In addition to being thrilled with what we have done here, they have been exposed to something called Agile Manufacturing."

Brian remembered Amy talking about Flexible and Agile while coaching them about Advanced Planning and Scheduling processes. At that time it seemed that, for Hayes, flexibility was more the business need. He had always expected Agile to raise its head at some point, but he kept quiet as Pete assumed the task of enlightening him, or so Pete thought, as he continued:

"I'll tell you more about that in a minute. Our plant here has led the way in process improvements with what we have done with Advanced Supply Planning and Lean. Some of our plants are still stuck in Stage 1 of Class A planning and control." (See Figure 12.1.)

"They have the Enterprise Resource Planning system, but they still haven't figured out what they need to do to get reliable material and capacity plans. They're in the same place we were in three years ago and haven't made real progress in plant scheduling or capacity management. The Toledo plant has been fiddling around with Lean for a while but doesn't have much to show for it.

"The corporate process-improvement initiative will encompass all of these things in what is called 'Agile, Lean, Six Sigma.' And, of course, this embraces the whole organization, not just production. But my concern is what the organization needs to happen in the manufacturing plants as part of the corporate program.

"The corporation needs someone to lead that initiative and coordinate all of the other fragmented projects we have going on. We want someone who knows what it's like to live in a crisis-management environment and has successfully made the transition to making a formal controlled environment where we make a good plan and make it happen, while virtually eliminate expediting.

"We also need someone who has the ability to look forward and implement new ideas. You have really impressed me and Mark Mac-Dowell with your abilities in both cases. So Mark asked me to make

Figure 12.1   Class A Planning & Control Journey

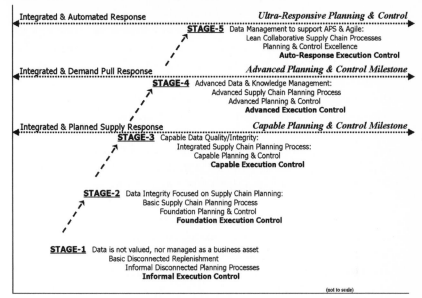

(not to scale)

you the offer. I would really like you to take that job so the corporation will be able to take better advantage of your skill sets. And since corporate is near the Georgia Plant, you will be close, to help Roy and me with the Georgia Plant. We want to be the first to start. It will be a big promotion, both from a responsibility and reward standpoint," Pete ended with a big smile.

Brian was floored by the offer. Mark MacDowell was the Executive VP of Operations for the whole corporation. He didn't know what to what to say, especially since he hadn't faced a challenge as big as Agile, Lean, Six Sigma before, although he knew roughly what it entailed.

Sensing Brian's dilemma, Pete spoke again. "Let me explain a little about Agile, Lean, Six Sigma as I understand it. I've only become aware of it recently myself, so I'm not going to try to give you the whole picture. I've got something for you that will help in that regard." Pete held up a book and then laid it back on his desk.

"The gurus and experts of the world, looking at current trends, are predicting that there'll be no let-up in global competition, where supply chains and innovation compete, not companies. And with much more knowledgeable customers they'll want the latest technology, and we'll need to keep up with their ambitions in design and manufacturing. Customers will want the product they want, not what we want to make. This is the age of Darwin: 'Adapt, or become extinct.' And we're not going to be extinct—it's corporate policy!"

Brian liked the idea of the corporate policy, or was it their vision, "We will not become extinct"? He imagined everyone at Hayes wearing t-shirts declaring this commitment. He smiled.

Pete wasn't sure what caused Brian to smile at that point, but continued. "Customers in the future will want to buy a far wider range of product options and specials, get delivery in a matter of days, and do it all for the same or lower price. This is already happening in the Fast Moving Consumer Goods sector, and even in the automobiles sector. Mercedes would love to sell just a few E-Class models—remember Henry Ford? 'Any color, as long as it's black'—but there are in fact around two billion possibilities through all the options the customer has. Probably the best example today is Dell computers who, it would appear, operate only on customized products offerings, at a good price, and fast.

"And the customer does not just go away with their purchases; they expect the manufacturer to be with them during the life of the product, often through to disposal and recycling. This 'care' aspect is now associated with what is called Total Cost of Ownership.

"Hayes, at this site, is one of the top 10% of companies in terms of its Capable Planning and Control status, which we've taken further toward a true Class A Excellence status in follow-on initiatives. But our competition is becoming wiser. I read in a business news flash that Gregory Tractors has bought the latest Enterprise Resource Planning software and is making brave announcements about how they're going to rule our industry. The rest of the competition isn't out making bold statements like that, but you can bet they're not sitting on their hands now we've taken market share from them."

"We have a little time to achieve our objectives, but not too much," Brian interjected.

Pete smiled, and continued, "There will have to be a revolution in technology throughout the industry. This revolution will include equipment that has such quick changeovers that, potentially, all products can be made in a single-part flow process. Then engineering will be redesigning the products to realize that potential, but also to enable customer choices of options without disruption to the flow. Have you heard of 'postponement'?"

Brian shook his head, "That's a new one to me."

"Well, I read that 'postponement' is designing products from the customer perspective, and that means delaying as long as possible the point in manufacture where customer choices are built in. So for example, we could delay fitting the gear box until we knew exactly which configuration the customer wanted, and deliver maybe the next day," Pete added.

"Wow!" said Brian. "The gear box goes in near the start of assembly today. I can see what you mean about a redesign."

Pete continued, "I read that for many major consumer products manufacturers, big name brands, around 70% of their output is customized! Imagine that and the agility capability they need to have. And this happens so fast they've got to be really smart at very short-term forecasting. They need to start sales of a promotion, go with the volume, and shut it down on a dime, all enabled by electronic point-of-sale technology, as the customers move elsewhere—hopefully the result of the next promotion!

"And parts we buy, make, and assemble must be near 100% right first time. It also means our processes must be variability and failure free; and that's where the values and methods of Six Sigma come in. And of course, we continue our Lean endeavors to seek out and eliminate nonvalue-adding activities anywhere in the organization."

Brian had never heard Pete in evangelizing mode before. It was amazing.

"And there's more," said Pete. "The key to getting Agile, Lean, Six-Sigma right is, first and foremost, how we treat our people. We'll educate teams, and managers, so the teams—shop floor, offices, design, and so on—can be empowered as self-managing units. The bounds of empowerment will be clear, and the teams will take responsibility for meeting their business objectives. Our main point of contact will be the Team Leaders, and we'll consider them part of our middle-management team."

"What about our supervisors? Where do they go?" asked Brian.

"That's gotta be handled real well," agreed Pete. "Some companies I've heard about got everyone to reapply for their jobs, and then selected the best-fit team they could. That was a very fast way to do it, but it hasn't really worked because they've got major trust issues, as you can imagine. I've asked Human Relations at the Georgia Plant to propose a modern, people-centered solution. I know some will be redeployed, but we'll do our best to minimize the impact."

"Well, people are our most valuable asset," said Brian.

"Oh no, they're not!" said Pete. "It's a nice thing to say, but it's not true. And that brings me nicely to the other cornerstone of our program. The good news is that you've already learned some of this, so it won't be completely new to you."

What's coming now, thought Brian?

"The missing piece of the jigsaw, the one we haven't paid enough attention to up till now, is Knowledge and Knowledge Management. I had a real good session with my new Human Resource manager in the Georgia Plant and he spent a couple of hours enlightening me."

"It's what?" exploded Brian. "How can that be more important than people?"

"Tell me, Brian," said Pete, "what would you do if Tony left, right now, today?"

"Well, I'd find a replacement real quick: Tony's a key guy." replied Brian.

"But your department wouldn't stop, or go out of business, would it?"

"Well, no," Brian admitted.

"But suppose I took away your routings and your Advanced Planning System rules?" asked Pete.

"I'd be dead in the water, Pete. You know we absolutely rely on. . . . I see what you mean now."

Pete jumped in, "Don't get me wrong, people make it happen. People are critical, and we've got to respect them, develop them, and get them to be high performers. They are the most important source of knowledge and ideas. But it's 'people,' plural.

"There was a study done in Europe—sponsored by the UK government—to advise on the most important asset in government and in business. I guess they expected it to be, officially, people. But the study concluded that without data and codified knowledge . . ."

"What's that?" said Brian.

"Sorry," said Pete, "Getting carried away, aren't I? So here are two questions about the essential skills and competencies of Hayes:

1. Are our key competencies held in your people, in your organization, or in your systems?

2. How secure is our knowledge and competence?"

"To the first," said Brian, "I know that they were in the people when I came here. Everyone was the local expert, but we've moved away from that. So I would guess it's now in our organization, today. We have policies and procedures, and they're followed."

Pete fired back, "What about where you use the Advanced Planning System?"

"Well, I guess it's no different, except. . . . Yeah, you've got me there," said Brian. "What we've done is to codify the knowledge people have, and often don't know they have, into master data and the rules."

"So now you're ready to answer my second question," said Pete.

"Okay. I can see how this works," replied Brian. "Where I've codified knowledge I am not vulnerable to people's moods, absences, or decisions to leave the company. I could keep the business running, in trim, and train someone else to take over the model maintenance stuff. In the old days, if two or three key people left, we'd probably stop until we regrouped; but that could hurt customer relations.

"You know, I've just had another insight: This is the message we started with some time ago. Time is the enemy. Without those rules, I'd spend time (= waste) trying to regroup to continue. But because of those rules—codified knowledge—I don't experience that waste."

Pete was pleased with Brian's new enthusiasm, and secretly knew he'd learned something too! "You're right. I don't want to downplay the importance of people. People operating in the mode that you have over the last three years are the key. They have to challenge the old paradigms constantly and be willing to listen to new thoughts and direction. This is not something we do naturally.

"Okay, then. As part of your new role you'll get education on all aspects of knowledge management. The top performers in industry, and there are plenty of examples from Japanese and U.S. automotive industries, survive through knowledge management. Obvious things such as automation and less obvious things such as auto-selling and auto-marketing are examples. Four hundred years ago Sir Francis Bacon wrote down what people have known from the beginning of time: 'Knowledge is power.'

"We're going to upgrade the corporate business systems to the latest version, and add in the knowledge-management modules. These information systems will be integrated across the corporation, and not only inside the company, but linked to key customers and suppliers as well. People throughout the organization will require enhanced skill sets. We'll see in some parts of Hayes 'Agile Manufacturing.' According to one published authority, in an Agile Manufacturing environment, custom products will be made as fast and as cheaply as mass-produced products. Our parent corporation wants to be part of that environment.

"As you are aware, Brian, overseas competition has hit the plant in Georgia hard. It's much like the Japanese impact on the U.S. auto industry. Overseas competition has not affected this plant too much yet, because we have become more effective, but it's only a matter of time before it does. The whole company needs to stay one step ahead and do everything we can to meet that challenge, like we have been doing here on the West Coast."

Brian conceded that maybe that could happen in some industries, but he thought that it would be a real stretch for Hayes. He thought about how tough it had been to make the changes that they had made so far, and this sounded like a giant leap from where they were. Pete had become known throughout the plant for his constant pushing for improvements, and this seemed like a step change. Brian was not particularly surprised that he was right in the middle of this one.

Pete handed Brian the book from his desk. "Here is some material on Agile Manufacturing. It will do a better job of defining what Agile Manufacturing is. Take the rest of the day to go home and look this over. Let me know tomorrow if you are interested," Pete said, smiling.

On his way home, Brian reflected back on his Chevy convertible. It was running well. But it sure didn't have some of the options available on the new cars, and it wasn't as reliable. It required more maintenance than the new models. His own new car went 9,000 miles between oil changes, 60,000 miles on a set of spark plugs, and didn't even have a carburetor to rebuild or points to change like the old Chevy did. If General Motors tried to sell a car like his convertible today, nobody would buy it because of all the maintenance and the lack of gadgets. The old Chevy couldn't go much more than 80,000 miles without rebuilding the engine and it had roll-up windows. That's called progress.

Reflecting on the differences between his old Chevy and today's modern vehicles, Brian realized that Pete was right about trying to improve the business continuously, whether through designing new products or improving the business practices. Brian knew, from talking with Rob Ericson of Mercury Electronics, that the electronics industry is even worse: If you don't stay up with technology in that industry, you can go belly up in just a couple of years. Brian was really starting to appreciate Pete's enthusiasm to keep the company on a path of continuous improvement.

Nobody was home when Brian got there, so he flopped into his favorite chair and cracked open the book that Pete had handed him. It was titled *21st Century Manufacturing Enterprise Strategy—An Industry-Led View, Volume 1.*[1]

Brian started to skim through the book. He learned about the way data become information, and information becomes knowledge. The winners in the 21st century will be those who capture knowledge and use it competitively. And that means the seamless flow of information between all parts of the organization. Having the right machines is a key part of this, but the ability of the organization to respond creatively to threats and opportunities, to rapidly change business models and even products and markets. Agility and flexibility are the winners. The role of knowledge management started to become clear to him. The integration of people and technology to create a flexible agile company was in line with his thinking. He also read that the technology was available today to enable information—something he had not been aware of. He promised himself he'd talk to Les, of Effective Management, about this. He considered Les to be his mentor and coach, and it was good to play with ideas with an independent expert.

What he was reading was fitting in with what the Effective Management coaches were saying and with the things that he had read in other publications.

Basically, that is what he did with his shop-floor system. With help from his coaches at Effective Management Inc., he had taken advantage of the available technology. It wasn't done by a bunch of technocrats, but rather by the people on the shop floor. No, it hadn't been easy, but the results were incredible. He began to recognize that what he had accomplished was small in comparison to what could be achieved.

---

1. Iacocca Institute, 1991.

The key technical factor behind Agile Manufacturing was matching the design of the products to the capabilities of the people, machines, and processes that built them. Product and manufacturing processes and design are done concurrently. The computer makes it possible to simulate total product design, process of its manufacture, can predict service needs and life-cycle, and the disposal cost implications.

When Brian finished reading, he started thinking about how applying these concepts to Hayes Tractor could achieve business stretch goals. He knew there must be business intent behind any program like this.

Perhaps they could rearrange the equipment to make custom cabs on the fly. In today's environment, some parts were made in Brian's and Dan's shops and some were made at the supplier. They were then stocked and picked as kits. By taking what they had done with manufacturing cells and Lean Manufacturing one step further, they could move some of Brian's and Dan's machines closer to Final Assembly and make all the components that they now purchased, except the molding and the glass. The moldings were standard parts for Hayes, and they could probably get the glass supplier to cut what they needed each day. Bingo! Instant cabs! The customer calls the day before and they can put a cab on a tractor.

Brian thought further. Engines and drive trains were the most expensive option problems. Hayes bought the engines and built their own transmissions. The current design had the transmission cases machined differently for each engine that they fit on. With three different transmissions and four different engine options for each tractor size, it resulted in twelve different part numbers for the transmission cases on each size tractor. With five differently sized tractors, this made 60 different transmission cases that they built.

The cases had to go through several manufacturing steps. Therefore, the Planning Department had to forecast the cases in advance to reduce the lead time to the customer. Trying to think "agile," Brian concluded that, with a new five-axis machining center equipped with loading pallets that could be loaded while the machine was running another part, he could machine whatever case that they wanted in a matter of minutes. Maybe they could put the machine right in the transmission assembly area. It took less than two hours to assemble and test the transmission. This would enable the customer to make changes on the transmission/engine combination the day before the tractor went on the assembly line. It would also reduce the inventory significantly.

As Brian's mind raced forward, he could see many other issues that they would have to work on, such as getting closer to flow, one piece at a time, but now it would be the right piece at a time, and putting together a crossfunctional team for quick design of specials. And now that they had their Advanced Planning System, they could expand its use through an update of the model. After all, the philosophy of continuous improvement and "one-less-at-a-time" had not been forgotten.

Brian realized that looking at the process from an Agile viewpoint meant a whole different look at order entry, master scheduling, material planning, capacity planning, buying, design engineering, manufacturing engineering, and more. Agile means people will have to be working in close-knit teams and have an in-depth knowledge of the systems, as well as the product. Commitments had to be made quickly with all functions, and that's where Capability-to-Promise came in. Through the model, auto- commitments could be made in near real time. It also emphasized the need to keep their knowledge (in the model and rules) correct and up to date. Knowledge truly is power.

The technology was available for them to become agile; the only question was could he get the people to change?

Brian called Pete first thing the next morning and asked if he could come up to talk with him about his offer of the day before. Ralph was in Pete's office when Brian got there. Pete motioned for Brian to come on in.

"I read that book you gave me, and I also looked at my notes from discussions with Effective Manufacturing. Some good stuff there too." Brian said. "I think I'm interested, but want to know more. I also have a few ideas of my own and want to see if they fit with what you are thinking." Brian then went through all of his ideas with Pete and Ralph.

Pete looked at Ralph. "This is the kind of thinking the company needs. I knew he was the right choice."

Then Pete turned to Brian. "Mark MacDowell and I would like you there as soon as possible. Discuss it with your wife and let me know by next week."

The day before Pete and Roy were to head off to Georgia, Pete gathered all of the employees together in the company cafeteria.

There were a few things he wanted to make sure they understood. A stage had been erected and refreshments were being served. You could see the change that had taken place at Hayes, not only in the faces of the employees, but even on the walls of the cafeteria. There were numerous displays that recognized and praised the results of the employees' hard work. A banner was draped across the front wall that indicated the change in company mind-set. It said simply, "The Hayes Team: Committed to Being the Best." Today, everyone in that cafeteria believed it.

Pete moved confidently to the microphone. "I must admit having this gathering is a bit selfish on my part," he said. "I wanted a chance to talk to you all one last time in order to acknowledge properly what we have accomplished in the last year. First of all, Team Hayes has not missed a single customer commitment in the last six months!" Pete began the applause himself, which soon echoed loudly throughout the room. "Productivity has increased by 23% and is still going up. We have installed some new computer systems in the past two years that have also played an integral part in our success. They are, however, only tools to aid us. It is the people using these tools who have made us a success, and that is every person in this room." Another round of applause briefly stopped Pete. "Thanks to our efforts in implementing Business Excellence in Planning and Control at Stage 3, and our efforts with Lean, we have also been able to reduce our lead time to the customer by more than 50% and our quality costs by over 65%. That is not only significant, it's downright amazing!" A ripple of applause again drifted across the room.

"What does this all mean? It means our profits are up 20%. It means that we have attracted the business of four major new customers, along with work from other plants for a total of a more than 28% increase in business. It means being more competitive and creating more jobs here at Hayes. It means that instead of the corporate offices phasing out this tired old facility, they're planning investment in machines and the construction of a new facility, right here, to take its place!" This announcement was met with thunderous applause. "This couldn't have happened without you. This could never have happened without your commitment to change and your willingness to make it happen. I know I owe my promotion to the hard work of every person in this plant, but especially to the people who make our product, from design engineer to assembler.

"As you all know, for the last few weeks you've been working with a team from Effective Management, who have been looking at our processes and asking you how you did your job. We invited them in to do a full assessment of where we were against all the tough criteria in their Class A Checklist. When I first saw this checklist I thought—impossible! To do this we'd have to learn to walk on water.

"We've learned to walk on water! I am very proud to show you this Class A Award—the first in our industry. We did it!"

Everyone was shouting and whooping at this news, but Pete called for quiet again. "I made a mistake." Everyone in the audience looked at each other, puzzled.

"I need to remind myself, the managers, and everyone," he continued "that when I said 'we did it,' my mind bucked back at me that truth—'achievement is the death of endeavor'—so let's all consider our Class A plaque as our official pass to continue the journey to perfection. KEEP GOING!"

The excitement took a while to cool down; Pete had struck just the right note.

"And now I've got one more special announcement to make."

Even Brian and his comanagers looked up at this.

"Seeing all the changes going on here on the West Coast, the senior management of the corporation realized that they may have become a constraint to progress." Pete was sure he heard a couple of voices say "You got that right," and he understood why they'd think that.

He continued, "So starting at the very top with the Chairman, we thought it was about time that we became the leaders again. And leaders should be at the front! We decided to commit the entire corporation to achieve the full Effective Management Business Excellence Class A. It all started with us here at this plant, based on the results we have shown. We're working on Strategic Planning first—that's our number one job. We haven't been very good at it in the past and we have 'knee-jerked' the corporation around far too much. We had no real focus or process. But now we have. We'll be driving changes in all areas of the company, supported by our friends at Effective Management, to achieve or establish the best practices in their Class A checklist."

At first the audience was just stunned but then broke out into loud applause as they realized just how much of a leadership role the plant had played.

Pete wrapped up his farewell address with a heartfelt "thank you" to all of the Hayes employees for their part in the company's success. "I owe my promotion to all of you, and I will never forget that."

As Brian made his way through the crowd and headed for his office, he began to think back over the path he and Hayes had traveled during the last three years. All he could think about was the hard work, followed by the heady successes. It had been fun. But there had to be an easier way to accomplish this kind of turnaround. He remembered that first day-long course that had introduced him and Joan to the ideas that seemed so much a part of his life today. Why hadn't someone told him about them sooner? And where would they be if he and Joan hadn't attended that course?

Then he began to think about Georgia and having to travel this path all over again. This time he would be guiding all of the other plants on their journey through shop scheduling, capacity planning, Advanced Planning Systems, Lean Manufacturing, and Agile Manufacturing. How could he get the change process to go faster?

Brian knew that one of the keys to making this process work better and faster was to educate everyone, from top to front-line workers, so they would take ownership of their processes in much the same way he had. Except, in this case, he wouldn't have the time and luxury of discovery. It all had to happen more quickly. The question that kept rattling through his head was *How*? He needed to find an education process that could aid him in teaching others the concepts he himself had fought and clawed to understand. He clearly remembered the resistance that Dan had put up when Joan first tried to present these new ideas to him and his department. As Brian thought about it, he realized that it wasn't until Dan had to explain it to his own troops that he finally came on board. Why? Because Dan had finally taken ownership. The process now belonged to Dan and his people.

It was obvious to Brian that the involvement of the people made the difference. Each department, team leader, and operator had to be committed to making things better, to understand the phrase "everyone has two jobs: the job you do, and doing it better." And then they had to be willing to do the work necessary to make it happen. The changes Hayes had to make were not only to the physical processes; they had to change culturally, too.

Suddenly, Brian asked himself whether or not he had ever really shown his appreciation to his people? He knew Ralph had never been one to acknowledge his gratitude openly, but that didn't mean Brian shouldn't. Brian made a mental note to be sure he would show his appreciation openly.

Brian stopped by Roy's office and found him packing a box of books. "I guess this means you're really going to Georgia?" Brian asked, as Roy placed a pile of well-read volumes into the box.

"You know, Brian, I asked Pete to have you join us in Georgia. I figured with the work you'd done here, I wouldn't want anyone else helping me start the process all over again. But I lost out to Mark MacDowell. Got you close anyway."

"That's what worries me, Roy. We worked so hard to get things right here: I'm not so sure I really want to go through all that pain again."

"You won't have to. We're not going to do things the way we did them here." He handed Brian a book. It was what they affectionately referred to as "the gold book." It was the Effective Management Class A checklist. He'd used it in their quest for Class A.

"In this plant, we sort of drifted through the implementation process. Mark MacDowell has recognized the importance of Class A and he has convinced the Chairman to make Class A certification a requirement for all divisions, but this time led from the top, the way it should be. It will, of course, be in stages, similar to the way we have done here at Hayes.

"I suggest you encourage each of the divisions to follow the process Effective Management has developed to help companies move through the journey to Class A. And don't forget, educate, educate, educate."

"That's great, Roy," Brian said, feeling a little better about the prospects, "but it took a lot of work putting the education and training packages together."

Roy sensed Brian's concern. "I suggest, instead of developing all the education training materials yourself, you use the Effective Management's material, but work with them to customize it to our needs and business language. In talking with Roxanne as this whole thing was developing, she also said they could help you train our own people to do the education. Then of course we will want to use their coaching. I think you agree it has been invaluable."

"You've obviously been doing some thinking about this, Roy. What you say makes sense. In fact, I've got some ideas of my own that may speed things along."

"I was counting on that," Roy said. "This is an exciting opportunity for you, Brian. That's why it's so important that you get down to Georgia as soon as possible."

"What about all our work here?" Brian asked. "You don't think as soon as we leave, it's all going to fall apart, do you?"

Roy laughed. "I don't think we have anything to worry about there. Joan will keep Ralph and Lenny on the right track. Lenny's been having a lot of fun running Sales and Marketing since he has all the advantages over the competition. And as much as Ralph complained about computers, he knows now that without them he'd be up the creek. You also have to realize this process has been ingrained in everyone who works here. They all know it's the best way to run the business. If Ralph ever tried to change things back, there would probably be an uproar we could hear all the way from Georgia."

"And we wouldn't be here to bail him out," Brian said. He suddenly realized that he'd already decided to make the move. "Well, I guess I'd better get to work on José. If he's going to be the new machine-shop manager, he's going to have to know where all the bodies are buried. Fortunately, he's already got a firm grip on how best to utilize our people's talents."

"More than that," Roy added, "he's got a clear understanding of the importance of planning and not just reacting. He's a good choice."

"I guess I'm going to have to work with Effective Management with regard to an ongoing education program also," Brian said. "That means we'll be enhancing the skills of the current employees. New employees will have a formal education and training program that they'll be put through, whether they're just starting with the company or moving to a new job."

"Listen, Roy, I'll let you finish up in here. I've got a Business Improvement Group meeting in a minute."

"All right, partner. We'll be in touch as soon as I get to Georgia."

Roy gave him a smile, knowing that, as sold as Brian was on the idea, he still wanted to check all the details. "I figure you'll have the Business Improvement Group on the right track quickly. Shouldn't be a problem since you can work on it full time."

"By the way," Roy said as Brian was walking out the door. "Joan wants you to stop by and see her. She has some news that she thought you might want to hear from her."

"Now what?" Brian thought as he entered Joan's office. "What's going on?"

"First of all, I want to know if you're going to take the job running the Business Improvement Group," Joan said.

"Well I'm not sure yet . . ."

"Don't play coy with me, Brian. I talked with your wife and she is ready to go. What are you holding out for?"

"Okay, Okay! I was just trying to make sure I have the right controls in place so I can really get the job done. I think I've got that, because I'll be reporting directly to Mark MacDowell. They just don't want to announce it until all the political issues are out of the way," Brian replied. "Now, what's the other thing?"

Joan gave a mysterious smile—she clearly had something juicy to tell him. "You know how everyone is trying to figure out what's going to happen to Mickey? Well, you remember what I told you about Amy Shinn and him about eight months ago?"

Brian nodded.

"Well, he is going to leave and go with Effective Management. Pete was angry at first, but Ralph talked him into letting Mickey go. What nobody knows is that Mickey and Amy Shinn have gotten real close, in fact, so close they are going to get married. They don't want to tell anyone until Mickey has left. What do you think about that?"

"I knew it," Brian said. "Mickey has been a different person since Amy showed up. Good for Mickey."

"You know, I'm going to miss you, Brian," Joan said.

"Same here, Joan," Brian replied. "We've come through a lot together. You've really been my partner in this whole process."

The two shook hands and then gave each other a very uncharacteristic hug.

"We'll still be working together," Brian said.

"Can't wait," Joan replied as Brian left.

Later that night at home, Brian thought back to what he had always envisioned for Hayes, a company that had what it takes to produce its products on time, without the craziness of constant expediting pressure, of missing parts, of inadequate labor supplies, or a continual tide of unscheduled surprises. Hayes had climbed the mountain of its own inefficiency and come up a winner. It took a lot of education, training, and a willingness to succeed.

Did that mean that all the change was over? Hardly. There was the never-ending job of continuous improvement and the whole new vision of Agile Lean Sigma. No matter how much Hayes had accomplished, there was always competition pushing them today to be the leaders tomorrow. Now, however, there was enough knowledge and information for them to be able to see what was coming their way and plan for what they knew would be happening. They also had the ability to simulate their options, to see with Rough-Cut Capacity Planning how their decisions might impact the plan and the factory if it were to change. Because they had the tools to plan with, they could spend their time making the improvements necessary to beat the competition, instead of spending all their time reacting to problems when it was too late for good solutions.

Brian recognized that there was a great difference in the quality of life at Hayes today versus his life when he stepped in as machine-shop manager. First, with capacity planning and shop scheduling operating the way they were supposed to, he wasn't working all hours of the day and night. Weekends were now spent doing what he wanted, like taking long, romantic drives with his lovely wife. He hadn't planned on the effect that getting his factory life together would have on his family life. But, most importantly, Brian felt that, when he went home at night, he had the satisfaction of a job well done, and now he had the results to prove it, too.

Had it been easy? No. Gaining control of the company by getting years of inadequate processes into shape is never easy. Was it the right thing to do? It was the *only* thing to do. Without the control and knowledge Hayes gained by becoming fully operational with its capacity management and scheduling techniques, the chances of surviving competitively on a national scale, let alone in the global marketplace, were next to none. It took hard work. It took change. It took a willingness and commitment to understand Planning and Control at capability and excellence levels, Integrated Business Management as the driver, Agile Lean Sigma as the challenge. They'd had to learn the importance of People, Process, and Tools—and the vital roles of leadership and education that brought out the best in people.

Most of all, it took integrity and guts to stand up and say, "Let's do it right!"

That night he watched a program on TV about upcoming technologies. They talked about nanotechnologies, and that today you can get self-cleaning glass windows . . . and Brian switched the TV off, and hoped that Mark MacDowell hadn't seen it!

Index